Reading Instruction that Makes Sense

by
Mary Tarasoff

 Active Learning Institute

Reprinted 2002

Canadian Cataloguing in Publication Data
Tarasoff, Mary, 1944–
Reading instruction that makes sense

ISBN 1-895111-08-0

1. Reading (Elementary).   2. Reading (Elementary)—Evaluation.   I. Title.
LB1573.T37 1993   372.4'14   C93-091882-7

Published in Canada by:

Active Learning Institute Inc.
P.O. Box 6275
Victoria, B.C. V8P 5L5
Tel: (250) 477-0105
Fax: (250) 477-9105

Distributed By:
Grass Roots Press
Toll Free: 1-888-303-3213
Fax: (780) 413-6582
Web Site: www.literacyservices.com

Contents

Introduction

The purpose of this book is to present a framework for planning, assessing, and evaluating children's reading development, and to make sense of suggested instructional strategies and programs for teaching reading. Traditionally, published reading programs based on different teaching and reading theories included teacher guides, reading texts, and student worksheets. Embedded in these programs was a hierarchy of knowledge, skills, and strategies presented for different grade levels. Teachers used these programs and materials as the basis of their reading instruction. Children were evaluated as to how well they did using the graded materials — above, below, average.

Over the years, as researchers learned more about teaching reading and children's reading development, various proponents argued for different approaches, resulting in programs changing in emphasis and appearance. However, the basic underlying philosophy continued to be the same; that is, by following a structured, hierarchical curriculum, teachers could help children learn to read. Within a classroom, all children used similar materials with some modifications in activities and pace of instruction for different reading groups. These reading programs were based on research and studies that analyzed reading, identified basic skills and knowledge needed for reading, and reassembled them in a logical sequence. It was assumed that if teachers followed these instructional programs, children would learn the skills needed to read competently. However, with each "new, improved" program there were still children who did not successfully learn to read. Curriculum-focused, teacher-centred programs were not providing the solution to help *all* children.

Traditional programs attempted to meet individual and developmental differences in students by providing more skill practice activities for "slower groups" and including some suggestions for extending "faster groups." However, because the program writers did not have information about the skills, learning needs and interests of the specific children who would eventually use the program, these programs could not provide the variety of resources and activities required to match the needs and abilities of all students in a particular class. Although teachers modified the programs as best they could, suitable alternative resources were not available, reduced by the expectation that all children would use one of the authorized programs in some way. In these programs evaluation strategies focused on establishing above average, average, or below average readers. Inevitably a certain number of children would be unsuccessful, failing to reach the set curriculum standards expected for each grade or age level at the end of a year.

Currently, there is a great deal of educational literature about children's reading development, individual differences in learning styles and preferences, and

Over the years, reading programs have changed in emphasis and appearance. With each new program, there still were children who did not learn to read easily.

Reading is an interactive process. You are encouraged to actively engage in this text, to reflect and make comments as you read.

the reading process. The concern about students dropping out of school and the focus on self-esteem emphasize the importance for all children to develop concepts of themselves as successful learners and readers. Today there is a greater acceptance of the diversity of children's abilities and talents. If reading is a major difficulty for some children, it should not prevent them from learning in other ways in school while continuing to develop their reading skills. This means that other ways of teaching and other resources for reading need to be employed with a focus on progress. Lack of success, or being labelled as a slow reader, does not contribute to a healthy concept of self as a reader.

There has been a shift towards what is called a learner-focused curriculum. Along with this is a holistic philosophy espousing the importance of the whole as well as the complexity of interaction between parts. Teaching about the relationships between parts (e.g. phonics and context clues) and between the whole and parts (e.g. reading and decoding skills) is just as important, if not more so, than teaching the individual parts (e.g. phonics knowledge) by themselves.

> The shift towards a more learner-focused curriculum reflects the consideration of students' interests, needs and abilities in choosing resources and activities that actively engage them in learning to read.

Current proposals suggest that there should be a wider variety of reading materials available (in number, genre, quality, and difficulty) in every classroom — rather than mostly basal readers and rather than centralized in the library. Instead of recommending one or two reading programs, a wide variety of trade books and anthologies of literature are becoming available and authorized for classroom use. This makes it possible to match daily reading materials more closely to children's abilities and interests than with a limited selection of basal readers. Current proposals also emphasize the importance of children actively learning to read by listening to literature, by discussing its form and content, by becoming aware of different reading strategies, and by engaging frequently in guided and independent reading. They recognize the value of ongoing assessment and evaluation of reading progress to determine the immediate instructional goals and suitable resources. Certainly, this is a step towards providing reading instruction and texts more appropriate for children's interests, abilities, and needs.

> Reading programs which use a wide variety of resources do not have teacher guides like those that accompanied traditional reading programs.

Teachers have traditionally relied on teacher guides to explain how and when to use program materials to teach reading skills. This overall framework is no longer provided when a wider range of resources is used. Presently, all that exists for teachers is their own personal framework assimilated over years of teaching from the traditional programs and from working with children. Many teachers have had experience with only a few levels (grades) of a program and, therefore, do not have an overall view of the reading process and the developmental and individual differences of children as they gain reading competency over a number of years.

In making the shift to learner-focused, literature-based programs, if the new resources for teaching reading are interpreted and used with the traditional philosophy and methods, there will be only an appearance of change. Taking a trade book and creating questions for each chapter, worksheets for phonics and vocabulary, and teacher-directed activities is the traditional program in new clothes. But having trade books that teachers and children can choose according to interests, abilities, and needs, and teaching decoding and comprehension strategies in a variety of ways guided by ongoing assessment indicate that a different philosophy is at work. However, a teacher guide for teaching reading using a wide variety of literature (both fiction and nonfiction) does not

🔆 I think . . . .

_____

_____

_____

_____

_____

exist. As well, expectations for goals of reading acquisition and evaluation are not identified for such programs. Thus to make this shift effectively is no easy task.

What is needed then, in order to make significant and essential changes, is for teachers to understand more clearly how to structure the classroom environment and how to facilitate reading development. As Adams (1990) states

> It is not just the presence of a variety of activities that makes a program of reading instruction effective or ineffective. It is the way in which its pieces are fitted together to complement and support one another, always with full consideration of the needs and progress of the young readers with whom it will be used. Good curriculum implementation depends on solid understanding of the principles and goals upon which it is built. To make the most of a set of materials, teachers need to understand why each activity is included . . . so that its importance can be assessed with respect to the particular needs of their own students . . . . They must be able to separate necessary from recommended activities. (pp. 122–123)

The purpose of this book is to create a framework for understanding the principles and goals of reading programs that include a wide variety of resources and a focus on learners and their success. This framework is meant to be a guide for planning, assessing, and evaluating children's reading progress as well as for deciding what needs to be done to facilitate this progress. The framework will provide a way to organize a cohesive program that acknowledges individuals in classes, incorporates effective teaching strategies, and recognizes the dynamic process of developing competent readers. It will provide a way to understand and to develop effective, successful reading instruction.

Making the shift toward literature-based programs will not be easy without understanding the principles and goals of effective reading instruction.

The purpose of this book is to create a framework for planning, assessing and evaluating children's reading progress.

My questions about reading & teaching

_____

_____

_____

_____

_____

_____

_____

_____

_____

Reading Theories and Models

Theories are insights that attempt to explain phenomena, in fact, the root of the word theory means "to see." Models attempt to depict connections between various theoretical concepts and processes. Reading theories and models are, therefore, generated to help us "see" better the relationships and influences of the various components of reading and to suggest what we can do to help children learn to read. Different reading programs are based on different models and theories.

In reality, events and situations are very complex. Predictions made by theories and models are often not borne out because the complexity is not represented in the models. As a result "theoretical" ideas often seem to be the opposite of "practical." "Don't give me the theory, just tell me what to do," sometimes seems to be the most practical approach to teaching.

We all have countless models and theories about how things work which, in fact, enable us to function in a complex world. The brain attempts to make sense (rather than nonsense, we hope) about what we see, hear, feel, smell, taste, and do. These personal theories and models whether intentionally or unintentionally developed are often referred to as "beliefs." We use them to explain events, interact with others, understand ourselves, and predict what might happen. However like maps, they only represent (re-present) reality and provide a guide. Like maps, they are not a substitute for reality.

Different maps highlight and represent unique aspects of the same thing. For example, one country could be mapped:

(a) from different points of view: as part of the universe, world, or hemisphere; in its entirety as a country; or as parts made up of regions, cities, munici-palities, and neighbourhoods, or

(b) to illustrate various characteristics, for example transportation routes, roads, geography, weather, economic regions, political divisions, population, density, flora or fauna.

As well, each of the above kinds of maps may provide different amounts of detail and accuracy.

Just as there are different kinds of maps for the same country showing different features, there are many theories and models of how we learn and how we read. Just as all the information about one country cannot be clearly represented on one map, it is impossible to represent a complex process such as reading and the variables that influence its acquisition in one model or program. Therefore, each model and reading program encompasses different perspectives, highlighting certain aspects and not others. Complex and important influences such as intelligence, interest, motivation, setting, purpose, emotional factors, personal self-image often are not incorporated.

Some models are descriptive, some predictive; some focus on skills, some on processes; others focus on hierarchy of skills (top down, bottom up); and still others focus on interaction of skills (parallel processing, schema theories). Over the years, accepted models of reading have reflected current understanding of reading and popularity of use. A few major approaches to teaching reading have been:

Theories and models are constructed to try to help us understand how to best teach students to read.

Different reading theories and models view the reading process from different perspectives. With complex processes, such as reading, not all aspects are included.

- Alphabetic — focus on letters of alphabet first and spelling words out loud
- Phonics — focus on learning letter/sound relationships first
- Whole Word — focus on learning words first
- Language Experience — focus on recognizing words in student's oral language written down
- Whole Language — focus on words and letters within whole texts and reading for meaning (see also Figure 1)

Theories and models can be useful if they are chosen appropriately. If the user is aware of their limitations and biases, they can be helpful in understanding how to teach reading. The key is not whether theories are right or wrong, but rather, do they increase or limit our understanding about what is really happening? Do they guide us to effective teaching practices? Do children benefit from the approach that the model suggests?

Theories, models, or beliefs which give rise to principles and goals of reading instruction must be recognized for what they are — *a framework from which to start*. They must be revised when new experiences and evidence dictate. They must be based on studies of individuals, not just of groups. Often research

Over the years there have been different approaches to teaching reading.

Theories and models are helpful if interpreted carefully and their limitations acknowledged.

☀ I think the strength of each program is

_____

_____

_____

_____

_____

_____

Programs Based on Different Approaches

Basal Reader
- series of graded texts organized in sequential order of difficulty

Individualized Reading
- wide variety of materials, individual teaching conferences and record keeping

Language Experience
- student-created (dictated or written) materials

Linguistic
- reading material emphasizing consistent letter/sound relationships and regular spelling patterns

Literature-Based
- wide variety of quality literature

Theme-Based
- areas of interest determine what texts and literature to use

Phonics
- reading materials emphasizing sound/letter relationships explicitly taught, programs varied in rate and sequence of introduction of phonics elements
  - Synthetic (instruction proceeds from teaching letter sounds, and blending sounds to form words), or
  - Analytic Approaches (instruction begins with words known to students to generalize phonics relationships in similar words)

Figure 1. Different Reading Programs.

underlying advocated approaches is based on studies done with groups of students in which the results are averaged and statistically analyzed. Although the results may indicate a statistically significant increase in certain reading measures, this does not necessarily mean *all* children in the group benefited from the experimental procedure. Procedures indicating success based on group results don't necessarily translate into success for individual learners. Because teachers have heterogeneous groups of students and need to teach each child to read, they need to know what will help every child progress, not just what will increase the class' average. Presently there is a growing body of reading research based on case study approaches and "action research" rather than the formal "scientific method." These studies provide insight into the effectiveness of instructional strategies and materials with individual students, their disadvantage being that they do not always generalize to group situations. However, each study does provide another glimpse into how a child may learn and contributes to enriching the variety of strategies and materials that could be used to meet the diverse abilities and needs of students in a classroom.

Without always realizing it, our beliefs and theories determine our daily interactions and decisions. Far from being "theoretical," they are the basis of our teaching practice. It is essential to know our own beliefs and models and how they influence our decisions. As Adams (1990) points out, "Effective reading instruction depends not only on what one does, but also on the depth and quality of the understanding by which it is guided" (p. 123).

The models of teaching and reading presented in this book will help to examine our beliefs and make sense of the sometimes overwhelming plethora of new ideas and information about reading. To avoid being torn in two by the Great Debate (Phonics vs Whole Word) we need a way to coherently approach decision-making in the classroom. When thinking about and teaching reading, we need to be aware that both a holistic approach and a skills approach can be involved at the same time. This makes sense because when children read, skills are intertwined into a complete process, the success of which depends on the interactions between skills and the effectiveness of each. Paradoxically, once it is realized that there is no one way nor one specific program for teaching reading successfully to all children, the way to teach becomes clear. Rather than continuing to search for *the* answer or *the* program, energy can be focused on learning about reading and how different children learn, and translating that understanding into practice.

Although this book attempts to present models of reading, learning, and teaching that I hope are more open-ended than most, remember that these, too, are only models. Take what is presented and use it to examine current philosophies, ideas, and programs. Then, using the framework that is developed, prove to yourself what really works in the classroom with children.

Research using groups does not always reflect accurately the effects on each individual.

Case study research can provide insight into strategies and materials which may be useful for certain students in a class.

Our beliefs and theories about reading and teaching influence our teaching practice.

Both a holistic and a skills approach can be involved in a classroom reading program.

 Right now my model of reading is . . .

Some Thoughts About Teaching Reading and Reading Programs

Modelling, demonstrating, guiding, facilitating, assisting, encouraging, choosing literature, organizing resources, selecting activities, interacting, instructing, monitoring, assessing, evaluating, reporting, creating an environment, responding, focusing, extending, enhancing, decision-making, interacting with learners.

Or, to put it more simply, teaching is a complex, creative act.

One of the most important aspects of teaching involves establishing a relationship with learners. The nature of this relationship in and of itself is instructive. Teacher as central authority figure — knowing the answers, controlling the tasks, providing positive and negative feedback, applying extrinsic motivation, preparing lessons, organizing learning activities, marking all tasks, evaluating achievements — teaches children that responsibility for learning rests with the teacher who will tell them what to do and when, whether they are right or wrong, clever or stupid, above or below average, good or poor readers.

On the other hand, the teacher who, also as a mentor or facilitator, acknowledges children's needs and interests, personalizes the instruction, encourages students' self-evaluation and reflection about reading, and involves them actively in reading will create a different relationship, with students becoming more actively involved in their own learning.

Another important aspect of teaching is realizing that children do not learn from lessons only what was planned or focused on by the teacher. In fact, they may learn something completely different. We cannot be aware of *everything* they learn. While the teacher is giving a lesson, children may be learning how to avoid answering questions or watching how the teacher and other students behave. (Children often can imitate their teachers with extreme likeness.) They may be deciding that they learn easily, that learning is hard, or that they are not very smart. They may not be interested in the stories they must read and conclude reading is boring. They may misunderstand what is involved in reading and try to sound out words without making sense. They may associate reading with having to answer comprehension questions and, therefore, avoid it whenever possible. This is some of the unplanned learning that may happen. If we are aware of this, we can try to ensure that this incidental, unplanned learning supports, rather than detracts from, the goal of children becoming readers. Thus in planning instruction, we need to focus on more than just the component reading skills as delineated by a logical and hierarchical analysis of reading. We need to be aware of the effect that instruction and nonverbal messages (the hidden curriculum) have on students. We need to observe carefully, talk with children about their understandings, and evaluate their progress on an ongoing basis.

Children will not learn exactly what we want them to learn just because we taught a lesson, motivated them, tried to keep them attentive, had them practice skills, and marked them right or wrong. We do not have control over exactly what each child will learn. However, knowing that active involvement, interest and success are powerful influences, we can structure the environment so that it is conducive to them learning to read. Within that setting a variety of suitable resources, activities, and experiences can be provided from which all children can learn to read in ways suited to their abilities, needs and interests.

Teaching is . . .

The nature of the teacher-student relationship is instructive in and of itself.

We are not aware of everything children learn.

When teaching, I could watch for

_____

_____

_____

_____

_____

Interest, success and active involvement are powerful influences.

Although reading methods and programs have seemingly changed over the years, their basic principles continued to stem from a scientific approach to research greatly influenced by behaviouristic psychology. Much of this research examined curriculum-based and teacher-focused instruction — what should be taught and what teachers should do to control the students' learning. The structure of lessons and behaviours of teachers were studied using a scientific experimental approach. The assumption was that if teachers carefully planned lessons with clear objectives, kept the children's attention, provided enough repetition and external motivation, children would eventually learn the knowledge and skills presented.

By analyzing what excellent teachers did, identifying and isolating activities, and then teaching other teachers to teach similarly, it was thought that better learning results would ensue. This reductionist approach applied to reading also resulted in the development of curricula and programs based on the belief that by analyzing the reading process, a set of basic skills could be identified and taught in a logical, hierarchical fashion to all children at particular ages.

As a result published reading programs included pre-made decisions about reading materials, teaching strategies, student activities, sequenced lessons, organization, motivation strategies, and assessment and evaluation. Inservice and professional development elaborated on these methods and materials, suggesting alternatives or new ideas. Educational authorities reviewed and recommended certain reading programs, thereby, making the decision about what and how to teach. Teachers were expected to use these methods and materials and adapt them, within the prescribed approach, to children in their classes. Educational research examined how children would learn to read best by using these materials and searched for reasons why some children did not learn to read.

As different methods were tried and still some children did not learn, causes of learning failures were ascribed to children's developmental stages, attention problems, learning disabilities, disadvantaged homes, second language deficits, and so on. While these may play some part in reading difficulties, they are not the complete answer.

Each program, it was hoped, would be more successful than the last by addressing what was lacking in other programs or by taking a different point of view (see p. 5). However, because each program tends to suit different styles of learners, none is as successful as hoped when used to teach a whole group of students with different needs and interests. "Within every instructional method studied, there were students who learned to read with thorough success and others who experienced difficulty" (Adams, 1990, p. 10). There is no one program or set of materials that will be suited to all children.

As programs were developed and changed, and leading educators and researchers strongly supported differing and sometimes conflicting points of view, it seemed to the classroom teacher that the pendulum just kept swinging back and forth. Actually, there had not been a fundamental change. Underlying each set of these "new" materials, methods, and programs was a model of learning and teaching that hadn't really shifted. Most continued to be based on a reductionist approach — analyzing the "whole" into constituent parts and reassembling it. The attraction was that in other research areas (such as physics and chemistry), this approach had given rise to a scientific-based technology

Reading methods and programs have seemingly changed over the years; however, their basic principles and goals are much the same.

With every method or program, some students learned to read easily and some had difficulty.

Is this another swing of the pendulum?

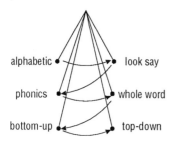

that has seemed to unlock long-standing secrets of the world, producing atomic bombs, computers, hi-tech communication, genetic engineering, and so on. However, the pursuit of this reductionist approach has given way to realizing some of its limits. The more learned about each part (of the whole), the greater the realization that there is, and always will be, more to learn. It is not just simply learning about the parts that's essential but also how they interact to create a functioning whole. For example, it was not just a matter of finding the basic particles that made up an atom. Each new particle, more "basic" than the last, was later found to be made of smaller bits. It was also discovered that some particles seemed to influence others even though a physical connection was not evident. Simply isolating and identifying the parts and putting them together did not make the whole. Rather the relationships between parts defined the parts and the whole. Parts are not separate in a functioning whole.

> Research-based models and programs hoped to identify the basic parts and skills that could be taught.

Although reading methods and materials changed in appearance over the past 70 years, the philosophical and research approach had not. Thus the foundation of teaching reading had not really changed, only its manifestations. Different programs were based on fundamentally the same principles. Minds trained or culturally submerged in a reductionist approach have a "tell me what I can do, so I can fix it" attitude (Briggs & Peat, 1989). The models and programs developed were mostly linear and causal. In dealing with the behaviour of complex systems, such models are unreliable. Forecasts don't emerge. Predictions based on these models don't work well for reading because these reductionist models do not take into account all the dynamic processes and factors involved.

> It is difficult to describe and include the dynamic relationship amongst the parts and between the whole and the parts.

> The models tend to be linear and causal, and are not accurate reflections of the complex reading process.

With complex systems such as learning to read and teaching reading, instructional models and theories need to shift from prediction and control. In teaching reading we cannot seek to control each step for each child. We cannot isolate every skill, monitor it to ensure mastery, and transfer it into daily reading. We cannot identify the precise reason why children can or cannot read easily. Therefore, we need to develop dynamic, nonlinear models that will guide our teaching, with the purpose being to increase our knowledge about teaching reading so we can interact more intuitively, as well as logically, and, therefore, more effectively with children as they become readers.

The changes over the past years are not about shifting from phonics to whole language programs but rather about balancing a quantitative, reductionist view with a qualitative, holistic awareness of the reading process. It is about the focus for instruction shifting from prediction and control of the process to understanding the dynamic interactions involved in learning to read. We will never be absolutely certain about how children learn to read — there are far too many variables. Realizing we cannot know everything (which is the truth of the matter), we need to have the same goal as we have children in our classes, that is, to be risktakers, to continue to learn and to rely on intuition as well as logic. "In interacting with complex dynamic systems we need to be in an experimental mode. This liberates the intellect to expand beyond set beliefs. In education it lets people operate in a learning mode rather than a fix-it mode" (Briggs & Peat, 1989, p. 180), which makes us more effective learners and teachers.

> The changes are not about phonics vs whole language, but rather about balancing a quantitative, reductionist approach with a qualitative, holistic one.

> ✓✗?
>
> I agree/disagree/wonder
>
> _____
>
> _____
>
> _____
>
> _____
>
> _____

It will be difficult to move from an authoritarian, reductionist view if we still hope that eventually experts will find the answers from scientific investigations. It will be difficult to understand holistic complexity and how to help children

There is no one program or way to teach all children to read.

Teaching involves making decisions and, in the end, these are governed by our personal theories and beliefs about reading and teaching.

It is necessary to examine our beliefs and how they affect our teaching.

read if, in the back of our minds, we continue to hope that at some point *the* way to teach reading will be discovered and will be embedded in a program with a teacher guide and a set of books. There is no neat, complete package outlining what to do each week that will be successful with all children. All children are not the same.

Teaching has always involved change and decision-making. With curriculum-based, teacher-centred programs the focus was on how to implement curriculum goals using certain prescribed resources and the current teaching methodologies. With learner-focused programs, we will need to know how to match the learning needs and interests of individuals more closely with materials and methods, and how to make informed decisions about resources, strategies and activities that allow each child to become a successful reader.

The starting point is a reexamination of our beliefs, models and theories about how to teach reading and how children learn to read. We need to realize that even if experts and researchers tell us what materials to use, which strategies to teach, and how to talk and interact with students, in the end our personal theory of learning and teaching governs what we actually do in the classroom. Helping children read, planning what to do, allocating time, organizing resources and activities, interacting with and responding to children, assessing and evaluating and reporting progress — all these are governed by our set of beliefs about learning and how to teach reading. Models of reading are not just theoretical, but, in fact, the most pragmatic aspect of teaching — the foundation of our decisions and actions.

Our beliefs have been moulded from previous experiences (our own schooling, teacher training, teaching children, cultural beliefs, emotional experiences, etc.). Quite often we are not really aware of our beliefs; they are so much a part of us. Because of this, it is difficult to change beliefs personally and culturally. Like habits, they are not in our conscious awareness. Thus, we first need to realize they exist and then be willing to clarify and revise them. Ordinarily, beyond clarifying and stating them, we are reluctant to alter them for we feel they constitute an integral part of ourselves and changing them may be admitting that what we believed in and what we did was wrong. However, living and learning means that our beliefs do change. By necessity they will be modified, extended, and refined as we live, experience the world and interact with others. Without learning and changing, we become nonadaptive, living in a world "constructed" from a limited point of view — a still-life version. We only need to look back through history to find an ample array of beliefs once held to strongly by people and cultures, which in fact now seem very quaint to us today. Thank goodness the world does change, although some would argue that "the good old days" were better.

Over the years we have come to realize that there is no one reading program or method that will be successful with all children in a class or at a certain age. Therefore, we will need to have a framework to assess and evaluate programs and methods in a meaningful way. With each child in mind we will need to examine closely the prevailing beliefs, research and ideas against the backdrop of the classroom reality. Without this reevaluation and subsequent refinement of beliefs, the current push for change will be yet another swing of the pendulum — that is, one set of materials replacing another.

Many questions arise as we move away from a curriculum-based, "reader"-sequenced program. No longer having a sequence of lessons and activities planned out in teacher guides, we are faced with answering these questions ourselves.

- What should we do on Monday?
- When should we refer a child for extra help?
- How can we prevent reading difficulties?
- What can we do to improve reading comprehension?
- How can we be sure every child is learning as quickly as they can?
- What should we do on Tuesday?
- How do we know if the basic skills are being covered?
- What are the basic skills?
- How can we meet different student needs?
- What should we do on Wednesday?
- Which strategy should we try next?
- Which method is best?
- How should we teach phonics?
- What will help this child learn more easily?
- How do we organize for instruction?
- How do we evaluate student progress?
- What are the expectations and standards?
- What should we do on Thursday?
- And what about Friday?

When reading the research literature and attending inservice sessions, we are faced with a dazzling array of "new", "reworked" or "renamed" ideas and teaching strategies, such as:

story maps   repeated reading   bubble thinking
ISL
webbing   literary letters   request   QAR
think alouds
reciprocal teaching   plot profiles   DRTA   graphic organizers
clustering
phonemic awareness   cloze   reading recovery

Do you still want to know what to do on Monday? What about having children respond to reading with drama, what about focusing on decoding skills, and what about teaching predicting as a reading strategy, or the 'Think, Pair, Share" strategy (Fogarty, 1990)? All these strategies and ideas, valuable or not, often seem like a bunch of brainstormed ideas quickly generated and randomly jotted down all over a piece of chart paper. We learn about them and are left wondering how to evaluate their contribution and role in reading instruction.

? Some questions I'd like to have answered

_____

_____

_____

_____

_____

! Other good strategies

_____

_____

_____

_____

_____

This infusion of new strategies is exciting for both teachers and children. It provides variety and alternative ways of learning to read and responding to literature — certainly a great improvement over having children read from a reader one story after another whether they wanted to or not and, after reading, write answers to comprehension questions. The spoonful of sugar to help that medicine go down was "free" time or something "fun" to do once the reading "work" was done. Work first, fun later — what were many children learning about reading?

Without some way to organize all these instructional strategies and the variety of materials and resources, decision-making becomes a difficult, overwhelming and sometimes random task. There is no teacher guide or schematic organization provided to bring these ideas together in a balanced, cohesive program.

How can these strategies, activities, and resources be coordinated in a balanced program?

The framework developed in this book is intended to help sort out, understand and organize newer strategies and resources, and to integrate these with effective techniques and materials already in use. Once developed, this framework needs to be continuously revised as new knowledge and practical experience is acquired from interactions with children on a daily basis and from professional development and reading. With this framework in "mind," effective decisions as to how, what, when, and why can be made confidently and for the benefit of each child in the class.

Instruction then becomes learner-focused, that is more personalized. Instead of using energy and effort to shape children to the curriculum, the same energy and effort can be used to shape instruction around the needs and interests of the children actually in the classroom. There is no doubt which is more rewarding both for the learners and for the teacher.

The foundations of this framework (represented in Figure 2) are based on understanding:

1. **Reading and its Role in Education**

   Why do we need to understand this?

   Six foundations to guide the development and teaching of reading programs.

   – to realize that the goal for learning to read is to be able to use reading as a tool for life-long learning

   – to remind ourselves that difficulty in reading should not stifle children's enthusiasm for learning or their chance for success with learning

   – to remind ourselves that there are many ways to learn

2. **Language and its Role in Reading Acquisition**

   Why do we need to understand this?

   – to remind ourselves that learning to read is closely interrelated with other language/literacy skills

   – to ensure that oral and written language skills develop in tandem with reading

3. **The Learning Process**

   Why do we need to understand this?

   – to identify factors that expand or limit learning and have positive or negative influences on learning to read

   – to identify a variety of ways to present and explain reading strategies

4. **The Reading Process**

Why do we need to understand this?

- to identify components of reading to focus on when helping children read
- to remind ourselves of the complexity of the reading process
- to realize we can't "teach" every specific skill needed in reading
- to guide planning, teaching, assessment and evaluation

5. **Developmental Patterns**

Why do we need to understand this?

- to guide realistic expectations for individual students
- to plan what might be focused on next
- to guide planning, teaching, assessment and evaluation of progress

6. **Individual Variations**

Why do we need to understand this?

- to recognize the role of individual talents, capabilities, interests in learning
- to remind ourselves of the individuality of learners and rates of progress
- to assess what helps an individual best

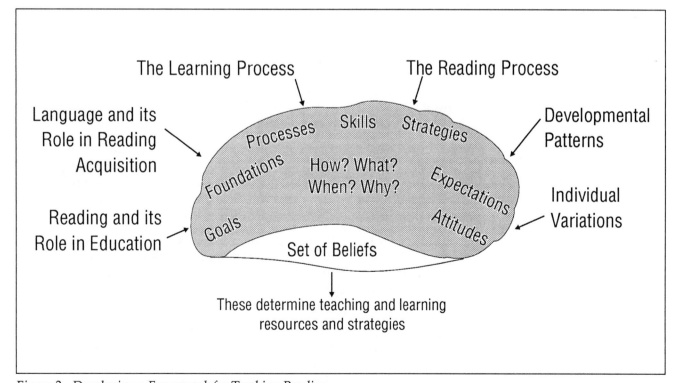

Figure 2. Developing a Framework for Teaching Reading.

Part I: Reading Instruction in the Broader Context

Reading and its Role in Education

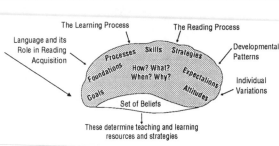

Why do we need to understand this?

- to realize that the goal for learning to read is to be able to use reading as a tool for life-long learning.

- to remind ourselves that difficulty in reading should not stifle children's enthusiasm for learning or their chance for success with learning.

- to remind ourselves that there are many ways to learn.

Learning to read is not a goal in and of itself. The real goal is to be able to use reading as a means of gathering information and ideas. At the same time, it must be acknowledged that reading is only one way of learning and communicating. Much knowledge about the world is obtained from hearing, observing, tasting, smelling, touching and so on. However, reading becomes a high priority in education because much of our culture is focused on and around literacy. In fact, reading has become an essential skill in our literate society and schools, and in the information-processing era.

Because of the heavy emphasis in school on learning to read and using reading to learn, the ease or difficulty and the success or failure of reading acquisition play a major role in defining children's earliest and lasting concepts of themselves as learners. Lack of success or difficulty in learning to read early in school can result in negative attitudes and impede further learning in school.

Where does reading fit into the larger view of life-long education? Why does the educational literature talk about a holistic approach to reading and "integrating reading across the curriculum?" What emphasis should be placed on reading especially for those who have difficulty acquiring the skill in an educational setting? What is the importance of reading?

To answer these questions let's consider a definition of education and how reading fits into that. Education in its broadest sense is a process of learning by experiencing, thinking and communicating (see Figure 3). The main focus of education should be to help people learn ways to think about and understand

---

⭐ Reading is important why? when? for whom? where?

_____

_____

_____

_____

The ultimate goal of learning to read is to be able to use it to acquire information and ideas.

How easily and early children learn to read can influence their concept of self as a learner.

Some questions to consider

experiences, and to act upon and to communicate their understanding and experiences. Education is a process of learning how to interpret, understand and respond to sensory input using both verbal and nonverbal modes; that is, how to use the mind, emotions, and body in concert to analyze, learn from, and respond to experiences (information, ideas, events, etc.).

In the broadest sense, education is learning through and learning about experiencing, thinking and communicating.

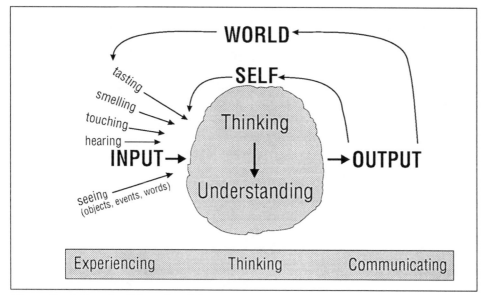

Figure 3. A Broader Educational Context.

The brain is predisposed to making sense out of the complex world in the interests of survival. Sensations from the environment and from within ourselves constantly bombard the body and its nervous system. These are the raw data from which meaning is made. Regardless of whether stimuli are perceived as verbal or nonverbal, or visual, auditory, or kinesthetic, they are actually encoded as electrical and chemical transmissions in the nervous system. From these encoded messages, in a process akin to magic, the brain carries out its function — "thinking." By naming this process thinking, its complexity is often forgotten. In fact, we talk about this very complex process knowing very little about it.

Having taken in sensations and impressions, having "thought" about them (see Figure 4), we then respond verbally and/or nonverbally reflecting back to the world and ourselves our understanding — actions often speaking louder than words. This process is the basis of daily living and learning. In this process, language is a powerful tool for mediating thought and interacting with one's self and others. It is *one* tool for representing objects and events (sensations) and their interrelationships so we can communicate with others and also "talk to ourselves" as we attempt to make sense of and control our environment and life.

Language allows us (a) to benefit from previously accumulated knowledge and vicarious experiences, (b) to mediate our own thinking, and (c) to communicate with others using a common vocabulary. Language has been the dominant mode for learning in school and communication in our society. However, as the model indicates, language (reading, writing, listening, speaking) is not the only way to experience, think and communicate.

The main focus is thinking about experiences and thinking to communicate.

Language, including reading, is a powerful tool for mediating thought.

However, language is not the only way to experience, think,

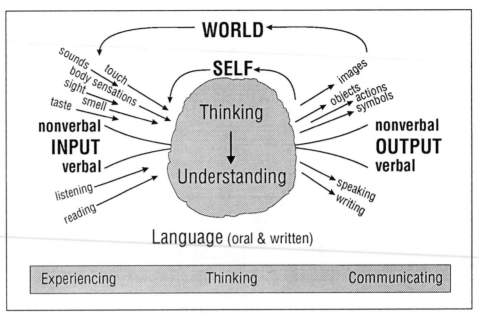

Figure 4. Language is One Aspect of Experiencing, Thinking, and Communicating.

✓✗?
I agree/disagree/wonder

_____

_____

_____

_____

Reading is only one way of
obtaining information.
However, it has become a key
asset because

_____

_____

_____

_____

Nonverbal thinking and intuition are essential as well. In fact many ideas and feelings can only be sensed, thought about, and expressed without words. Many insights have been gained through nonverbal and intuitive thinking and then later associated with language or symbols in order to verify and communicate the thoughts and images. Daily living for all people involves intuition (e.g. being sensitive to others, understanding one's own feelings, solving problems). Education needs to focus on developing both intuitive and nonverbal thinking in addition to logical thinking and language-mediated processes.

Language attempts to represent thoughts and reality using words and only roughly approximates a true understanding of phenomena. Language, in fact, is like a model; it only *re-presents* real meaning. To learn a language is to learn how that language represents meaning. To use the language effectively is to understand its power and its limitations in depicting reality.

In this view of education, reading is only one way of obtaining information, and in fact, second-hand information. However, its advantage over other language and first-hand experiences lies in the fact that meaning is embedded in a form (print) that can be easily produced in multiple copies, stored in books and computers, and transmitted over time without being changed.

Written language is a vehicle for transmitting thoughts over time and space. Knowledge and ideas can be accumulated and built upon over hundreds of years. Therefore, since the invention of the printing press, reading and writing have become dominant means of communicating knowledge and thought. Competency in reading can give members of a society unbiased and full access to a wealth of written knowledge and the power of that information. Books are accessible to everyone; theoretically, if you can read, you can access information. Being able to acquire knowledge and skills throughout one's life contributes to one's success and standard of living. Today in our society, reading is a key asset.

Although accessibility to audio-visual and computer technology for use as learning tools is increasing compared to printed materials, more equipment is required, cost is higher and portability is less. Also reading is faster than listening to a story. At the same time, it needs to be remembered that the kind of information transmitted by writing and reading is different from that of actual experience, speech/conversation, viewing art/drama, listening to music, and so on.

For students who have incredible difficulties in learning to read and, in fact, for all students, we need to remember that listening, viewing, and experiencing are other valid and important ways of obtaining information. While children are in the process of becoming competent readers, we need to ensure they are learning through these modes as well. This is how they learned in early child-hood before they learned to read. In other words, although some children learn to read later than others and, perhaps later than, or not as well as, hoped for, this should not be a barrier for them to continue to learn about language, other subjects, and the world. It is essential that difficulty with reading does not adversely affect their concept of themselves as learners and does not limit their capacity and opportunities to learn in other ways in school.

In summary, reading is one way of obtaining information, albeit an important one in our literate society. However, there are many other ways of learning. These need to be acknowledged and developed as well, often providing the key modes of learning for children with more severe reading difficulties. We need to realize that in reality helping children learn to think and to make sense of the world is the core curriculum and reading is just one way of getting information into the thinking process.

Thinking is central to education, and reading is one way of accessing information and ideas to think about and respond to.

Ways to obtain information/ideas

_____

_____

_____

_____

_____

_____

_____

_____

_____

_____

_____

Ways to communicate information/ideas

_____

_____

_____

_____

_____

_____

_____

_____

_____

_____

_____

Language and its Role in Reading Acquisition

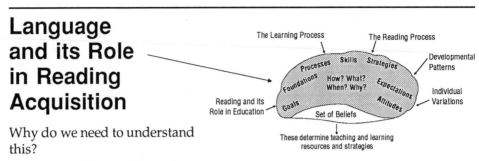

Why do we need to understand this?

- to remind ourselves that learning to read is closely interrelated with other language/literacy skills
- to ensure that oral and written language skills develop in tandem with reading

Figure 5 focuses on the language (verbal) aspects of experiencing, thinking, and communicating. Listening and reading are input modes; speaking and writing, output modes.

Oral language develops as children interact with their environment. They learn to differentiate language from sounds and to communicate meaning by using speech and other (sometimes rather demanding) noises. This learning results from frequent experiences using language while trying to express themselves. Through these meaningful interactions with others, children gradually become more competent in their native tongue. Thinking, which also incorporates nonverbal input and output, again is central to the learning process whether it is focused on language or not. Individual variations in general developmental trends are demonstrated as children learn to associate objects and events with words and to interpret their relationships through language. By the time they become aware of print in the environment, children are using oral language with varying degrees of sophistication.

In the preschool years many children begin to read and write. In a process similar to how they learned to understand speech and to talk, these children

Children's competency with oral language develops as they interact with others.

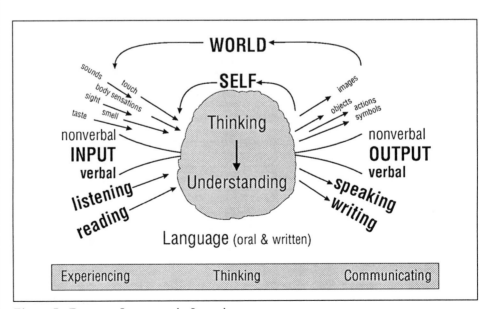

Figure 5. Focus on Language in Learning.

have had many opportunities to interact with print. Engaging in reading and writing activities and pursuing them with interest, they have asked questions and received answers. Their familiarity with the sounds and the structure and function of language provided the foundations upon which they could continuously build their understanding of written language. Their environment provided materials and assistance; their inherent capabilities facilitated the learning.

Some children learn to read later than others; however, it does not necessarily mean that they have learning difficulties or are slow learners. It may be that they have not had the many opportunities to learn about language that other children have had. The more experience and competency with oral language, the more support it gives to the process of learning to read and write. Expecting all children to read at about the same age implies that we expect they have had similar opportunities to interact with language and have similar capabilities to benefit from those opportunities. Children may take longer to learn to read because they have had less exposure to and fewer opportunities to use oral language and explore written language. There are also individual differences based on each child's unique physiological, psychological, and cognitive capacities.

In learning to read, oral language acts as a scaffold, making the task easier (see Figure 6). For example, words in print can be related to spoken words and the meanings associated with them from personal experiences; the sequence of printed words can be related to the structure of speech. Since speech patterns differ from those in written language, reading literature out loud to children helps them become familiar with written language patterns. Just as they learned to understand and structure oral language by listening, responding and receiving feedback, they also can assimilate the syntax of literature through listening and discussing it with others. Later when beginning to read, they can use what they have learned aurally to help them predict the syntax of written text.

 I have noticed that early readers . . .

_____

_____

_____

_____

_____

Oral language provides a scaffold for learning to read — words in print can be related to spoken words and their meanings.

Stories read aloud provide models of written language patterns and structures.

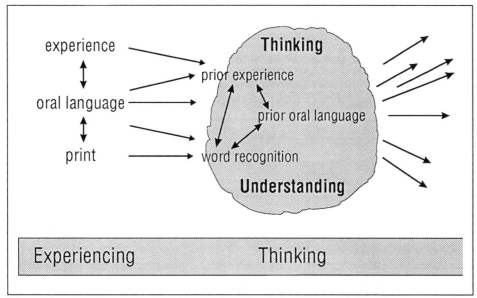

Figure 6. Learning to Read: Associating Words in Print with Oral language and Prior Experience.

Thus long before being able to read independently, children are learning how to understand literature. By reading literature to children and discussing ideas and strategies, children learn comprehension strategies and ways to communicate their understanding of a text they cannot even read.

Oral language and experiences are key foundations for reading.

Through life experiences children learn about things and events along with the associated vocabulary and patterns of thinking. When print is read to them, they use these experiences and language background to help them understand. Eventually when reading by themselves, the strategies and knowledge already acquired can be utilized. Thus other aspects of language are interrelated with reading acquisition. Reading, both recognizing words and generating meaning, is more difficult without this previous experiential knowledge and oral language.

Reading-Writing Connections

✓ Reading-Writing similarities

Learning to read can be facilitated and enhanced by learning to write and vice versa. It's not a matter of one happening before the other, but the fact that both deal with the written form of language — reading is recognizing meaning from words in print, writing is generating meaning with printed words. Knowledge about one process helps with learning the other. For example, knowledge of the relationships between letter patterns and sounds is necessary for both spelling and decoding (reading) words.

When listening to or reading literature, children are also learning about the structure and forms of written language. Each text, either heard or read, provides a model of the different elements which contribute to effective writing, including descriptive language, powerful vocabulary, purpose, voice, style, structure and forms of writing, syntax, punctuation, spelling, and so on (see Figure 7).

✗ Reading-Writing differences

An instructional emphasis on integrating reading, writing, listening, and speaking is really just a recognition of the natural connections between these language processes. In reality these are mutually supportive and cannot be separated, no matter how separately curricula and lessons treat them. For example, consider spelling and learning to decode words. Both of these involve understanding the relation between sounds and print. As letter/sound relationships are learned to help with spelling, it can be pointed out that they will also help with decoding words. Young children become aware of words in print both through learning to read (matching spoken words to print) and to write (constructed spelling). In fact much of the sense and ease of learning is lost by teaching decoding and spelling separately.

Direct teaching of spelling and phonics can be integrated into reading and writing lessons and activities.

Integrating phonics and spelling into writing and reading programs does not mean that they are never taught directly. Rather integration of phonics and spelling means ensuring students see the connections between these skills and learn by using them both in reading and writing activities. That is, lessons may focus directly on graphophonics relationships, and explicitly discuss example words. At the same time, these phonics patterns are also used in reading and writing activities occurring in the classroom. However, rather than using prepared programs, phonics workbooks, and spelling texts to structure the lessons, more active ways can be incorporated to help children make connections between reading and writing and internalize phonics. To do this effectively we must know what can be taught and the general developmental and structural sequence. This information was embedded in traditional reading and spelling

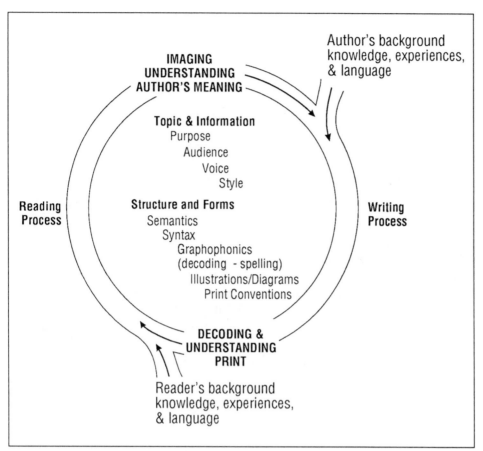

Figure 7. Reading-Writing Connections.

programs; it was the basis of their scope and sequence of skills. However, when traditional programs are not used, we need to have on hand ourselves the information needed to guide learner-focused programs incorporating a variety of resources and active learning strategies. The intent of the following chapters is to provide such information for reading (for spelling, see Tarasoff, 1990, 1992).

Current emphasis on teaching "integrated language arts" is a recognition of the learning about language and language use that has always occurred during any activity involving language. For example, when reading a story to children, they are in fact learning not one or two skills, but many aspects of language simultaneously. They are learning about story structure, meaning of words, pronunciation of words, reading comprehension, illustrations, plot, and so on. There are strong reading and writing connections whether or not a "holistic" approach is advocated. This trend towards acknowledging the interrelationships and integrating reading, writing, listening and speaking curricula makes sense. All forms of language are extremely important foundations for reading acquisition.

Integrating language arts with content areas is a recognition of the natural connections between learning through experiences and through language.

The Learning Process

Why do we need to understand this?

- to identify factors that enhance or limit learning and have positive or negative influences on learning to read

- to identify a variety of ways to present and explain reading strategies

The Oxford dictionary defines learning as "knowledge, understanding, skills, behaviours as a result of experience, study or instruction." But how does learning actually occur? In the early 1900s, the brain was thought of as a "black box." Behaviourists concerned themselves with trying to predict the relationships between input and output. There was no way of knowing what went on in this so-called "black box." Since the 1950s great advances have been made in our understanding of the brain, recognizing at the same time there is a vast amount that we still don't know. We have literally only scratched the surface. Theories have been proposed about differences in left and right brain functioning, different kinds and locations of memories, different areas of brain specialization, and so on. New techniques and equipment are giving us a peek into the brain. Undoubtedly models of brain function will continue to undergo radical transformations.

In using some of the current models of learning and brain functioning, we must remind ourselves that more is unknown than known. As well, whatever is expressed in terms that nonspecialists can understand is a gross simplification of how the brain really works. In applying these theories we must therefore exercise caution.

> The frontier of the brain is a vast territory and explorers have only begun to wind their way into the wilderness. Brain models shift in popularity with the frequency of rock stars, and it's likely that in a hundred years' time the current maps of the neurophysiological land-scape will look as quaint as the sixteenth century charts of the New World. But a map has to start some place and among the map makers is a growing number of scientists attempting to sketch in the big picture. (Briggs & Peat, 1989, p. 168)

Much of our learning occurs without us being aware, for example, walking, talking, habits, attitudes, beliefs. Actually most of what we know and do has been learned without self-awareness. Only in making efforts to observe and reflect on our learning (metacognition) can we become more aware of how we learn (see Figure 8). In thinking about the learning process, we begin to realize that some learning occurs through imitation without conscious attention, some requires focused attention, some needs repeated practice to gain mastery, and still other learning happens instantly and indelibly the first time (especially that associated with a high level of emotion, interest, or pain — remember that embarrassing moment when you . . . ? You only need to step on the end of a rake once. . .).

Over the past 50 years our understanding of the brain's functioning and role in learning has greatly increased. However, there is still much to be learned.

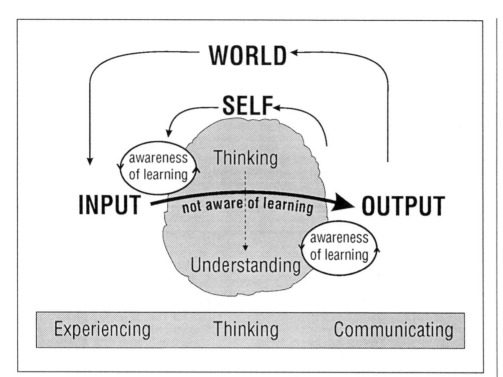

Figure 8. Learning and Metacognitive Awareness.

Few of us can remember exactly how we learned to read, although we usually remember the emotional flavour of the process. As a result we cannot rely on our own experience to help us understand how children learn to read. Perceptive observations of children as they read and conferences with them about what they understand and what they are doing can give us some hints if we know what to look for. However, our knowledge and beliefs about reading can limit our vision. We may not know what questions to ask and what to observe, or how to interpret the answers and observations. Conferencing with children will provide only some answers because children are not aware of how they read nor do they have the vocabulary and understanding necessary to describe how they learn. Also, because of the complexity and interactive nature of the reading process, all the components and intricate interactions cannot be observed or described. There are too many aspects and relationships, and many have no detectable signs.

How do we know what to observe and talk about with children? How do we know what to examine in the classroom environment and in our teaching activities? Knowing about the current theories of learning and reading is a starting point.

Since learning refers to acquiring, retrieving and understanding knowledge and to using new skills and behaviours, assessing learning involves not just asking children what they know and what they understand, but also observing their attitudes and use of skills and strategies (their behaviours). Analyzing these observations helps identify the learning that children themselves are not aware of and the learning that cannot be easily and empirically measured.

Many things are "learned" by the brain and embedded in our memory without us realizing it. Some are more obvious and when brought to a conscious level

---

Usually we are not aware of everything we learn and how we learn.

How do we know what to notice and assess in order to understand how children learn?

Assessing learning involves not just finding out what children know and understand, but also observing their attitudes and behaviours.

can be identified and described (e.g. facts, songs). Other memories, however, are "trapped" in the brain, reflected by our beliefs and behaviours or retrievable only with focus, attention and effort. (Surgical studies of brain function using direct electrical stimulation of brain cells indicate that memories we thought were long forgotten are stored in the brain but are not retrievable by usual means.) All these levels of learning occur simultaneously and affect our daily processing of information and consequently our behaviour and potential for further learning. Memory is the key to learning. Learning has not taken placed if some knowledge, skill, strategy or attitude is not "remembered" in some way. Some researchers have conceptualized the memory process using terms such as iconic, short term, and long term. Long term memory is further categorized into semantic, episodic, and procedural (see Figure 9).

Memory is key to learning.

One model of the memory process describes different aspects of the memory process

The term *iconic* refers to short-lasting images produced by the reception of sensations (e.g. a word is "seen" by the eye or "heard" by the ear and that image lasts for a short time as a nerve impulse). For example, when you don't "quite hear" what someone said and you ask "What did you say?", if they don't immediately reply, often it seems as if you can actually "hear" an echo of the words and you realize that you do know what they said. Then, the sensation quickly disappears.

iconic memory

The concept of *short term memory* is used to explain why some sensations are remembered for a short time and then forgotten, such as remembering a phone number long enough to use it. Remembering new information requires active processing, such as repeating it, actively trying to visualize it, or some other way of directing attention to it. Once the active effort stops, the information is forgotten.

short-term memory

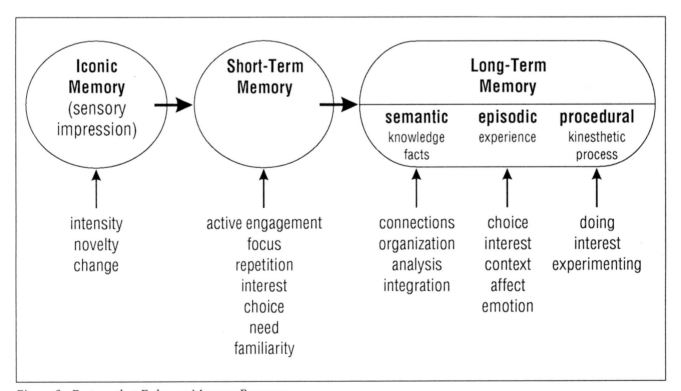

Figure 9. Factors that Enhance Memory Processes.

Through greater attention and active processing, information and skills are stored in what is called *long term memory*. This memory has been categorized into three kinds:

(a) semantic (knowledge — e.g. recognizing words, meanings),

(b) episodic (information and images linked to events and personal experiences or emotions — e.g. learning words with personal meaning, such as birthday, Christmas, mom, dad), and

(c) procedural (complex motor patterns controlling actions and processes — e.g. oral reading, eye movements during reading).

The process of learning (remembering) involves encoding and retrieving images (auditory, visual, kinesthetic, tactile, tastes and smells). The brain encodes sensations and retrieves "memories" with and without our conscious attempts. Through this process referred to as "thinking," meaning is created, new information added, and understandings and skills modified or reinforced. "Thinking" is a word to denote what happens in the brain.

There is no linear hierarchy of skills or strategies for thinking; many processes happen simultaneously. The labels used in this model (Marzano et al., see Figures 10 and 10a) to describe the thinking process are only attempts to explain in words how meaning is generated. Note that the skills listed are similar to those often referred to as comprehension skills and are the basis of reading strategies and activities. Many other words are also used. "Higher Level Thinking Skills" programs have their own terminology. Lists of words have been generated and categorized into higher and lower level skills for reading comprehension or thinking-skills programs (e.g. Bloom's taxonomy). However, if the purpose of identifying "thinking skills" is solely to teach them, they can easily just become the categories and concepts of a reductionist approach. As Smith (1990) points out in his book, *To Think*, thinking cannot be taught. The brain's function *is* to think. Nothing can stop it. From day one children use what we categorize as

Margin notes:

long-term memory

semantic
episodic
procedural

Thinking is a word to denote what happens in the brain.

Thinking skills have been categorized in different ways.

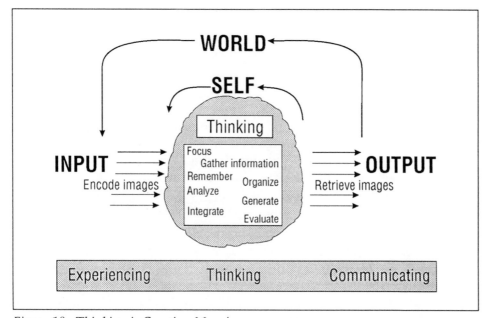

Figure 10. Thinking is Creating Meaning.

Many of the words used to describe thinking skills in Marzano et al.'s model are similar to those used for reading comprehension skills.

Thinking Skills

  Focusing Skills

    Defining Problems   Setting Goals

  Information Gathering Skills

    Observing   Formulating Questions

  Remembering Skills

    Encoding   Recalling

  Organizing Skills

    Comparing   Classifying

    Ordering   Representing

  Analyzing Skills

    Identifying Attributes   Identifying Relationships

    and Components   and Patterns

    Identifying Main Ideas   Identifying Errors

  Generating Skills

    Inferring   Predicting   Elaborating

  Integrating Skills

    Summarizing   Restructuring

  Evaluating Skills

    Establishing Criteria   Verifying

  Source: Marzano et al.

Figure 10a. Thinking Skills.

"higher" and "lower" level thinking skills. They can evaluate, assimilate, analyze, generalize and integrate ideas. How else do they know how to get what they need and want? (A fact that parents will quickly attest to.)

We cannot teach the brain to think any more than we teach the eyes to see, or the stomach to digest. However, we can learn to influence thinking by deciding what to focus on and how to interact with the process as it occurs. We can learn to become more aware of our thinking and use certain kinds of logic or approaches. For example, when looking at an object we can learn to notice different shadows and textures rather than looking to identify it (aesthetic or scientific frames of reference). When solving problems we can become aware of an intuitive process — gathering information, focusing on the problem, attempting to solve it, and then leaving it, knowing that often later when least expecting it, solutions "pop" into the mind.

We cannot teach the brain to think, but we can learn to influence thinking.

Thus what children need to learn is how to use language to mediate, create and clarify thoughts. They need to learn to approach different domains of knowledge with both nonverbal and verbal strategies of thinking and various frames of reference, and to use oral and written language to think about and represent different ideas and problems. Education in different subject areas (e.g. science, social sciences, history, fine arts) helps students develop different thought patterns and frameworks for thinking, and different perspectives and beliefs with which to approach learning and living in the world.

The "thinking skills" in this model (see Figure 10) are meant to be used as a reference to plan instruction and activities focusing on thinking about reading and strategies, rather than as topics or skills to be taught one by one in lessons. This framework is a reminder of the kinds of thinking patterns to ensure they are incorporated into a balanced program focusing on active reading.

Using these models of memory and thinking (combined in Figure 11), we can begin to examine the process of learning to read. In learning to read, children learn to associate print with meaning from previous and concurrent learning. As the eye focuses on print, visual sensations are transformed into electrical and chemical signals that travel to the brain. Other sensations occurring concurrently with learning to read can become paired with the learning experience (in episodic memory) and enhance or detract from it (e.g. success or failure, embarrassment, enjoyment of the activities).

To process information during reading, these sensations must first be attended to and then remembered. Sensations (images from print) are received in what is called the iconic memory. Attention directed to these sensations will increase the chance of them being processed into short term memory. Attention can be enhanced by creating a "set," or expectation (see p. 92). For example, having a question about or an interest in a subject will focus attention on certain aspects and thus determine what will be learned. Once this input is received, it needs to be processed by the short term memory, which can be enhanced by:

(a) familiarity (making connections with prior knowledge/skills),

(b) active engagement (such as repeating or using the information needed, daily reading),

> The models of memory and thinking skills can help us examine our beliefs about learning and the reading process.

> Reading and memory

> Directing attention influences what is remembered.

> Memory is facilitated by
>   familiarity
>   active engagement
>   interest/need
>   unusualness/novelty
>   meaning

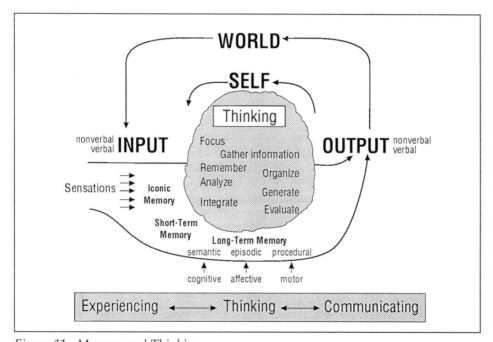

Figure 11. Memory and Thinking.

Notes about types of memory and reading knowledge, skills and strategies

_____

_____

_____

_____

_____

_____

_____

_____

_____

_____

_____

_____

_____

_____

_____

_____

_____

(c) interest or need (activated by creating purpose, set, asking questions, allowing choice), and

(d) attraction to unusual, different, or meaningful parts.

Semantic memory, one aspect of long term memory, is enhanced through associating new with prior knowledge, connecting with an interest, and fulfilling a purpose or need. Some experiments on memory in the early 1900s focused on learning syllables. This research indicated that if people could make sense of the syllables or relate them to each other, they were easier to recall. Researchers felt that this was not really studying "memory" since subjects were using prior knowledge which was a factor difficult to control experimentally. So they constructed a learning task in which the material could not make sense — the subjects were asked to remember nonsense syllables. This gave rise to learning and forgetting curves indicating the number of repetitions needed to learn and not forget *nonsense* syllables. These results influenced educational models of learning which suggested that repetition and drill was essential in learning. The crucial observation that was not given due consideration at the time is that learning is easier and more permanent when the material makes sense and can be related to prior knowledge and skills. Learning syllables in which connections can be made is easier and requires less repetition than nonsense syllable learning. We all have personal examples of "one-shot" learning in our own lives; it does not always take 10-20 repetitions to learn everything. The current focus on integrating curricula, accessing prior knowledge before learning, and building on what children already know is based on these observations and does make sense.

Of all the myriad sensations impacting simultaneously on the brain, those that are changing, those that are unusual, and those that are meaningful are attended to. We are not aware of all these sensations and the choices made by the brain. However, making efforts to attend to certain things increases the success of learning. Situations affecting our emotions and our safety tend to enhance our awareness and memory whether we intend it or not. A near accident needs to only happen once for you to never forget it.

Personal experiences and their associated emotions have a direct and strong impact on memory, referred to as *episodic* memory. Pleasant and unpleasant events may be easily and vividly remembered. Successful experiences encourage and stimulate further learning; embarrassment and failure can limit it. Learning to read will more likely be pursued if children are interested and experience success.

Procedural memory is enhanced by doing, experiencing, moving, and using processes, thus enabling the kinesthetic patterns to become engrained and performed automatically and smoothly. Certain procedural aspects of reading can be improved by reading more often, just as handwriting and typing become easier and faster with use, and running improves by running, and tennis improves with practice. Focusing on certain procedures and attempting to modify and learn new strategies does lead to improvement. In reading we need to distinguish which skills have more of a procedural component, and those that have more cognitive (semantic) or affective (episodic) components. The approach to teaching these will differ. Is learning phonics (letter/sound relationships) a procedural task (requiring repetition and practice) or a semantic task (needing understanding)? How can the concept of episodic memory be used in helping children learn to read? — perhaps by providing for student choice, interests, and enjoyment.

Assessing and evaluating children's reading ability or progress involves observing what children do while reading, talking with them about their understanding and their reading strategies, and observing their assimilation of ideas and knowledge extracted from reading. We must infer much of this because understanding is constructed within the brain.

When assessing and evaluating reading comprehension, we need to distinguish between competency in comprehension and in communicating that understanding (see Figure 12 and Appendix H). Children may have an understanding of the text, but their writing skills may not be competent enough to thoroughly demonstrate it (e.g. children who read at a very young age, children with physical handicaps). To truly assess reading comprehension, a variety of ways must be used to ensure children demonstrate their real understanding. Standardized reading tests provide only partial information about a child's reading competency because they focus only on certain aspects of reading and use short written or multiple choice answers to reflect their understanding. Measuring comprehension through written answers to questions focuses on writing ability, not necessarily understanding. More accurate assessments and evaluations of reading and comprehension can be obtained by providing alternative ways, both verbal and nonverbal, for children to demonstrate their reading strategies and understanding (see Figure 13 and Assessing and Evaluating Reading, pp. 96-110).

In summary, knowing more about memory and thinking processes and connecting these to learning to read helps us identify factors that will enhance or limit children's progress. The importance of choice and interest, active engagement, variety of strategies, making connections with prior knowledge and personal experiences, reading meaningful texts, and so on becomes evident and demands consideration in planning and teaching reading. These provide guidelines for making decisions about teaching strategies, learning activities, resources and students' involvement in their own learning.

Assessing and evaluating children's reading

Knowing about learning and thinking processes helps identify factors that enhance or limit children's reading progress and provides guidelines for teaching and evaluating.

Figure 12. Ways to Communicate Understanding.

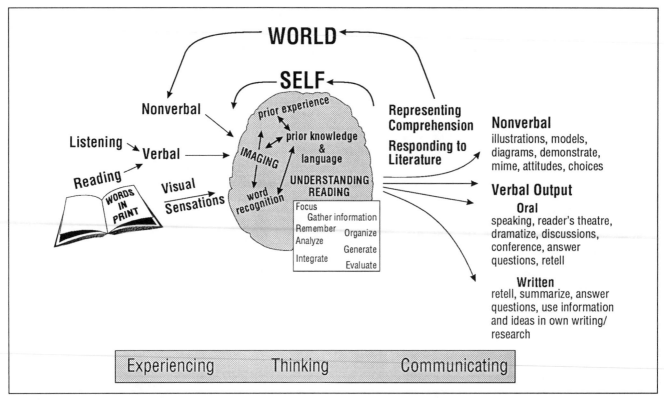

Figure 13. Some Ways to Demonstrate Reading Strategies and Comprehension.

The Reading Process

Why do we need to understand this?

- to identify components of reading to focus on when helping children read
- to remind ourselves of the complexity of the reading process
- to realize we can't "teach" every specific skill needed in reading
- to guide planning, teaching, assessment, and evaluation

It is difficult to describe the reading process fully because of its complexity and because we really do not know exactly how it happens. However, by observing and conferencing with children who are learning to read, by reflecting on our own experiences, and by analyzing the process, we can identify some important strategies and components. These can then be included in a cohesive framework that includes an understanding of how children learn. This can provide guidance for how, what, why and when to teach, assess and evaluate.

A model of the reading process establishes the framework for making sense of, and knowing how to use, the myriad of reading programs, materials, strategies, and teaching suggestions. It guides the utilization of energy and time in the most effective direction. It is a starting point for focusing on students learning to read rather than on following a prescribed reading program. It becomes the "teacher's guide" that can be kept "in mind" for easy reference and revision as current knowledge and experiences dictate.

Teaching is an active decision-making process. The purpose of developing a reading model is to aid in deciding what works, what needs changing, and which strategies, resources, and programs will be appropriate for children. Far from being theoretical, developing a model of the reading process is a very practical approach to "What to teach on Monday" or any day of the week for that matter. A model attempts to highlight key aspects of a system and indicate intrinsic relationships. If a system being studied is simple and linear, models can be used fairly successfully to predict or approximate outcomes. In complex, nonlinear systems, the rate of success is less impressive since all the factors and their relationships are intricately interwoven, and many cannot even be identified. Because reading is a complex, active process, a model cannot prescribe exactly what to do.

In any complex process, such as learning to read, there are many components which interact — some being the procedures, knowledge, and understandings about reading, and others being the environment, physiology, psychology and cognition of the individual. Bottom-up (skills-based) models attempt to identify and isolate reading skills and then synthesize them into what appears to be a logical hierarchy: letter/sound relationships, synthesis of letters into words, words into phrases, phrases into sentences and so on until meaning is perceived. From a superficial point of view this seems to describe reading. The implication of these models for reading instruction is that beginning readers need to focus on

A model of the reading process can provide guidance for how, what, why and when to teach different reading knowledge and skills.

Models highlight certain key aspects and their inter-relationships. However, as with all complex processes, models are not comprehensive.

Bottom-up (skills-based) models

31

the recognition of words, with emphasis on phonics and structural analysis as main word identification strategies. Activities for skill development might include flash cards, readers with controlled vocabulary, skill-focused worksheets, and unrehearsed oral reading.

Top-down (holistic) models

Top-down (holistic) models view reading as a constructive process beginning with the reader's prior knowledge and experience. Words are recognized and meaning constructed by the interaction of prior knowledge (language and the topic) and the visual clues from the text. Word recognition, using the least amount of energy and time, relies on the reader's ability to use meaning and phonics to recognize words, predict subsequent text, and confirm meaning and accuracy. The implication of these models for teaching beginning readers is that reading skills, such as word recognition, should be taught using intact, meaningful texts. The top-down models suggest that if children understand that reading is meaningful and enjoyable, they will more likely be able to make sense of specific strategies, knowledge and skills. This is analogous to learning a game. Knowing the overall "game plan" and goals of a game makes it easier to remember the rules and strategies.

The "Great Debate" focuses on which method should be given emphasis in learning to read — but really there is no debate, both points of view have valid contributions to understanding reading.

The "Great Debate" (Chall, 1983, 1992/93: Goodman, 1992/93) focuses on which method should be given *emphasis* in the beginning stages of learning to read — the making of meaning (Top-Down, Holistic, Whole Language) or the decoding of print (Bottom-Up, Skill Based, Phonics). The problem with the debate is that there really is no debate. Both points of view have valid contributions to understanding reading instruction. There is no *either/or* method for teaching any complex process to a variety of learners. And there is no one correct method. Each method is based on beliefs and principles about reading, and activities are developed without familiarity with the students who may eventually be subjected to them. One method cannot meet the individual needs of all students in a class nor the needs of a particular student as he or she progresses. At all times in developing reading competency, both word identification and meaning play important roles, although the emphasis may shift back and forth from one to the other at different stages of development. Perhaps the discussion should centre on *when* the shifts in emphasis occur for different children and what the effective instructional methods are for focusing on phonics and on meaning.

✓✗?

I agree/disagree/wonder:

_____

_____

_____

_____

_____

_____

Top-down and bottom-up models present different views of the same process, each emphasizing different aspects of reading. As teachers we need to look beyond dichotomous representations of complex processes. We need to view reading from many perspectives simultaneously and particularly from that of the learners in classrooms. It really doesn't matter if some current educational specialists claim that phonics is the first thing children need to learn in order to read if a child is not progressing with that strategy. It doesn't matter if Whole Language proponents emphasize that phonics be taught within the context of a story, if the child is not beginning to read with that approach.

Given a classroom of 20 to 30 children, teachers need to be able to decide, within a manageable system, how to facilitate each child's learning and attend to the wide range of learning styles and capabilities. There are many instructional alternatives beyond (a) choosing one program for the class and perhaps varying the pace for different reading groups, or (b) trying to manage and teach 30 different individual programs. Likewise there are many variations in reading models between the Bottom-Up and Top-Down models. One program or model will not be appropriate for all children even if presented at different rates nor be suitable for one child from prereading through emergent to competent reading. At the same time 20–30 different programs, one for each child, is very difficult for one teacher to manage effectively.

Rather than starting with programs that can be modified or individualized, effective reading instruction in classrooms needs to begin with structuring an overall environment which encourages children to engage eagerly in experiences, and in language and literacy interactions, building on their successes and focusing on progress. Within this active setting, rich in language and experiences, different reading strategies can be presented using a variety of reading materials matched to the interests and needs of the children (groups, individuals, whole class). In whole class activities, learning can be "personalized." Specific needs (interests, abilities, learning styles) can be accommodated through activities which are open-ended and encourage a variety of responses, and thereby provide a range of challenges and learning experiences (discussed in Part II: Reading Instruction in the Classroom).

Reading is one source of sensory information which the brain receives and uses. It differs from listening to a story in that visual clues (the print) rather than sounds trigger and interact with the thinking process. Therefore, learning to read involves developing fluency and accuracy in word identification. The words, once identified, are connected with previously stored knowledge of written language, oral language and prior life experiences in order to make meaning. This process is called reading comprehension but, in fact, it is thinking (stimulated by printed words). Other sensory clues (verbal and nonverbal, and visual, auditory, kinesthetic/tactile, etc.) are part of the same thinking process. What is learned from these other sources of input (prior or background knowledge) is also associated with the input from reading. Learning to read involves learning to make the associations between print and accumulated knowledge/images stored in the brain, adding to and modifying them in the process (see Figures 14 and 15, note similarities between reading and listening).

Predicting and confirming meaning based on previous knowledge and experience (that is, thinking while reading) decreases the dependency on print clues. Nevertheless, the graphic clues are essential for reading accurately. Words must be correctly identified and this decoding process needs to become automatic. Competent reading can be described as a dynamic interaction between print and nonprint clues as the reader self-monitors the process for meaning. In other words, as words are recognized, thinking must occur, just as it does when we listen to a story or discussion, or carry out a physical task.

Children possess varying degrees of reading competency from novice to expert. Each time children read, they learn more about how to read as well as learning from what is read. Reading competency develops by building upon previous experiences. As described in the learning model, what makes sense or is somewhat familiar is easier to learn (see pp. 22-30). As well with each reading experience, fluency (ease of using mechanical processes and reading strategies — procedural memory) increases as does the familiarity with words and written language structures (semantic memory). The more familiar the words and procedures of reading, the more attention can be focused on understanding the text and learning from it.

In teaching reading I think it is important to include

_____

_____

_____

_____

_____

Reading differs from listening in that visual sensations from print, rather than auditory sensations, must be associated with meaning — word identification skills are essential.

Reading and listening are similar in that the same thinking skills process the language to construct meaning.

Automaticity in recognizing words allows more attention to be focused on understanding while reading.

LaBerge and Samuels' (1985) concept of automaticity emphasizes the importance of being able to identify words automatically so that most attention can be focused on thinking about what is read. This is analogous to automatically recognizing the sounds of words when listening (see Figure 15) with the result that thinking can focus on understanding the speaker's meaning rather than perceiving the words. If many new or unfamiliar words are heard, understanding is more difficult because attention needs to shift to recognizing new words and searching for meaning. Competent readers know how to shift their attention back and forth between print clues and thinking. They achieve a degree of automaticity not only in word recognition as suggested by LaBerge and Samuels, but also in shifting between strategies.

Competent readers shift their attention between print clues and thinking. They also gain automaticity in word recognition and in using strategies flexibly.

As is often said, reading is more than recognizing words (although this is an essential component). It also involves understanding the meaning of the words, phrases, sentences, paragraphs and whole texts as intended by the author. This process of understanding print (reading comprehension) is related to the same verbal and nonverbal thinking processes by which we create all meaning in our lives. Understanding of what we read, hear, and see occurs in the brain. All prior verbal and nonverbal information is accessed and influences the

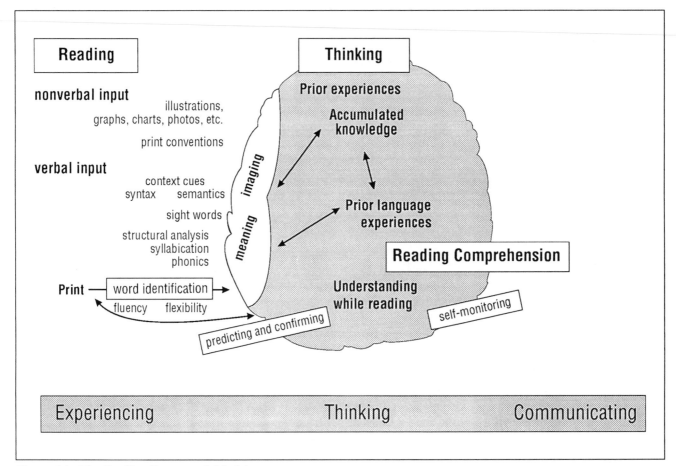

Figure 14. The Reading Process: A Model

interpretation. While listening to stories, children also learn about the structure of written language and story grammar. By speaking they learn about the sounds of words, their meanings, how to construct language. By writing stories they learn about story structure, organization, syntax, semantics, phonics, decoding skills, and so on. All that is learned in these other activities is accessed during reading and contributes to their developing reading competency. Integrating Language Arts instruction, therefore, makes sense because previous learning is accessed whether we are listening, reading, or experiencing. If we attempt to identify all that is taught, intentionally and unintentionally, in one lesson, we begin to realize that reading comprehension is being taught even when we are not actually teaching what traditionally has been called "reading comprehension skills." For example, children listening to a story are learning about life experiences, the world, and concepts; about oral language and literature; and about how to understand and respond. Without actually reading, they can learn strategies for understanding literature which they will use later as they read.

Ways that I think teaching reading and science (for example) are connected:

_____

_____

_____

_____

_____

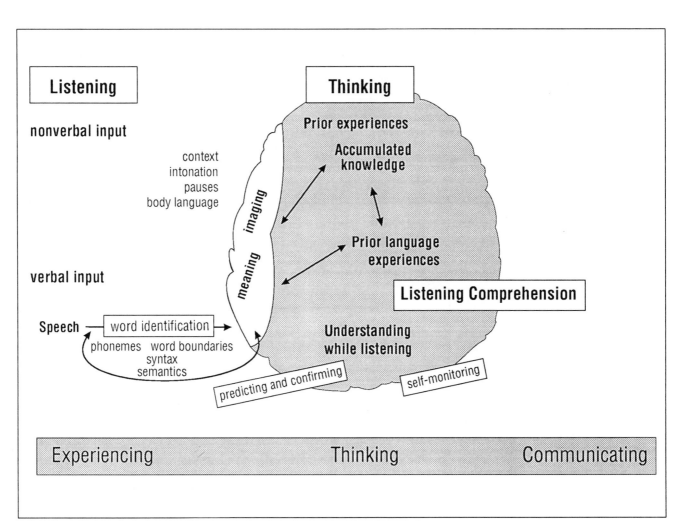

Figure 15. Listening (note processes similar to Reading).

Role of phonics

Initially, using what they know about language and print, children attend to the more general aspects of reading. With each experience, their understanding increases and they are able to attend to more detailed aspects of reading. Since reading, by definition, does involve interpreting *print*, children do need to focus on phonics clues, and use them effectively and fluently. This is not to say that phonics is the only strategy that is used. When used alone, sounding out words is a slow and tiring process. On the other hand, without using graphophonic clues, children are left to guess the words. If children are unable to easily decode new words and unfamiliar words, they will be limited in their scope of reading, detracting from the ultimate goal which is to be able to learn new information and new words from the text.

Phonics clues are thus helpful in recognizing words but are most effective when used along with context clues in an active process of making meaning. In beginning reading, children cannot recognize many words by sight (just from graphic clues). Thus they are limited to using picture clues and relying on what they remember from a story read to them. Children often begin to read by "imitating reading" using stories they have heard many times or stories with a predictable pattern or repetitive phrases and by recognizing one or two words from memory. By doing this "memory reading," they have opportunities to learn about certain aspects of the printed text without having to decode or recognize every word. "Memory reading" and predictable pattern books support the beginning reading process in a similar way that background knowledge, prior experience, and context clues support the reading of more experienced readers. Frequent experiences matching the memorized words with the print and many writing experiences are necessary for children to gain knowledge about phonics and to develop a bank of sight words. As children develop an expanding sight word vocabulary and are able to use context clues and phonics more effectively, there is less need for previous exposure and memory, and less need for predictable, repetitive, or familiar language.

Role of memory reading

Some children seem to easily learn sight words and use graphophonic clues along with context clues. These children progress quickly from memory and supported reading to independence. However, some children do not move easily to independence without specific help focused on phonics, sight words, and/or context clues. Without focused instruction they seem to become stalled in their early reading development.

In my class I have noticed

_____

_____

_____

_____

_____

Thus it is not a matter of which side of the "Great Debate" will be upheld as *the* way. The real question is what knowledge and strategies need to be focused on, and when and how for different children. Not all children need to focus on the same components and strategies in the same way; it will depend on their individual capabilities and previous experiences.

The model of reading presented in this book depicts a close relationship between reading, thinking, oral and written language development, and life experiences. To help children learn to read, this model points out the need for all children to be in an environment rich in experiences, oral language, and print. Children need some opportunities to choose their own reading material, to read for their own purposes, and to read meaningful texts. Some children will need more specific instruction focusing on phonics and context clues or on recognizing words by sight. These can be focused on as children read on their own and as they participate in lessons structured by the teacher. These lessons are based on knowing what certain children need to learn and what they already know. The rate of acquisition, the degree of competency, and the types of strategies will vary depending on the children's general capabilities, potential, and developmental rates. Within a class, groups of children needing similar strategies and materials can be established as needed. Whole class instruction can be used to introduce topics or strategies, followed later with small groups or one-to-one conferences or feedback. A learner-focused program can be regarded as personalizing, rather than individualizing, the reading program for each child. It means the program activities and organization develop from knowing student needs and from understanding the components of the reading process.

Components of the Reading Process

This section identifies and describes some of the components of this reading model. These are some of the components that may be focused on during instruction and assessment.

Components of the reading process

1. Sight Words.

This term refers to:

(a) **nonphonetic words** — those needing to be recognized by sight because they can't be sounded out (e.g. was, through)

(b) **frequently occurring words** — those needing to be recognized easily because they occur so often

(c) **high interest words** — those recognized by sight because they have special interest and or emotional overtones for child (e.g. mom, dad, love, birthday, Christmas, dinosaur, etc.).

(see Appendix A: 1044 Most Commonly Occurring Words)

Sight words

Interconnections

- Sight words and context clues — students need to know enough words by sight in order to have enough context to help identify other words:

    The _____ went to the _____ to _____ and had a _____ _____.

    For the above sentence it is more difficult to predict the words than in the following:

    The child went to the _____ to play and he had a _____ _____.

- Sight words and prior knowledge — already knowing the pronunciation and meaning of spoken words makes it easier to recognize and remember written words.

Importance of sight words for independent reading

Enables use of context clues. Increases fluency and ease of reading. Children can read greater amounts and for longer periods. Focus can be more on comprehension than on decoding.

Context clues

Syntax

Semantics

2. **Context Clues**

(a) **Syntax**: the structure (grammar) of the language puts constraints on the order of words, thus in predicting what might come next the number of possible words is reduced. For example:

Unfamiliar word order makes it difficult to give possible words for those unknown.

> Boy dog _____ the _____ to the _____ after

Familiar order makes it easier to predict the unknown words.

> The dog _____ after _____ boy to _____ the _____

Initial consonants reduce the number of possibilities even more and make it still easier to identify the unknown words.

> The dog r____ after t___ boy to g__ the b____.

Interconnections

- Syntax clues, oral language, and prior experiences — having a large oral vocabulary associated with experiences helps children think of possible words.

- Syntax clues and prior experience listening to stories —familiarity with patterns and structure of written language helps children predict what words might be next in a written text.

- Syntax and phonics clues — reliance on phonics is decreased if children can predict some possible words and then choose the correct one based on print clues (e.g. initial letters, final letters).

(b) **Semantics**: the words and phrases that will occur in a text are determined by the topic. If a sentence is describing boats then certain words connected with boats and water are expected and others, such as lawnmower, car, street, are not expected.

e.g. The boat's billowing _____ shone over the sparkling _____.

Interconnections

- Semantics, oral language, and experiences — children need to have developed vocabulary related to experiences so they can understand what they are reading. In other words, familiarity with the topic (vocabulary and experience) makes it easier to identify words and bring meaning to the words read. In the example to the left, they would need to know the meaning of billowing and sparkling; having these words in their speaking vocabulary makes it easier to recognize them, and having experience with sailing would enhance their understanding.

- Semantics and familiarity with written language patterns — children need to understand figurative use of language and literary phrases, idioms, figures of speech, and so on.

- Semantics and graphophonic clues — as they sound out unfamiliar words, children will be able to relate them to words they already know are associated meaningfully to the topic. If they do not pronounce the word correctly, it may be close enough so that it prompts them to remember the correct word from their own vocabulary.

> **Importance of context clues for independent reading**
> - focus is on understanding while reading
> - increases the ease of word recognition

3. Phonics Clues

(a) one-to-one letter-sound relationships — strategies children use include articulation clues, letter names, and phonics

(b) letter sequence-sound patterns — sounds associated with common letter sequences (e.g. ou, ai, tion, -le, affixes) Some sight words can also be considered to be in this category because there is a certain sound related to the specific letter sequence e.g. was, once) rather than to the individual letters (see Appendix B: Phonics Patterns).

> **Interconnections**
> - Phonics and context clues — using phonics (e.g. initial and final consonants) puts constraints on the possible words that would make sense in the context (Many more words are possible for "I like to eat _____" than for "I like to eat b___d.")
> - Phonics and learning to spell and write — the same knowledge about letter/sound relationships is used to decode words and to spell words.

Phonics

To be able to use phonics children must have some degree of phonemic awareness, an awareness that words are a blend of speech sounds (phonemes). It is not expected that children explain this awareness of speech sounds, but rather that they develop and use the skill. Phonemic awareness is reflected in their ability to manipulate speech sounds when rhyming or playing with the sounds of words, and when decoding words and spelling. For example, rhyming involves the ability to identify and separate the initial sound (onset) from the vowel and final consonants (rime) and to combine new initial sounds with the same ending (rime). Some children will need more experience with rhyming, sounding out and blending sounds in order to effectively and easily manipulate speech sounds, a skill needed in using phonics to decode words.

> **Importance of graphophonic clues for independent reading**
>
> Children are able to decode new words or at least get an approximate pronunciation to help identify and learn new words. They do not need to know every word before reading the text and do not need to rely on help from others. Freed from reliance on having to recognize every word by sight, children can begin to read independently. Also they are able to learn new words and information from reading.
>
> Using phonics clues, children can monitor the accuracy of their reading based on the print, not just on context and background knowledge.

Syllabication

4. Syllabication

— decoding words by chunking longer words into smaller bits so they are easier to decode. Children need to learn common syllable patterns (e.g. tion, ture, age; see Appendix C: Syllabication Patterns).

Interconnections

- Syllabication and phonics clues — phonics is necessary to help sound out the syllables.
- Syllabication and prior language — when blending syllables together, readers must be able to recognize the pronunciation of the whole word. At first the pronunciation may not be quite right. However, if they have heard the word before, it will be easier to recognize it from a mispronunciation.

Importance of Syllabication for Independent Reading

Children are able to independently identify unfamiliar multisyllabic words, and learn new words and ideas from a text.

Structural analysis

5. Structural Analysis

— identifying parts of words and relating them to meaning (prefixes, suffixes, endings, roots, combining forms; see Appendix D: Structural Analysis).

Importance of structural analysis for independent reading

Children can independently figure out the meaning of new multisyllabic words which helps with understanding the text and learning from reading.

Interconnections

- Structural analysis and phonics — helps with identifying pronunciation by chunking longer words into parts so they can be more easily sounded out.
- Structural analysis and comprehension — knowing the meaning of prefixes, endings, roots, and so on helps with determining the meaning of words and understanding the text. It also helps readers construct the meaning of new words.

Print conventions

6. Print Conventions

— punctuation, paragraphing, font type and size, hyphenation

Importance of print conventions for independent reading

Children can gain fuller meaning from the text if they understand these conventions.

Interconnections

- Print conventions and understanding — print conventions embody nonverbal aspects of communication, for example, ? represents tone of voice when asking questions, ! for exclaiming, " " for conversation, **bold** for emphasis. Periods and commas help indicate thought units and pauses in speech.

7. Prior Experiences and Background Knowledge

Life experiences provide children with their own images and memories of sounds, sights, tastes, smells, feelings, textures, events that can be called upon and related to the meaning engendered by the text. Prior experiences make it easier to visualize and to understand while reading. The diversity of individual experiences account for the differences in understanding the same text; each reader personalizes the text as they read.

Interconnections

- Life experiences and word recognition — oral language develops as children experience life. As they read, a larger oral vocabulary will help them recognize printed words more easily.

- Life experiences and comprehension — as words are identified the images and memories associated with them from personal experiences contribute to the depth and quality of meaning obtained from the text.

Prior experiences

Background knowledge

Illustrations in picture books serve the purpose of providing background knowledge or context for children who may not have had any related experiences or may not be familiar with the topic. As children gain experience in reading, their own imaging and visualizing replace the need for illustrations. In more advanced reading, illustrations, graphs, photos, diagrams, tables, and so on serve both to elucidate the text as well as to supply images and information that readers may not have in their prior knowledge or experience.

Interconnections

- Illustrations, word recognition, and comprehension — as mentioned, illustrations provide the context for beginning readers helping them to predict words that may be used in the text. For more advanced readers, they provide alternative ways to present information difficult to explain in words.

Illustrations

While acquiring *oral language,* children have learned to associate meaning, events, objects, concepts with words (sounds). Later these are associated with print as they learn to read. The first introduction to literature (its language and forms) is usually through listening to stories read orally.

Interconnections

- Oral language and comprehension — from oral language experience, children bring the meaning and images associated with words and also nonverbal emphasis, tone, and expressions used in conversations. Print conventions (punctuation, font, size, and boldness) attempt to signal these nonverbal aspect of oral language.

- Oral language and word recognition — already knowing words and their pronunciation helps with recognizing words as they are decoded using phonics and context.

Oral language

8. Thinking.

Thinking skills

Reading comprehension is thinking stimulated by decoding print. It involves creating images as one reads, construction meaning, making connections with prior knowledge and language; refining, expanding, and modifying prior understanding. Children need to understand that the text should make sense as they read, just as speech should make sense as they talk and listen. They need to think about what they are reading and make corrections, if necessary. With beginning reading, the material needs to be familiar in language structure and content, so that the focus at first can be on learning to decode and recognize words while still understanding what is read. Once they know many words and have decoding skills, less familiar material can be used because less attention is focused on decoding and more can be given to thinking and understanding.

Reading involves recognizing words and associating meaning with those words. Word recognition involves an active *thinking* process which uses context and print clues. Sometimes the focus is more on context, other times it's more on print.

Strategies using context and meaning

- Rerun — return to the beginning of sentence or phrase and read again using meaning to help decode words
- Read on — skip word and continue to read to see if following information will help
- Illustrations — these may provide clues just as background and prior experiences do

Strategies focusing on print

- Sight words — recognition based on visual clues
- Phonics — blending sounds based on graphophonic clues
- Syllabication — chunking into syllables
- Structural analysis — identifying roots, endings, affixes

9. Aspects that influence the rate and efficiency of the reading process

Rate and efficiency

- Ease of word recognition
- Purpose for reading — for entertainment or for information
- Familiarity of content — vocabulary, concepts, events
- Familiarity with elements of written texts — see Figure 16

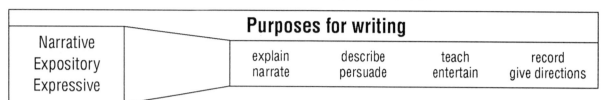

Elements of Written Texts

Purposes for writing

Narrative		explain	describe	teach	record
Expository		narrate	persuade	entertain	give directions
Expressive					

Components

Theme / Content
Voice
Style
Point of View
Mood / Tone
Audience
Paragraph Organization
Main Ideas
Supporting Details

Genre and Form

Picture Books	Plays	Biography	Journals
Stories	Reports	Mystery	Prose
Fairy Tales	Articles	Historical Fiction	Letters
Myths	Tragedy	Science Fiction	Journalism
Rhyme	Irony	Autobiography	Songs
Verse		Poetry	

Fiction Story Grammar

Plot
Character (Main)
Character (Supporting)
Setting
Opening
Problem
Events
Conclusion

Story Patterns

Repetitive
Cumulative
Linear
Circular

Nonfiction Text Organization

Classification
Cause-Effect
Chronological/Sequential/Episodic
Descriptive/Thematic
Comparative/Contrast
Scientific Report

Literary Devices, etc.

Figures of Speech

e.g.   Idioms
Metaphor
Onomatopoeia
Hyperbole

Stereotype
Bias
Prejudice
Testimonial
Bandwagoning
Appeals to Emotion

Flashback
Foreshadowing

Foreign Words

Fact
Fiction
Opinion
Fantasy

Humour

Word Play
Pun
Exaggeration
Understatement
Incongruity

Text Features

Title	Chapters	Glossary	Italics	Punctuation	Graphs
Author	Subheadings	References	Boldface	Illustrations	Charts
Table of Contents	Index	Bibiography	Paragraphing	Diagrams	

Figure 16. Elements of Written Text. This can be used as a guide to what can be focused on when teaching children about reading and writing literature.

Implications for Teaching

1. Expose children to a wide variety of life and language experiences — this develops vocabulary and practical background knowledge.

2. Expose readers to wide variety of story forms and good literature above their reading level and provide opportunities to read literature at their level of competency

3. Teach reading using texts and activities of interest to the students.

4. Teach students a variety of reading strategies. Ensure they learn to use the strategies effectively and easily. (Focus on phonics, sight words, context clues, background knowledge, structural analysis, thinking skills, etc.)

5. Have children set own purposes for reading.

6. Develop silent reading as first priority.

7. Encourage readers to read by themselves for longer periods.

8. Ask readers to substantiate assertions about text by reference to specific parts of text.

9. Emphasize what they are able to do and help them set further goals to be developed and refined. Ensure children do not stall at a certain stage.

10. Understand that although general developmental trends can be observed as children learn to read, there is no absolute hierarchy to the knowledge, skills and strategies that need to be learned. Rather it is a process of becoming aware, refining, modifying, and mastering the many skills and strategies as they experience and learn more about reading.

Teaching involves exposing students to knowledge and strategies they are not aware of, teaching them how and when to use them, helping them modify and refine what they know. Providing them with frequent opportunities to read, ensures they use the knowledge and skills in their reading as they learn them.

Reminder: The Reading Process model (see Figure 14, p. 34) does not list every component skill that is involved in competent reading. It is a beginning framework that highlights many aspects that are commonly thought to play an important role in the reading process. The format of the model is only one way to organize the components. Other ways to organize these concepts are presented in Figures 17 and 18.

⭐ Things I am already including in my teaching:

_____

_____

_____

_____

_____

_____

_____

❗ I need to find out more about

_____

_____

_____

_____

My Reading Model now . . .

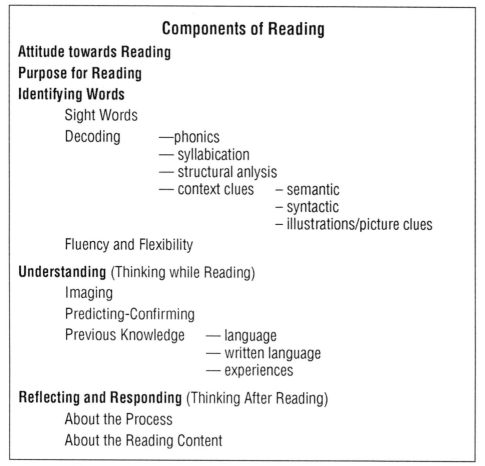

Components of Reading

Attitude towards Reading

Purpose for Reading

Identifying Words

    Sight Words

    Decoding
        —phonics
        — syllabication
        — structural anlysis
        — context clues
            – semantic
            – syntactic
            – illustrations/picture clues

    Fluency and Flexibility

Understanding (Thinking while Reading)

    Imaging

    Predicting-Confirming

    Previous Knowledge
        — language
        — written language
        — experiences

Reflecting and Responding (Thinking After Reading)

    About the Process

    About the Reading Content

Figure 17. Reading Components — Another View.

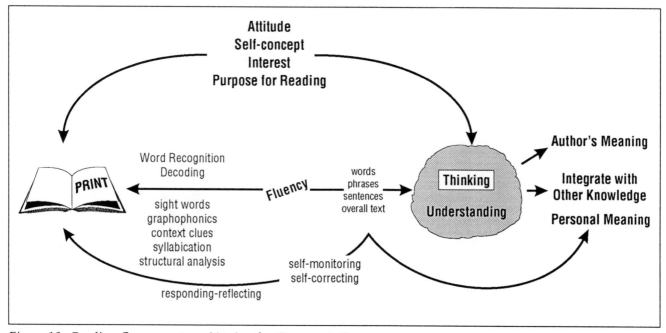

Figure 18. Reading Components — Yet Another Representation.

Developmental Patterns

Why do we need to understand this?

- to guide realistic expectations for individual students
- to plan what might be focused on next
- to guide teaching, and assessment and evaluation of progress

Although there is no strict developmental hierarchy of reading skills, observation of children's reading acquisition indicate such trends as:

- developing oral language
- developing print and phonemic awareness
- relating print to meaning
- learning about letters, letter names and sounds
- beginning to read independently
- becoming more fluent and independent
- increasing competency

Looking at reading development in this way reflects the underlying belief that reading acquisition occurs gradually, emerging from and supported by other language skills and by a growing awareness of how print encodes language. Using these developmental trends as a framework helps establish realistic expectations and guidelines for what a child might learn next, and helps differentiate between transitional and ineffective use of strategies. For example, in the early stages children need to be familiar with the story and language to support word recognition. This familiarity helps them figure out what words might be used. Later they need to be able to read text with unfamiliar language and ideas using phonics along with context and relying less on background knowledge. Relying on memory reading, an effective strategy for beginning readers, becomes an ineffective strategy for independent readers.

Realizing the presence of a developmental pattern places the focus on learners rather than on a curriculum (see Figure 19). This suggests learning will occur more easily if instruction is matched to children's abilities and builds on what they already know and on what makes sense to them. The foundations for beginning independence in reading lie in the development of oral language, life experiences and familiarity with literature and patterns of written language. These are not stepping stones, but rather foundations that need to be laid before children begin to read and need to continue to grow concurrently as children learn to read. Through continued exposure to experiences in the world and through increasing familiarity with oral language and literature above their speaking and reading levels, children's reading can be fostered, supported, and led towards competency and independence.

I have noticed in my class

_____

_____

_____

_____

_____

General developmental trends can be used as a framework for establishing realistic expectations and guidelines for setting goals.

Developing Oral Language and Life Experiences

Familiarity with world, people, concepts, knowledge, information

Daily living experiences

Foundations

Familiarity with Sound of Literature and Patterns of Written Language

Listening to stories and looking at books
Reconstructing stories in own words
Developing phonemic awareness

Awareness of Print and its Function
Emergent Reading

Exhibiting reading-like and writing-like behaviours
Tracking print while retelling story
Matching words to memorized story (1:1)
Understanding concept of word
Recognizing and naming letters
Learning letter/sound relationships
Matching sounds to letters and to letter sequences in words

Refining and expanding awareness of written language and reading

Beginning Independence — Identifying Words

Beginning to remember words from memory (sight words)

Beginning to develop various strategies for decoding unfamiliar words

Reading new text independently at a beginning level

Increasing Competency — Increasing Fluency

Increasing sight words
Increasing ease of decoding
Understanding wider range of genre and unfamiliar texts

Competency and Independence

Increasing ability to read and understand wide range of unfamiliar text using variety of strategies effectively

Increasing ability to evaluate and reflect on the reading process and comprehension

Increasing knowledge of aspects of written language

Figure 19. Developmental Patterns.

Foundations for beginning and developing reading lie in **oral language and life experiences.**

Developing oral language supports reading by

_____

_____

_____

_____

Personal experiences support reading development by

_____

_____

_____

_____

Integrating language arts throughout the curriculum makes sense because

_____

_____

_____

_____

Developing Oral Language and Life Experiences

Oral language is used to (a) interpret and mediate thinking about experiences, (b) to represent and communicate experiences to others through words, and (c) to create vicarious experiences. Children gain oral language competency by interacting with others who model and demonstrate competent functional language use in daily living experiences (see Appendix E: Functions of Oral Language). Life experiences refer to nonverbal and verbal interactions with the world and within one's self.

In developing oral language, children are learning about:

(a)   the verbal aspects (how to use words, idioms, common expressions to refer to objects, concepts, actions, relationships, etc. and how to put words together to have utterances make sense to others)

(b)   the mechanical aspects (how to produce phonemes, individual speech sounds, and combine them to form words)

(c)   the nonverbal aspects (how tone, pitch, stress, intonation, actions, facial expressions, and the context of the communication affect meaning).

While personally learning about the world and themselves, children expand their command of vocabulary in relation to objects, concepts, events, actions, and experiences in various domains of knowledge. They continue to increase their competency in understanding and expressing ideas and information through oral language. In developing oral language children are also developing images that correspond to the sounds of the language. This provides the basis for understanding while they read because, as words are identified from print, meaning is created by associating them with the images already created in memory and connected with words (oral language).

The development of oral language provides the foundation for written language acquisition. If vocabulary and concepts are already familiar to children, then reading for information and writing to communicate about a particular subject will be easier. The goal, as children develop and acquire more knowledge and reading competency, is to enable them to learn from reading with less oral language and experiential background than was needed in the beginning stages. Integrating language arts throughout the curriculum makes sense because it is a recognition of the connection that exists between understanding oral language, learning about a particular subject, and reading. For example, learning about science involves learning the vocabulary used to identify, name, and classify things and concepts, as well as learning about the pattern of logic/thinking used to organize, analyze, evaluate information in that domain. Reading and understanding scientific texts requires familiarity with the vocabulary, concepts and methods which at first can be learned through oral language and experience.

Familiarity with Literature and Patterns of Written Language

Children gain familiarity with literature and written language structure by listening to stories read aloud and responding to what they hear, and by interacting with books themselves. Their previous oral and aural language experiences provide the foundation for introduction to books and print.

Reading literature to children and talking about it lays the foundation for independent reading because these activities:

- make children aware of the world of literature.
- demonstrate the value and enjoyment found in literature.
- extend their interests in new topics, stories, ideas.
- provide motivation for learning to read.
- provide an emulative model of competent reading.
- build familiarity with the structure of written language compared to oral language.
- build familiarity with structure of literary forms.
- provide opportunities for children to learn to create meaning and images from literature and to develop strategies for responding.
- provide opportunities for children to memorize a familiar story, which can become the first step to reading print (matching memorized words to print).

Continuing to read to children at a level just beyond their reading ability, even after they have begun to read independently, provides opportunities to lay foundations for increasing competency. Since children can understand text beyond their own reading level, reading aloud and discussions are ways to orally and aurally introduce reading strategies, vocabulary, idioms, forms, genres, and other aspects of written texts (see Figure 16, p. 43). In this way, as their reading vocabulary and experience increase, they can "grow into" independent reading of more complex literature, the strategies for understanding and responding to literature read aloud being incorporated into their emerging independent silent reading.

As children discover books and interact with them, you will notice the following:

- they listen to stories and enjoy handling books and looking at pictures.
- they begin to reconstruct stories using their own words as they look at pictures, demonstrating an initial grasp of meaning based on their own experiences and what they notice in a book.
- with stories that they have heard frequently, their retelling becomes more fluent and closer to the original text in language and sequence of events.
- they begin to memorize word for word idioms, phrases, sentences, sections, and entire stories, joining in with the repetitive or predictable parts as they listen.
- they fill in missing words and phrases from familiar stories (oral cloze).
- they begin to make reasonable guesses for words that might come next in an unfamiliar story.
- they can suggest what might happen next in the story.
- they use pictures to interpret the story.
- they demonstrate a concept of self as a reader.

Developing Oral Language and Life Experiences

Familiarity with Literature and Patterns of Written Language

Reading literature to children helps them learn to read.

I have noticed this:

_____   ✓✗?

_____

_____

_____

_____

_____

_____

_____

_____

Developing Oral Language
and Life Experiences

Familiarity with Literature
and Patterns of Written
Language

Awareness of Print and its
Function

Children become aware of
print in their environment
(books, signs, writing) and
become interested in learning
to read and to write.

I have noticed this:

✓✗?

_____

_____

_____

_____

_____

_____

_____

_____

_____

_____

_____

Awareness of Print and its Function

As children become familiar with listening to stories and handling books, they exhibit reading-like behaviours that reflect their awareness of print and its function. They look at pictures, turn pages, and tell the story in ways that indicate both their understanding of the story and their command of language. Building on prior experiences with literature, children use their oral language experience to help them delve into the way print encodes speech and meaning. In the early stages, they point to the pictures or the general area of the print as they tell the story. Later they point word by word as they repeat a memorized story ("memory reading").

Listening to stories
- develops experience with reconstructing meaning
- provides exposure to vocabulary and written language patterns

Looking at books
- develops awareness of print
- develops matching of print to words and letter/sound relationships

During this phase, children gradually become able to:
- ask what signs, words, labels and letters say.
- tell what print and/or symbols mean.
- look at books and tell a story about the pictures.
- reconstruct stories previously read to them by looking at the book and using some of the language and structure of the story.
- turn the pages at the appropriate place when listening to a story (they will not let you skip a page!).
- reconstruct or retell the story turning at the correct page if they are familiar with the book.
- point to the print if asked where to start reading.
- memorize a story word for word, and attempt to match spoken to printed words (voice/print matching); multisyllabic words may pose a difficulty at first as they want to point to a new word for each syllable.
- "memory read," match spoken to written words accurately reflecting an understanding of the concept of word (multisyllabic words are now matched accurately).
- locate a specific word by matching voice to print in a memorized story until they come to the word.
- identify a specific word using the initial letter as a clue, indicating knowledge of letters, letter names, and letter/sound relationships.
- identify frequently occurring and/or high interest words by sight because of experiences with reading and writing.
- demonstrate their concept of self as a reader ("I can read by myself." "I can read this book without even looking!").

Word identification skills are acquired not only from learning to decode print but also from learning to write (using phonics to construct words). Along with their reading development, children demonstrate their growing understanding about print in their drawings and writings as they:

- develop control over drawing shapes and become aware of print, children make letter-like shapes and ask, "What does this say?" or tell you, "This says . . . ."

- print strings of random letters to represent their name, other people's names, and messages; their drawings are an integral part of their writing.

- begin to draw pictures, separating the letters and words from the pictures. Messages may or may not relate to the drawing, indicating their emerging understanding of the function of print.

- learn words of interest to them such as names of friends or words they use frequently (mom, dad, love, to, Santa, nintendo, hockey, . . .).

- begin to spell words using letter names and initial letter sounds to represent words.

- begin using initial and final letter sounds and letter names to represent words and leaving spaces or putting dashes (-) or dots (.) between words, indicating an awareness of the concept of word.

- begin to spell more words correctly and from memory (sight words, e.g. **to the go like can is it me at**).

- demonstrate their concept of self as a writer by initiating writing activities and commenting, "Look what I wrote all by myself! Let *me* read it to you!"

During this phase, children's reading and writing begin to reflect their memory of frequently occurring or high interest words and their understanding of:

Some of my students who show this are

- the concept of word (spaces between words, voice/print matching).

- constancy of print (unfamiliar words are spelled similarly each time and identified in the same way each time).

- phonemic awareness (number of sounds in words represented by same number of letters).

- graphophonic knowledge (letters related to sounds, rather than to letter names and articulation clues).

- use of context clues (language, prior knowledge/experience, pictures).

Reading stories to children and discussing them prior to independent reading is a way to provide some background knowledge of both the topic and the vocabulary. This supports a meaning focus in beginning independent reading by ensuring the children know something about the topic and have heard some of the specific vocabulary. Another activity for beginning readers is to have them listen to part of a story, then predict what will happen by drawing pictures. This helps them focus on visualizing and making meaning while listening or reading. Learning to visualize and to create their own images as they listen lays the foundation for understanding as they read, particularly stories without illustrations.

Developing Oral Language and Life Experiences

Familiarity with Literature and Patterns of Written Language

Awareness of Print and its Function

Beginning Independence

Many children move easily into beginning independent reading. However, some seem to stall at the memory reading stage.

In becoming independent readers, children need to focus on decoding print accurately while reading for meaning.

Notes to myself:

_____

_____

_____

_____

_____

_____

Beginning Independence

"I can really read all by myself!" "Don't tell me that word."

In order to become independent readers able to read unfamiliar stories, children need to learn to use phonics clues to identify words. During the beginning reading stages, they need to increase their sight word recognition along with using context and phonics as they read.

Many children move into this phase easily. They have developed their own strategies for decoding print as they listened to stories, played with books, and followed the print while someone read the story. They actively sought answers to their questions about print, and their capabilities and thinking processes enabled them to figure out how to decode and remember words without direct teaching intervention.

However, some children seem to "stall" at the memory reading stage. Perhaps they have the perception that reading is memorizing a story and pointing to words. They may find remembering sight words difficult. They may have difficulty learning letter/sound relationships or blending sounds together easily. These children will need more explicit instruction focusing on print and decoding words. They may need more direct teaching to become familiar with letters and with letter/sound and letter sequence/sound relationships. They may need to develop phonemic awareness and fluency in blending sounds so they can easily decode unfamiliar words and gain automaticity in word recognition.

In becoming independent readers, children progress from reading familiar books to reading those they have not seen or heard before. At first when reading "memorized" favourites, they fluently repeat words while following the text. As they become more aware of words, their reading of these same stories becomes slower and word for word, indicating close voice to print matching. This is a sign that they are focusing on the printed words and are moving from memory reading towards beginning independence. In their writing at this time, they begin to leave spaces between words, another indication of their awareness of words as units.

To become independent readers, children must be able to use phonics clues, context clues and prior knowledge easily and in concert. In beginning reading instruction, opportunities to develop these strategies is key. Books suitable for beginning reading need illustrations, since the latter compensate for lack of background knowledge, serve to help children imagine what is happening in the story, and stimulate their interest in books. Beginning reading books need short sentences with familiar vocabulary and structure so that prior language knowledge can support word recognition. They need a level of vocabulary such that beginning readers can easily recognize most (90% to 95%) of the words. With these books, children can get the gist of the story while learning to decode a few words. Too many unfamiliar words requires too much effort and makes the reading too laborious. In addition, children need books they have read before available for rereading. Rereading familiar books several times increases reading fluency because words are more quickly recognized each time.

In this phase children become able to:

- match the spoken word accurately to the printed word (voice pointing or voice/print matching).
- identify words in and out of context.
- use phonics clues to sound out words, matching letters and sounds accurately (reflecting phonemic awareness).
- use context clues to identify unfamiliar words.
- use a variety of strategies concurrently.
- self-correct reading miscues.

I have noticed this:

_____ ✓✗?

_____

_____

_____

_____

_____

Strategies being used:

- Sight words — frequently occurring words, high interest words, non-phonetic words
- Phonics clues — initial and final sounds, similar parts, and middle sounds
- Language clues — syntax, semantics, and vocabulary of familiar topics
- Previous knowledge/experiences and pictures — accessing language and associated images

---

Moving from emergent reading to beginning independence, the reader shifts from creating meaning from what was remembered about the story and from pictures to being more focused on the print and being concerned with reading the words correctly as well as with making sense. At this stage it is important for children to develop facility with sounding out and blending sounds to decode words. Children who do not acquire phonics knowledge and skills continue to over-rely on context and prior knowledge to identify words. They seem to "stall" at the memory reading stage, continuing to guess new words as best as they can. At the same time, over-emphasizing phonics may result in children relying too heavily on phonics to decode words (see p. 104 for Wade's (1990) and p. 107 for Phinney's (1988) descriptions of readers who over-rely on one particular strategy).

Increasing Competency

"I can read a chapter book."

Once children have moved from memory reading into beginning independence, they need to continue developing competency by expanding their use of reading strategies into a wide variety of literature for various purposes. They demand "chapter" books which seem to signal to them that they are real readers. During this phase children need to develop an increasing ease and rate of word recognition so that the mechanical processing of print into meaningful words and phrases occurs with as little attention as possible (Samuels, Schermer & Reinking, 1992). As they become more independent, their own visualizing of the text replaces the need for illustrations. In more complex texts, graphs, maps, illustrations, diagrams, and charts serve the purpose of elucidating new concepts and information that are better presented by those formats ("a picture is worth a thousand words"). Children need to learn how to interpret these new tools. Thus it makes sense to integrate reading instruction with the traditional "content areas" because expository texts often include graphs, maps, diagrams, and so on.

Developing Oral Language and Life Experiences

Familiarity with Literature and Patterns of Written Language

Awareness of Print and its Function

Beginning Independence

Increasing Competency

I have noticed this:

✓✗?

———
———
———
———
———
———
———
———

I agree/disagree/wonder:

✓✗?

———
———
———
———
———
———
———
———
———
———
———
———
———
———

Developing Oral Language
and Life Experiences

Familiarity with Literature
and Patterns of Written
Language

Awareness of Print and its
Function

Beginning Independence

Increasing Competency

Competency and Independence

During this phase, children's oral and silent reading indicate that they are developing:
- an expanding repertoire of sight words.
- a variety of strategies for decoding words.
- effective and fluent use of strategies.
- self-correcting/self-monitoring for meaning.
- ability to deal with less familiar topics and genre.
- less reliance on illustrations, using their own imaging to sustain and enhance text.
- varied rates of reading depending on reading purpose and difficulty of text and content.
- reading for longer periods of time.
- ability to obtain meaning from longer passages, identifying main ideas and themes.

Instruction throughout this phase must focus on continued exposure to and understanding of:
- word recognition strategies and ease of use.
- language (vocabulary and expressions).
- print conventions.
- various literary forms and genre.
- organization and structure of texts.
- the world and themselves.
- integrating prior knowledge.
- thinking and imaging when reading.
- learning from reading, connecting with other knowledge.
- evaluating the ideas presented in the text.
- self-monitoring and self-correcting.
- author's purposes, point of view, sense of audience, and style.
- the importance of purpose for reading.
- reading rate related to purpose (skimming, scanning, normal reading, studying, memorizing).

Competency and Independence

Children can be described as competent and independent readers when they:

(a) easily read unseen texts dealing with new information (new topics and vocabulary),

(b) think about the information and make connections to prior knowledge/experiences and language skills,

(c) choose to read for enjoyment and information, and

(d) vary reading rate depending on their purpose for reading.

Once the basic meaning (decoding words) is obtained from the text, the reader needs to think about what is read. As mentioned earlier, the word "think" refers to all the processes used by the brain to make sense of the world. Input, or information, from the sensory organs must be focused on, organized, analyzed, synthesized, evaluated, recalled, and so on. Reading comprehension is really thinking, that is, making sense of print (sensory input) while reading by associating the written words with knowledge and images stored in memory from prior experiences with life and language. It is through this active thinking process that the reader understands what is read.

> Reading comprehension is really thinking, that is, making sense of print.

Developing comprehension strategies for reading, therefore, is actually a process of developing thinking skills (see Figures 10 and 10a, pp. 26-27). Developing competency and independence in reading also involves extending reading strategies into more advanced texts and into a wider variety of genre. Since prior knowledge is essential for understanding, continued success in reading relies on students continuing to learn about the world through a variety of experiences.

Since different disciplines or domains of knowledge have distinct ways of categorizing and communicating information, students need experience with their various literary forms (e.g. Fine Arts, Science, Social Studies, Math). They will need instruction to help them learn about the concepts and logic of the disciplines and the structure and forms of their associated literature. For students to learn from reading content area texts, it is essential the texts are suitable to their reading level and that they have the background knowledge to support their reading. Reading instruction in the traditional content areas will need to involve not just reading texts, but also hands-on experiences, listening and speaking activities, and activities focusing on the different genre, organization and features of the literature.

> Reading instruction integrated with traditional content areas

There are general developmental patterns that can be observed as children become independent and competent readers. These trends provide guidelines for assessing and evaluating readers' progress as well as planning for and teaching children at different stages. These trends suggest what can be expected next for children who exhibit certain abilities and skills. The rate of their progress and specific instructional goals are also guided by these trends but will be different for each student. The next section briefly outlines aspects to consider when adjusting and "personalizing" programs for individuals.

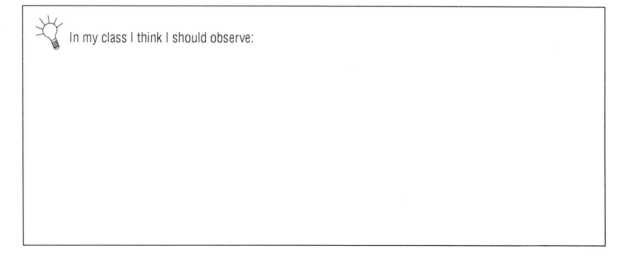

In my class I think I should observe:

Individual Variations

The Learning Process | The Reading Process

Language and its Role in Reading Acquisition

Reading and its Role in Education

Developmental Patterns

Processes · Skills · Strategies
Foundations · How? What? When? Why? · Expectations
Goals · Attitudes
Set of Beliefs

These determine teaching and learning resources and strategies

Why do we need to understand this?

- to recognize the role of individual talents, capacities, and interests in learning to read

- to remind ourselves of the individuality of learners and rates of progress

- to assess what helps an individual best

The intention of this section on individual variations is to present in diagrams and outlines some of the aspects and dynamics that need to be considered in helping specific children. Due to the diversity of children's abilities and capacities and to the myriad of factors involved in reading, helping *all* children become successful readers will always demand creative problem solving in planning and teaching. This is why it is essential to know about the reading process, about how children learn, and children's reading development, keeping in mind individual differences. It is not a matter of nature *vs* nuture, but rather nature *and* nuture and their interaction.

In teaching reading it is necessary to keep in mind that individual variations in needs, abilities, and interests do exist and influence the way children will learn to read. It does not mean developing individualized programs, but rather personalizing the materials and learning activities considering the factors presented in Figures 20 to 22. These can be used as a checklist as you think about a particular student and what may be possible factors interfering with the ease and rate of learning to read. The factors presented in these figures suggest questions to keep in mind such as: Does the child have difficulties with sensory input, perception, integration of sensory/motor/perceptual processes, memory, attention, self-concept, interest, and so on? What prior educational, cultural, and social experiences has the child been exposed to or immersed in? What are the child's preferred ways of learning? What needs to be changed? What is possible to change? What aspects of the reading process need to be explicitly taught? By observing, asking questions, evaluating, and then responding by modifying instruction, activities and materials, individual differences can be acknowledged and incorporated into classroom instructional activities. The next section describes how to provide differentiated focuses for learners in classrooms.

Some key individual variations I have noticed with my students:

_____

_____

_____

_____

_____

_____

_____

_____

Some questions to consider in assessing and evaluating individuals

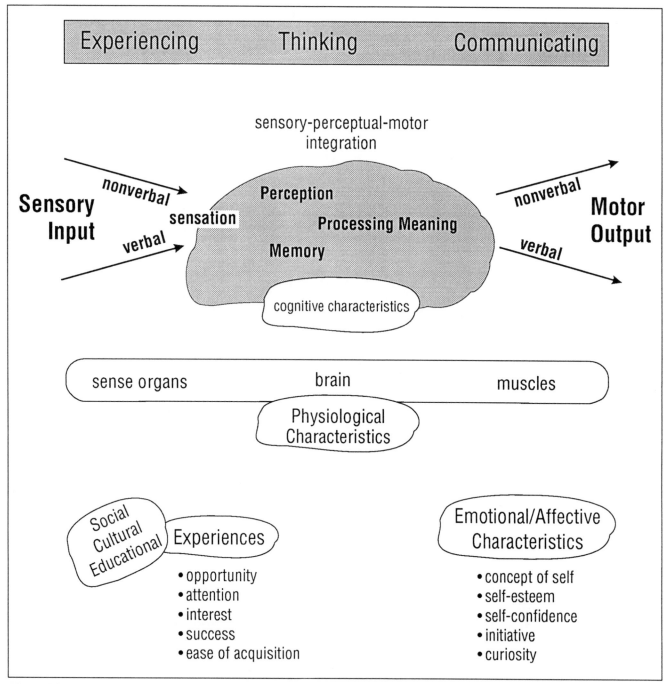

Figure 20. Factors Contributing to Individual Differences.

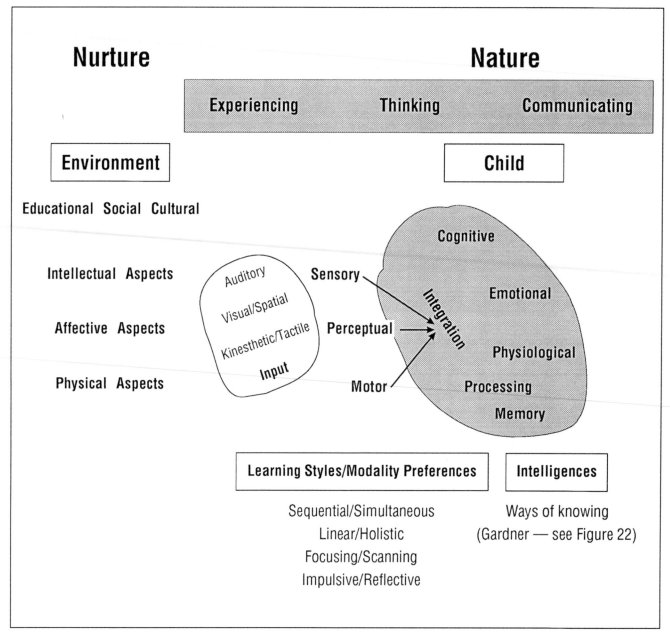

Figure 21. Factors Contributing to Individual Differences — Another Perspective.

Linguistic Intelligence

- has highly developed auditory skills
- learns best by verbalizing, hearing or seeing words

Logical–Mathematical Intelligence

- thinks conceptually
- constantly questions and wonders
- experiments to test out things, loves computers

Spatial Intelligence

- knows where things are located
- thinks in images
- designs, draws, builds, ponders

Musical Intelligence

- responds in many ways to music
- has strong opinions about music
- is sensitive to non-verbal sounds
- is sensitive to rhythms in language and sound

Bodily–Kinesthetic Intelligence

- processes knowledge through doing
- may be physically able
- may be gifted with fine motor coordination
- learns by moving, acting things out

Interpersonal Intelligence

- understands people — empathetic
- organizes, communicates with others
- learns best by relating to others

Intrapersonal Intelligence

- may possess a strong personality
- may shy from group activities
- shows deep awareness of inner feelings
- may be very self-confident

from Gardner (1983)

Figure 22. Gardner's "Seven Intelligences" Suggests Variations in the Ways Individuals Learn.

Part II: Teaching Reading in the Classroom — Putting It All Together

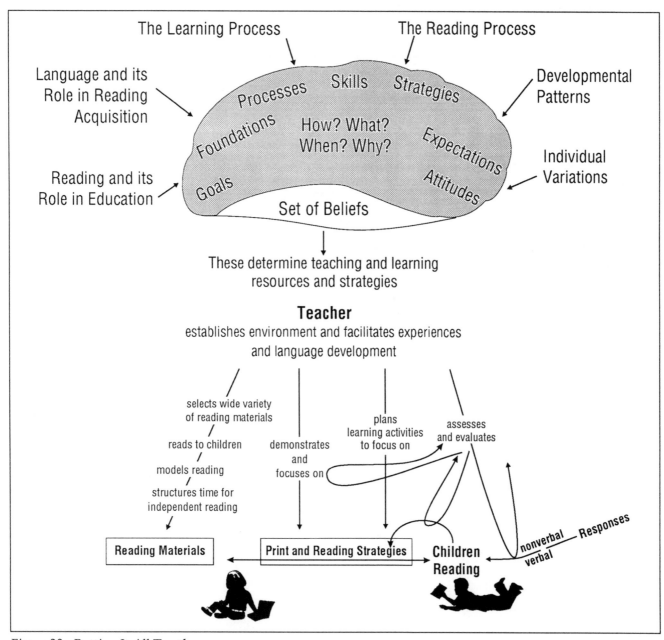

Figure 23. Putting It All Together.

1. Creating an environment for all learners
2. Providing differentiated focuses for learners within the classroom

Teacher

Teacher creates environment

- Selects and organizes resources and plans time to provide
  - Oral and written language activities, and
  - Experiences (world, others, self)

Teacher interacts with children

- Assesses, evaluates, and teaches
  - Engages interest/attention, models process,
  - Demonstrates strategies/knowledge
  - Focuses strategies, knowledge, attitudes
  - Provides Feedback — encourages, guides, extends, reteaches/refocuses

Grouping
- whole class
- small group
- one : one

Children

- Participate in lessons and demonstrations given by teacher or others
- Individually read and write   (on own and cooperatively)
- Self-monitor and self-correct, self-evaluate
- Use approximations moving toward competency

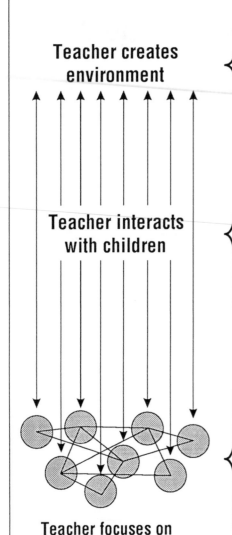

Teacher focuses on learners and provides lessons based on assessment of children's needs

Figure 24. Teaching Reading in the Classroom.

Creating an Environment for All Learners

Within a nonschool environment, many children learn to read and write without formal educational intervention. Studies of these children indicate the process to be similar to other language learning. It occurs through social interactions in an environment with many sources of language and print in which someone (e.g. parent, sibling, friend) more knowledgeable is available to respond to children's questions. Children are naturally curious about print and want to learn to read. Those who read early seem to instinctively pursue this task with great interest. The act of reading is demonstrated to them through socially meaningful use (bedtime stories, magazines, letters, signs, directions), and oral language promotes their learning as they begin to figure out how print relates to meaning. Through a complex, self-regulated process involving successively refined approximations, these children develop competency in reading as best and as quickly as they can. Growth progresses along a path influenced by developmental patterns, personal experiences, and their individual talents and capabilities, rather than strictly by age and intelligence.

> Many children learn to read and write before coming to school, without formal teaching.

At school age, of those children who are not reading, some are on the verge of becoming readers and others are just beginning to become aware of print and its functions. Whether the children who are not reading at school entry just need more time in a language rich environment is the subject of much discussion. Is it a matter of developmental and individual growth? Is it a matter of the amount of time and attention they gave to literacy activities in the preschool years? Regardless, with their entry into school comes the expectation that formal educational intervention will help these children learn to read within one or two years and will continue to challenge and engage those already reading.

> Of those children who are not reading upon school entry, some are just beginning to read, others are just becoming aware of print. Are these variations the result of developmental or environmental differences?

In studies of children who were early readers, researchers have attempted to identify factors contributing to their learning to read at home. Generally these children had home environments where many books and writing materials were available to choose from, where they were read stories, where their questions about reading and writing were answered, and where the use and appreciation of reading were evident in daily activities. This certainly suggests some of the things that should be emphasized in the school setting to ensure the language environment of the school emulates and enhances rather than detracts from the best settings available out of school.

Because children vary in their capabilities and interests and because reading is more than a hierarchical accumulation of skills, the school environment needs to have embedded in it language and cultural complexity, and open-ended activities. In this environment, children can be actively engaged, challenged, and successful according to their individual and developmental qualities.

> The priority in school is to create an environment conducive to enhancing the language development of all children. Within this setting, different focuses and varied approaches can be used.

The first priority in the classroom is to establish an environment conducive to enhancing the language development of all children (see Figure 24). Within this overall environment, there needs to be different focuses for children as they develop. As well there needs to be a variety of focuses and approaches so that the different needs and interests of all children can be met concurrently. Different children will have different ways of learning and will need to focus on different aspects of the reading process.

⭐ What I am doing to create an effective environment

_____

_____

_____

_____

_____

_____

_____

_____

In the classroom setting the teacher is the guide, instructor, encourager, and facilitator. Aware of how learning occurs and what is involved in learning to read, the teacher shapes the environment, creates the tone, gathers resources, instructs and interacts with the learners, and also encourages and assists children in engaging in tasks. These tasks need to challenge present abilities and enhance knowledge. They need to encompass goals that extend the children's achievement but are within their reach. Effort is required from the children and, in turn, they are rewarded with the satisfaction of learning and becoming better readers. Overcoming challenges that require effort and energy is satisfying and self-motivating. However, if faced frequently with impossible tasks that have little meaning or interest for them, children will direct their energy in other directions.

Thus, classroom teachers need to make decisions about what to do, how to interact, and what to demonstrate, focus on, and explain. They need to reflect on how children respond to the lessons and what the children are really learning from the lessons and tasks. To give a series of lessons and expect each child to learn the goals set by the teacher or the program at a specific time in a certain way is not reality. What children learn is determined by their needs, interests, talents, abilities, past experiences, emotional state, and so on. Learning, scheduled by the learners' interests and abilities building on their prior experiences and knowledge, develops intrinsic motivation.

In creating this environment teachers need to:

- ensure the resources and activities reflect rich and varied language, both oral and written, with open-ended opportunities to demonstrate understanding and competency.
- engage students in interactions with print, providing frequent opportunities to read and write.
- recognize the importance of interest, choice, enjoyment, background knowledge, past experience, self-regulation, and self-concept for children's self-motivation and engagement in reading.
- demonstrate and model reading strategies and purposes for reading.
- expand children's awareness of what reading competency entails, helping them to establish their own goals for progress.
- determine what each child knows and can do, and what aspects of reading need more indepth instruction, more guided practice, specific feedback, more frequent individualized feedback, and so on.
- demonstrate the knowledge, skill, and/or strategy clearly by using the following procedure:
  - state what the knowledge, skill or strategy is used for.
  - review previous experiences and lessons connected with it.
  - demonstrate and discuss what it is, how it is useful and why it works.
  - demonstrate again.
  - use it together with students, provide feedback.
  - have students use it collaboratively and/or individually.
  - provide feedback (encourage, extend, or redirect as specific needs are recognized).
  - model with other texts and let students take turns as the "teacher."

– provide opportunities for independent and individual use in a variety of texts.

Within the environment created to foster growth in reading for all learners, the teacher focuses on three aspects when planning activities (see Figures 25 and 26):

(1) Foundations for reading

(2) Learning to read

(3) Independent reading

Development needs to occur simultaneously in these three areas.

For example, all readers need to continue to be exposed to oral language, life experiences, and stories read aloud. These lay the foundation for understanding increasingly more complex texts and information. At the same time, children need to continue to acquire a variety of decoding/reading strategies and knowledge about print conventions and text structure; they need to continue to learn more about reading. As well, opportunities to read independently for sustained periods helps them develop fluency in decoding texts and provides opportunities to use reading for self-directed learning.

> Daily lessons and activities should include a focus on each of three key aspects . . .
>
> Foundations for reading
>
> Learning to read
>
> Independent reading.

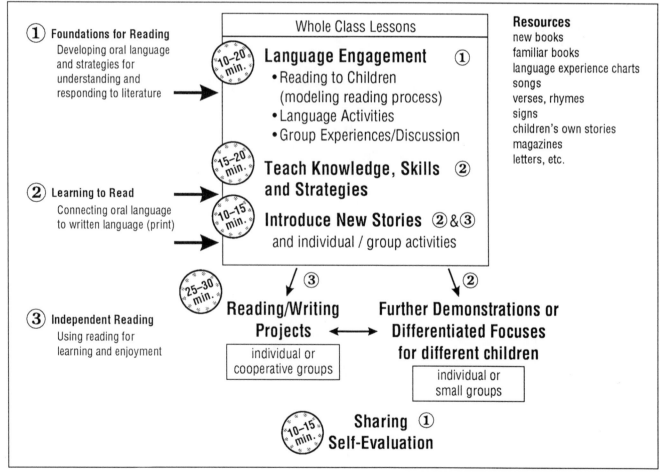

Figure 25. Teaching Reading.

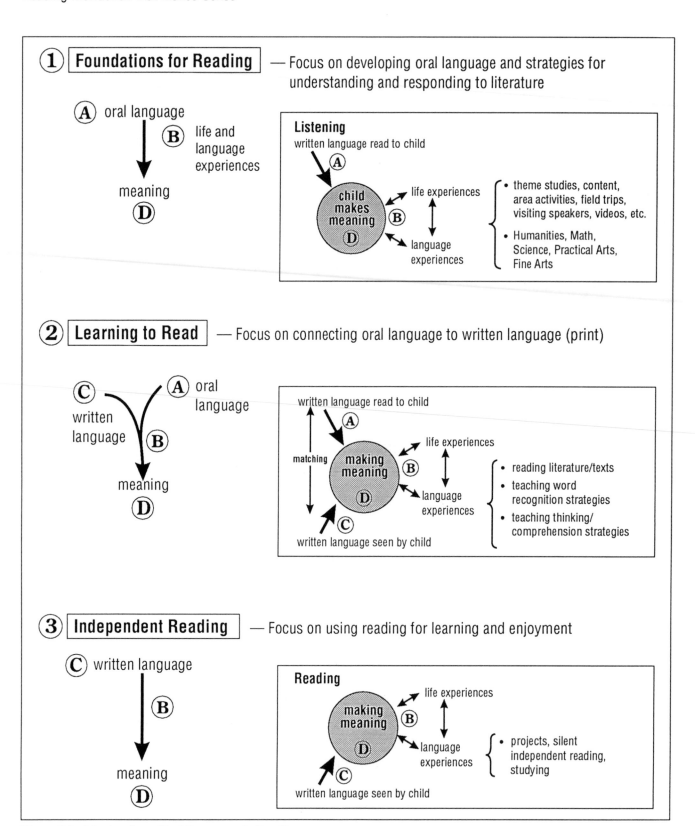

Figure 26. Moving from Oral Language to Reading.

Foundations for Reading

The teacher develops the foundations for reading and encourages children to become readers by ensuring they participate in a variety of life and language experiences attuned to the children's interests, needs and choices. The children learn to:

- understand spoken language.
- associate words with meanings and images (vocabulary development), interpret experiences using language.
- use language to mediate thinking.
- use oral language to communicate thoughts (express understanding).

The teacher also develops the foundations by reading to children, thereby:

- exposing them to wide range of literature, engaging and generating curiosity and interest.
- familiarizing them with vocabulary and written language models.
- demonstrating a variety of purposes (enjoyment, learning; skimming, scanning, memorizing, studying, reading "normally").
- modelling reading/thinking strategies (decoding print, predicting, confirming, self-correcting, thinking aloud, summarizing, analyzing, etc.).
- familiarizing them with conventions of books/print.
- encouraging a variety of responses.
- establishing a basis for evaluating written language.

Activities to Promote Foundations of Reading

As children participate in learning experiences and listen to stories read to them, they learn many different things about the world, themselves and language simultaneously. Many examples of activities that promote language development in a literature-based reading program are described in Brownlie, Close and Wingren (1988, 1990) and Johnson and Louis (1990).

To enhance and focus learning goals, teachers and students need to establish the purpose for participating (experiencing, listening and responding), for example:

- developing vocabulary and concepts.
- listening for exciting language.
- predicting what might happen.
- finding out information.
- comparing to other stories.
- creating images as they listen.
- responding by extending or finishing the story.

To help children understand, children need to draw on their previous knowledge and experiences to predict what might happen or what they might learn, for example, by:

- creating images from their experiences.
- listing vocabulary and language they know.
- brainstorming what they already know.
- predicting what might happen.
- asking questions about what they would like to know.

Daily lessons and activities need to include a focus on:

Foundations for reading

⭐ Ways I do this:

_____

_____

_____

_____

_____

_____

_____

Activities:

Establish purpose

Draw on prior experience and knowledge

Develop familiarity with language

To establish a foundation for context clues, children need to gain familiarity with language vocabulary and structures, for example, by:

- joining in with familiar phrases, verses, and repetitive parts.
- participating in choral activities — rhymes, verses, songs.
- participating in oral cloze activities — fill in missing phrases, words, and word parts.
- brainstorming vocabulary associated with the topic/idea.
- finding and discussing examples of powerful language, idioms, expressions, and so on.

Develop familiarity with literature

To develop familiarity with literature and its forms, teachers can present a wide variety genre and focus on different aspects of literature (see Figure 16, p. 43).

Model and discuss thinking strategies

To lay a foundation for understanding oral and written language, teachers can model thinking strategies (see Figure 10a, p. 26) by thinking out loud while reading and teaching, and focusing on, for example:

- gathering certain information
- predicting and confirming
- questioning
- organizing
- analyzing
- self-correcting
- going to other sources.

Daily lessons and activities need to include a focus on:

Foundations for reading

Learning to Read

Learning to Read

As children begin to read and continue to develop their reading skills, they are learning about:

- decoding written text,
- connecting written language with oral language and meaning, and
- using the conventions of written language.

Teachers facilitate emerging reading competency by:

- reading and rereading literature, thus providing the repetition needed for familiarity, assimilation, and solid acquisition of vocabulary and language patterns that are the foundation of context clues, text structures, and understanding
- demonstrating use of print and language clues, modelling both phonics and context to predict and confirm word identification and meaning
- demonstrating reading strategies that focus on the print (phonics clues, syllabication, print conventions, context clues . . .) when matching oral reading with written language
- discussing meaning, identifying author's message and purpose, relating to what children already know and have learned
- modelling ways of thinking and responding

Activities to Promote Beginning Reading

Using familiar stories or language to begin to teach reading ensures that meaning plays a role in learning to read. Familiarize students with the text by reading and rereading it to them and with them. The difficulty of independent follow-up reading tasks can be modified by:

- the number of times the children have heard the text before
- the familiarity of the topic
- the familiarity of the language structure
- the amount of support given by the teacher

Materials:

- Big Books
- Teacher made text on charts/chalkboard/overheads (e.g. morning message, language experience, classroom news, poems, rhymes, songs, jokes, theme charts)
- Individual copies of same text

For group activities, "enlarged print" allows the teacher to demonstrate reading strategies. Multiple copies of the text can also be used but it is more difficult in a large group to direct every child's attention to the same spot. Not all children can focus well in a group, and unless the teacher is very clear about where attention is to be focused, some children will not be attending to the same print or feature as the teacher. It is essential to ensure children can easily and clearly see the print focused on. In identifying parts of the text, it must be highlighted and apparent. Just pointing to a word or framing it with one's hands may not be enough. It may be necessary to use cardboard with a cut-out window to frame the print, or to print the word or phrase on cards or on a chart.

General Procedures (Attention focused on print)

- First read the whole text, as children follow along. If children are familiar with the text, they can read along. If children are more advanced readers, they can read the text first. (The focus is on the overall meaning of the text and activity.)
- Cloze — leave blank or cover up phrases, words, parts of words; children can read along and fill in blanks orally. (The focus is on context and/or phonics clues — see Part III: C5, Cloze Procedure.)
- Rearrange sentences in text — using pocket chart and sentence strips, students read changed sentence order and restore to original. (The focus is on meaning and sequencing ideas.)
- Make changes in text — students find incorrect word/words part. (The focus is on the print and specific words.)
- Rearrange words in sentence — students read rearranged word cards and then arrange them to make original or other sentences. (The focus is on recognizing and decoding words, ensures students have not just memorized words in a sentence, but can actually recognize the words.)
- Find similar words in the text (e.g. ones that rhyme, end the same, begin the same). (The focus is on phonics patterns.)
- Read a sentence starting all words with same sound. (The focus is on phonemic awareness and phonics.)

With beginning reading, using familiar stories, topics or language ensures meaning plays a role.

Enlarged print enables the teacher to demonstrate reading strategies to a group of students.

Activities focusing attention on the print help children become independent readers.

I might try

_____

_____

_____

_____

_____

_____

_____

_____

_____

_____

- Find words that are repeated in text. (The focus is on constancy of words and word recognition.)
- Find sight words in text, choosing ones you have taught before. (The focus is on repeated exposure to sight words.)
- Finish with children rereading text; this can be done in unison (whole class, small groups, or individuals) or divide text into parts and different groups or individuals read parts. (The focus is on meaning and fluent reading.)

Other Activities to Focus on Specific Decoding Skills/Strategies Using Enlarged Text or Individual Reading Activities

a. **Letter Recognition and Phonemic Awareness**
  - learning letter names (recognize letters, name them, then print them, find words with specific letters in them).
  - recognizing sounds within words (phonemes).
  - identifying words with certain sounds or with same initial/final sounds (see Appendix B for suggestions about teaching sequence).

b. **Concept of Word**
  - voice/print matching.
  - pointing smoothly but slowly to each word.
  - unmasking words slowly as read.
  - matching word cards to words in sentence from story.
  - taking sentence from story — cut into words, reassemble into sentences that are the same as or different from the original, then read.

c. **Use of Context Clues**
  - using aural/oral cloze procedure, children learn to listen to sentence with missing word, then fill in missing word as the sentence in the story is reread from beginning (see Part III: C5, Cloze Procedure).
  - using oral cloze along with phonics clues, children learn to begin saying word using initial sounds, and then continue reading to end of sentence. This helps them focus more on print than with aural/oral cloze alone. The difficulty can be varied by the kinds of words omitted, for example:
    - common phrases, idioms
    - signal words, connecting words (*however, but, then, next, first*)
    - referential words (those referred to by words such as *it, he, those, the latter*).
    - verbs, nouns, adjectives, adverbs, pronouns.
  - brainstorming words and increasing vocabulary (homonyms, synonyms, antonyms, shades of meaning) develops children's ability to generate a number of appropriate possible words, a skill needed for using context clues.

d. **Use of Phonics Clues**

  – using cloze procedure, leave out or cover up word, leaving only initial one or two letters or initial letter and final letters.

  – changing letters in words in text (initial letters, final letters, digraphs, blends, vowels, endings, etc.), students then attempt to read changed text, find the mistake, and explain how to fix it.

  – replacing words with rhyming words, read, and fix.

  – beginning all words with same letter/sound, read, and fix.

  – finding words that are similar in spelling.

  – finding patterns in different words (e.g. digraphs, blends, diphthongs, and vowel patterns; see Appendix B for phonics patterns and teaching sequence).

e. **Sight Words**

  – having students find certain sight words (see Appendix A).

  – having them find how many times the same word is used in the passage.

  – having them find certain words elsewhere in the room, in reading books, in their writing.

  – visualizing words.

f. **Prior Knowledge/Experiences and Illustrations**

  – thinking out loud to demonstrate how prior knowledge and experiences plus phonics and context clues help predict what words may be used.

These teaching activities can also be used by the children during independent times as they imitate on their own the teaching activity. Similar activities can also be done individually by preparing smaller versions of cloze and word cards for children to use at their tables or centres. Using syllabication, structural analysis, and conventions of print are also necessary for fluent and independent reading. Activities focusing on these are given in the next section, Differentiated Focuses for Learners in the Classroom.

In these teaching activities the teacher is providing demonstrations of how reading uses print, language, and meaning clues to make sense. By "thinking out loud," the teacher models thinking processes, and students can verbalize and reflect for the benefit of others and themselves about the role of language, decoding strategies, and thinking in reading. (For other ideas see Part III: C1-5, Focusing on Print, Phonics and Beginning Reading.)

Daily lessons and activities need to include a focus on:

Foundations for reading

Learning to Read

Independent Reading

★ Ways I do this:

_____

_____

_____

_____

Independent Reading

Teachers facilitate growth in reading competency by:

- promoting individual reading for enjoyment and learning.
- engaging children in reading and writing activities.
- providing suitable assistance and encouragement.
- helping children use what they know about language and print to make meaning.
- promoting self-monitoring, self-correcting, and self-evaluation.
- extending their reading abilities and time engaged in independent reading (and writing).

Teachers need to plan ways to:

- ensure frequent opportunities for children to read silently and independently.
- provide appropriate reading material with which they can interact meaningfully.
- provide suitable feedback — encouragement, extension, redirection (Cambourne, 1988).
- allow students choices in reading materials so they can become fully occupied with reading because of their own interests and capabilities.
- encourage children to respond in a variety of ways and to share their understanding and appreciation of reading experiences.

Activities and Materials to Foster Independent Reading

Books with a wide range of difficulty, genre and topics need to be available in the classroom for children to choose from (see Appendix G). In many cases children will choose appropriately, but sometimes the teacher needs to narrow the choice so students will choose books so they can successfully engage in independent reading. Some children may consistently choose books that are too long and difficult, perhaps reflecting their image of a reader as someone who is able to read a "real" book, not a "little kid's picture book." Others continue to choose only familiar picture books with little print or books they have memorized. For these students it is beneficial to allow these choices, but as well it is important to ensure some of their reading involves books more closely matched to their level of word recognition.

The following list suggests ways to create varied levels of support for individual reading time. Children can choose from:

- Familiar text (heard many times or their own stories)
  - Children imitate strategies demonstrated by teacher and focus on print as they reconstruct or repeat memorized text.
- Familiar text (heard a few times, their own stories, or summaries of stories read to the class)
  - Children need to focus more on the print to decode words accurately. Memory of the story helps with recognizing many of the new words.
- Familiar text (heard once)
  - Having heard the story may have generated an interest in reading it or provided some background information to provide context for reading and decoding words.

- Unseen text with familiar language, structure, and/or topic
  - Children need to be able to recognize about 95% of the words easily if they are to read independently and successfully.
- Unseen text with unfamiliar language, structure, and/or topic
  - This is the goal for competent, independent readers.

Daily, children need opportunities to read on their own and to apply the knowledge and strategies they have been learning. During the time while children independently read, write, or work on projects or at centres, the teacher may choose to work with a small group of children to provide extra instruction based on their needs. The teacher may also choose to conference with an individual or small group to assess reading or to provide feedback. This creates opportunities to extend or reteach a strategy or to provide encouragement and reassurance. The next section suggests ways to provide differentiated focuses for learners within the classroom environment.

Choosing Literature for Beginning Reading

Increasing Difficulty ⟶

many illustrations	⟶	no illustrations
larger print	⟶	smaller print
few words/page	⟶	more words/page
smaller vocabulary	⟶	larger vocabulary
controlled vocabulary	⟶	no control
repetitive sentence structure	⟶	no repetitions
simple plots with repetition	⟶	complex plots
familiar concepts	⟶	unfamiliar concepts
simple sentences	⟶	complex sentences

Appendix G lists beginning reading books for children who have learned a few sight words and have some phonics decoding skills. Beginning novels are also listed for 7- to 9-year-olds who are keen to read "chapter" books .

As I read about different focuses, I want to think about the following students:

_____

_____

_____

_____

_____

_____

Providing Differentiated Focuses for Learners within the Classroom

⭐ Examples of this in my classroom

_____

_____

_____

_____

_____

_____

Within the classroom setting, teachers can provide for different student needs and abilities by:

- planning wide based themes so that students can
  - choose a particular aspect based on their interests
  - read and share different books
- planning the focus for whole class activities based on ongoing, daily observations and assessments of what the children are doing and need to learn
- using open-ended questioning, which allows students to
  - respond with different points of view and for a variety of reasons
  - extend or modify their response
  - ask questions, not just give responses
- allowing for varying kinds of response, for example, students can
  - respond alone, with others, or with support from teacher
  - respond verbally or nonverbally
  - respond by participating or by watching and listening
- gearing the type of feedback to specific children within the group
- being aware that each child is learning different things
- conferencing with small groups or helping individuals, the specific focus being based on the teacher's assessment and evaluation of what is needed (see Figure 27).

Providing for individual needs during independent reading time can be accomplished by allowing students choice in their reading material, encouraging them to read for their own purposes (for enjoyment, for projects), and providing reading material at an appropriate level of difficulty. To meet these needs the classroom will need a wide range of reading material in difficulty, topics and forms.

Assessment and evaluation are integral parts of the instructional and learning process. It is necessary for teachers to find out what each child knows and can do — What strategies and knowledge are being used? Do the children understand the text as they read? What aspects of reading are they aware of? Evaluation involves considering their prior experiences with reading, and their developmental level, individual capabilities, and talents together with their demonstrated reading strategies and competency. An essential part of evaluation is to observe and assess over time. Is growth occurring? How quickly? Is this rate of growth usual for this child?

In evaluating children's reading, a sense of how well the different strategies and knowledge interact is also valuable. It is important to note if children are overusing, underusing, misusing, or not using different aspects of the reading process. Perhaps they are focusing too much on the print or too much on prior knowledge or illustrations. Perhaps they have developed a habit of reading word-by-word or slowly, without realizing they can read faster (see also Assessing and Evaluating Reading, pp. 96-110).

Ongoing assessment and evaluation are essential to planning for and facilitating success with reading for all children.

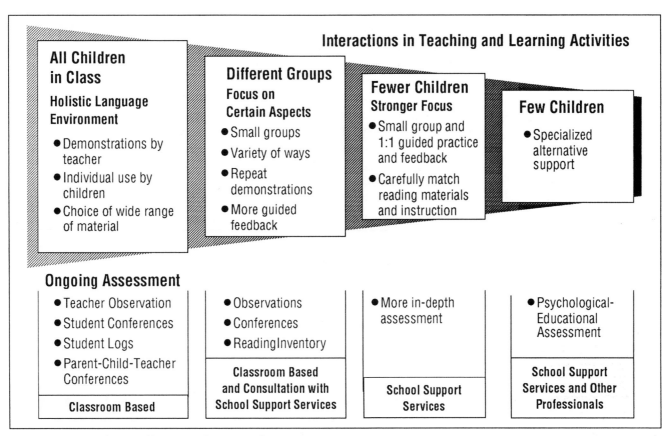

Figure 27. Providing Differentiated Support for Learners.

To decide what to assess and evaluate and, therefore, what to teach next, the *reading process model* provides guidance. *Developmental patterns* help establish realistic expectations of what might be developed next, and *individual differences* suggest the amount and kind of instructional intervention, and the use of different approaches (e.g. auditory, visual, kinesthetic/tactile; sequential, global; small group, individual instruction; focus on phonics, meaning, context, etc.).

Making decisions about different focuses for specific children needs to be based on:

- **Model of Reading Process** which indicates components of competent reading

- **Developmental Patterns** which indicate what children may be able to learn at a certain time

- **Individual Differences** which indicate aspects to consider for specific children

- **Prior Experiences** which contribute to children's attitudes towards learning and reading (concept of self) and to their present level of knowledge and competency

Providing Guidance and Support as Learner Moves Towards Independence

Students need varying degrees of guidance and support which will depend on their abilities, interests and prior experiences. Figure 28 represents the kinds of instructional support that may be provided. Starting from the left in the diagram, instruction for different students will involve one or more of the steps indicated. Some students may just need exposure to a strategy or idea, others will require a fuller explanation while it is modelled, and others will also need encouragement to use the strategy. Still others will need further step by step modelling with guided feedback, and so on. For some tasks one student may need little support, but for other tasks the same student may need much more support.

The following is a list of ways to vary the amount of support given to students:

- number of demonstrations of strategy/knowledge
  - some students will need to have more lessons/demonstrations or explanations.
- variety of approaches
  - some students will need visual, auditory, and/or kinesthetic/tactile strategies.
  - a particular student may learn certain tasks more easily visually, whereas the same student may learn other tasks better auditorily.
  - some students will be able to demonstrate their understanding better in writing or discussions, or by role-playing, drama, drawing, etc. (see Appendix H: Reading Responses).

⭐ Examples of this in my classroom

_____
_____
_____
_____
_____
_____

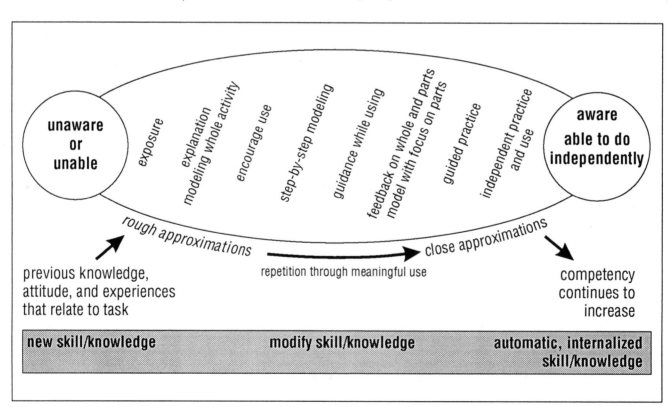

Figure 28. Providing Guidance and Support as Learner Moves Towards Independence.

- frequency of feedback
  - some students will need less feedback; others will need it more often.
- support given during practise/use
  - some students will need help after group instruction, as they actually try out the strategies; others will be able to implement them on their own.
- repetition and opportunities to use strategies/knowledge
  - some students will need more time and opportunities to use knowledge or skills in order to master them.
- selection of reading material
  - teacher or student choice, stories with familiar subjects allows students to relate reading to prior knowledge, level of vocabulary, language structures, illustrations, etc.

_____

_____

_____

_____

_____

_____

O'Brien (1987) poses the question, "How do we define having difficulty in a whole language context?" (p. 165). She states that "to some purists, no children will be in trouble in whole language classrooms" while others acknowledge "there will be some troubled or ineffective readers . . . but there will be a lot fewer" (p. 165). She states that although teachers are quick to notice children who are not developing, they are not certain how to act on their observations. In her article she describes three types of children who are referred for help:

- **Type I** — those developing at a significantly slower rate than peers in the class
- **Type II** — those who seem to stall at a particular level
- **Type III** — those who exhibit unusual development or unexpected ways of processing and responding to text.

She suggests that for Type I no changes are necessary; whereas for II and III the required changes may be accommodated in the class or in a pull-out setting. If the major cause seems to be, for example, a medical or emotional difficulty, a referral for a more indepth assessment is necessary. O'Brien (1987) categorizes intervention strategies along a continuum from low to high considering the degree of teacher direction, control and choice involved. Intervention may range, for example, from a low degree such as providing suitable reading material (high interest, easy reading novels) for student choice; to suggesting strategies as student reads text; to choosing the text, modelling strategies and guiding the reading (high degree of intervention). She also lists ways of intervening as: changing reading materials; before, during and after reading activities; dialogue and questions to focus and extend thinking; student discussing reading strategies; direct and indirect modelling; and scaffolding.

Low intervention
- providing reading materials
- modeling strategies
- _____
- _____
- _____

High intervention
- direct instruction and immediate feedback
- structured reading lessons
- _____
- _____
- _____

What to Focus On
- Strategies for word recognition
- Strategies for understanding and responding to literature
- Fluency in using strategies and recognizing words
- Flexibility in using strategies and monitoring comprehension

(see Figure 29 and box on pp. 79-80)

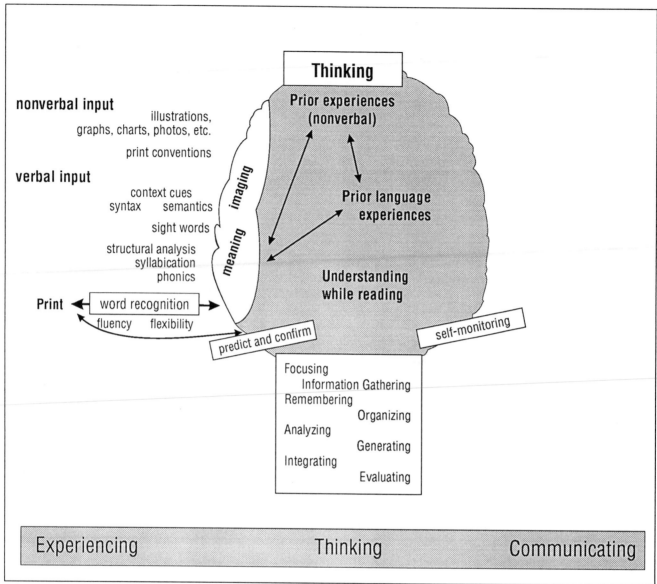

Figure 29. Focuses for Helping Children Learn to Read.

FOCUSES FOR HELPING CHILDREN LEARN TO READ

1. WORD RECOGNITION

FOCUS	PURPOSE
a. Awareness of letters and phonemes	• begin to use phonics clues • decrease reliance on memory reading and picture clues
b. Concept of Word	• decrease reliance on memory reading • begin to use sight words and phonics clues to identify words
c. Sight Words	• decrease reliance on memory reading • decrease reliance on phonics clues • enable better use of context clues • improve fluency
d. Context Clues	• decrease reliance on phonics • decrease reliance on sight words • enable combined use of phonics and context clues • improve fluency • focus on meaning and prior language
e. Phonics	• decrease reliance on memory reading • decrease reliance on context clues • decrease reliance on prior knowledge • enable combined use of phonics, context, and sight words • increase ability to decode new or unfamiliar word
f. Syllabication and Structural Analysis	• decrease reliance on prior knowledge • decrease reliance on sight vocabulary • decrease reliance on context clues • enable identification of new and unfamiliar words • obtain meaning of new or unfamiliar words

2. UNDERSTANDING (before, during, after reading)

FOCUS	PURPOSE
a. Establishing purpose for reading — e.g. learning, enjoyment	• decide whether to skim, scan, read "normally," study, or memorize the text • know what to focus on
b. Active processing	• monitor comprehension, predicting, confirming
c. Prior knowledge	• access, connect, revise language and experiences
d. Literal and inferential interpretations	• understand fully author's meaning
e. Thinking strategies	• focus, gather information, remember, organize, analyze, generate, integrate, evaluate
f. Using text features	• enhance focus on understanding
g. Evaluating ideas/text	• determine — fact/opinion/fiction, quality of writing, etc.

Focuses for Helping Children Learn to Read (cont'd.)

3. COMMUNICATING UNDERSTANDING AND USING INFORMATION

FOCUS	PURPOSE
• writing — notes, lists, words, summaries, reports, clustering, overviews, outlines, essays • sketching, diagramming • dramatizing • discussing, talking about • representing • demonstrating through one's actions in life • revising own ideas and thoughts • enhancing one's knowledge • modifying and establishing attitudes • visualizing, imaging (see Appendix H: Reading Responses)	• provide variety of ways for children to demonstrate understanding and to develop communication skills

At each grade or level strategies for word recognition, understanding, reading fluency and flexibility need to be focused on in lessons and activities with emphasis on those areas indicated by the needs of the students. What changes over the years and grades is the difficulty and length of the reading materials, the degree of independence in reading, the increased use of reading for learning, and the depth and complexity of understanding.

Effective readers use a combination of strategies, the reliance on each varies depending on the complexity of the text, the purpose for reading, and the reader's preferred strategies. If the reading material is familiar, the focus will be on context clues and meaning. If meaning is not disrupted, miscues will go unnoticed. The types of miscues made will reflect effective use of print and context to gain meaning.

If the vocabulary and concepts are unfamiliar, effective readers vary their reading rate, using print clues more when needing to decode unfamiliar words and rereading to make sense or to understand a new idea. Competent readers exhibit flexibility in using different reading rates and strategies as they monitor their understanding.

Difficulties arise if readers do not have the knowledge and variety of strategies to apply, do not take risks in predicting and confirming which words might come next, and do not concurrently self-monitor and self-correct their reading to maintain sense.

Difficulties arise if the process of integrating known strategies and adjusting their use does not happen automatically and fluently.

Difficulties arise if the reader relies too much on one strategy, or misuses or does not use a strategy, or does not use strategies flexibly.

Process for Deciding What to Focus On

- Assess and evaluate students' competency

  e.g. what they know and can do already, what they need to learn next to become more competent, and how they learn best.

- Decide on the purpose and focus of the instructional activity

  e.g. word recognition skills, comprehension strategies, ways to demonstrate understanding, independent reading, introduction of a new strategy, reinforce or reteach a strategy, develop fluency in reading or using a strategy.

- Once a focus is chosen, decisions can be made about which text to use and which learning or instructional activities would be best.

  e.g. If the purpose is to teach a strategy that will be applied to independent reading later on

  - students listen to a text and participate in activities to demonstrate understanding (text can be above students' reading level; this can be a whole class activity).

  e.g. If the purpose is to provide independent practice of strategy that has been taught (e.g. summarizing)

  - students choose own reading text and respond by summarizing story (text needs to be at independent reading level, student choice enhances interest for student, summarizing has already been taught; this can be an independent or paired activity).

  e.g. If the purpose is to teach word recognition strategies

  - students read text chosen by teacher and focus on decoding skills (text needs to be at instructional level and chosen so that particular decoding skills can be highlighted).

  e.g. If the purpose is to develop fluency of reading, enjoyment of reading, and sustained reading time

  - students read easy, familiar texts chosen by student (text choice is monitored by teacher to ensure it is easy and student input into choice ensures interest).

  - some students might use a repeated reading activity to increase fluency (see Section III: G2, Repeated Reading).

Strategies for Word Recognition

Once the purpose and focus is decided, the teaching and learning activities need to be selected. Teaching activities refer to those that the teacher carries out along with the children. Learning activities are those that the children will be doing to ensure they acquire the desired skills, knowledge, or strategies. Many of those activities used with the whole class are also suitable to be used again for specific children in small group or individual sessions. These children may find it more difficult to focus in large groups, or they may need more explicit instruction or more practise and review. Teaching some children a lesson before it is taught to the whole class (pre-teaching) helps them focus better in a large group lesson. Attention is enhanced because they already are familiar with the activity or task, they feel they can successfully participate, and they can show their peers what they know. This is also another way to provide review and repeated experiences within the class setting.

⭐ Some things I need to focus on in the class lessons:

_____

_____

_____

_____

_____

_____

Selecting teaching and learning activities

Strategies for word recognition

1. Familiarity with Letters and Phonemic Awareness

Phonemic awareness is a strong predictor of later reading achievement.

Phonemic awareness tasks

Developing phonemic awareness

⭐ In my class children who may need more direct instruction in hearing and manipulating sounds are:

_____

_____

_____

_____

1. Familiarity with Letters and Phonemic Awareness

Materials

Familiar texts, letter and picture cards, letter tiles, alphabet/letter games

Activities (The focus is on letter recognition and sounds in words.)

- Read and make up rhymes and alliterative phrases/sentences, tongue twisters.
- Listen to and repeat text that "plays" with language.
- Develop phonemic awareness.
- Use alphabet games and puzzles that involve matching and naming letters.
- Find letters in text being read out loud in class lessons, have children individually and in pairs do similar activities.

Phonemic awareness is the recognition of the basic speech sounds in spoken words (Griffith & Olson, 1992). Although it is not essential for being able to speak or for understanding speech, it does play a critical role in the ability to manipulate speech sounds. In a language that uses an alphabet, phonemic awareness is essential for decoding and spelling words. Because speech sounds are represented by letters and letter sequences, children will need to be able to separate the sounds in words in order to understand how letters represent the sounds. Phonemic awareness involves learning about the component sounds in words, whereas phonics involves recognizing and using letter/sound relationships to decode or spell words. Thus phonemic awareness is a prerequisite to being able to use phonics and is a strong predictor of later reading achievement (Beck & Juel, 1992; Juel, 1988).

Easy phonemic awareness tasks involve recognizing rhyming words and generating rhymes. Blending speech sounds into words (*m-a-n, sh-i-p*) and isolating speech sounds (e.g. asking child to give the first, middle, or last sound) are more difficult tasks. Tasks requiring the complete isolation of all phonemes in a word are even more demanding for young children (e.g. asking child to give the different sounds in a spoken word). The most difficult task is to remove a phoneme and say the remaining part (e.g. saying cat without the /t/ sound, saying house without the /h/ sound) (Griffith & Olson, 1992; Juel, 1988).

The development of phonemic awareness begins before children recognize letters because it deals only with speech sounds, not with letter/sound relationships as does phonics (see box on pp. 83-84). In fact, it is part of what children do naturally in playing with the language. Listening to and repeating literature that has rhymes, alliteration, or assonance (repetition of vowel sounds in a series of words) are activities children enjoy. Using these, they love to make up silly sentences saying each word beginning with the same sound, or to make up rhyming words. Many children's books play with words, for example, *Sheep in a Ship* (Shaw, 1989), *Don't Forget the Bacon!* (Hutchins, 1976). Besides listening to text that plays with language, frequent opportunities to write using constructed (invented) spellings develops phonemic awareness as children attempt to isolate the sounds in words and match them to letters.

Some children may require more direct instruction in hearing sounds in words. Activities can be structured to help children focus more explicitly on sounds in spoken words. For example, using picture cards and bingo chips or coloured tiles, the teacher models sounding out the word, putting down one chip/tile for each sound. Gradually the children take over the process, first putting

Phonemic Awareness (awareness of different sounds in words)

Materials: 5 each of 6 different coloured squares or blocks

Sequence of lessons — the following includes a number of activities that take would place over a number of weeks, progressing from one type of activity to the next as students demonstrate understanding and mastery.

① **Represent the number of sounds**
Children place one tile for each sound heard.
Begin with 2- and 3-letter words (e.g. **cat** **Hi** **hop**)

ⓐ use same colours for each sound
ⓑ use different colour for each different sound

② **Represent changes in sounds** (focus on sequencing and noting differences)

ⓐ change initial consonant

Children represent a word, e.g. **cat** ▨□▩

then represent rhyming words below this word using same colour tiles for same sounds and different colour tiles for different sounds, e.g.

fat	▨	□	▩
hat	▨	□	▩
mat	▦	□	▩
rat	■	□	▩

This is repeated using different word families (e.g. -an, -ad, -ap) until children can easily work with initial consonants. Similarly spend enough time with each of the following.

ⓑ change final consonant, e.g.

cat	▨	□	▨
can	▨	□	▩
cap	▨	□	■

ⓒ use word pairs that change order of sounds, e.g.

top – pot ■□▩ — ▩□■
mat – tam ▨▩■ — ■▨▩

ⓓ use nonsense syllables

ⓔ use words that change only vowel sounds, e.g.

pet	▨	□	■
pat	▨	▨	■
pit	▨	▩	■
pot	▨	▦	■

ⓕ use words with 4 sounds, including blends

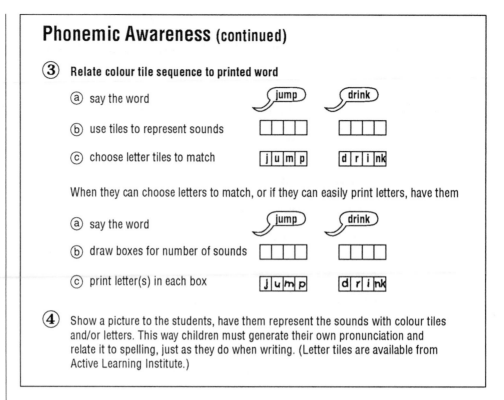

down the chips as the teacher says the word slowly; later saying the words themselves, separating the sounds, and independently matching each sound with a chip (see Figure 30). The words can be chosen from the stories being read to the class, daily "morning messages" or themes being developed in other class activities. Later, as phonemic awareness grows and letter recognition and printing develop, the children can print letters for the sounds, leading them to beginning phonics.

Figure 30. Developing Phonemic Awareness and Beginning Phonics.

2. Concept of Word

Similar to an awareness of speech sounds in words, children need to become aware of words in a spoken utterance. In speech, words are not distinct units. However, in print, words are separated. Both for reading and writing, children need experiences with text that help them develop an understanding of what a word is.

Materials

- Familiar verse, story or text enlarged for shared reading or individual copies
- Language Experience Approach, using child's language

Activities (The focus is on word boundaries and matching spoken to printed words)

- Read, pointing to or unmasking words as they are read.
- Find certain words, match word card to words on chart, frame word, circle word, point to word.
- Print sentence on a strip and word cards, match words below sentence strip
- Cut words from sentence strip, rearrange and read, arrange in different orders and read
- Collect their own interest words on cards, in personal dictionary, on tag-board strips taped on desk.
- Cloze activities using memorized text to focus on matching one-to-one spoken to written words, or orally fill in missing word in the sentence (see Part III: C5, Cloze Procedure).
- Writing activities
    - Provide feedback that directs attention to beginning and final sounds of words and relate these to child's constructed spellings.
    - When their spelling includes beginning and final consonants and some sight words, encourage children to leave spaces between words.
    - Have children read their own writing, matching spoken words to print and making some corrections.

3. Sight Words

As mentioned earlier, this term has three different meanings:

- Words that occur frequently in reading, and therefore, must be known by sight for fluent reading
- High interest or personal words — words learned by sight because of personal interest
- Nonphonetic words — cannot be sounded out, therefore, need to be recognized by sight

Activities (The focus is on recognizing words easily and quickly.)

- Match printed sight words to words in chart, book, or their own writing.
- Find specific sight words in charts/stories (e.g. ask children to locate "was"), have "word of the day" that they look and listen for during the day's activities.

Strategies for word recognition

1. Familiarity with Letters and Phonemic Awareness

2. **Concept of Word**

Strategies for word recognition

1. Familiarity with Letters and Phonemic Awareness

2. Concept of Word

3. **Sight Words**

- Add frequently used sight words and children's "interest" words to their own dictionary or cards (personal collection), these can be used in games and referred to when writing.
- Sentence scramble — using familiar and unfamiliar words, print sentences on cardboard strips, have children cut them into words, scramble, make new sentences and read.
- Easy reading for enjoyment, reread stories during independent reading time.
- Repeated reading — reread the same short story or passage three times to increase fluency (see Part III: G2, Repeated Reading).
- Teach children how to visualize words (Tarasoff, 1990).
- Have children write frequently — this helps them become familiar with commonly used words.
- Have games using sight words chosen from classroom reading activities for children to use — bingo, fish, memory.

4. Context Clues

As mentioned earlier semantic clues are based on meaning (only certain words will make sense because they relate to the topic) and syntactic clues are based on grammar (words can occur only in a certain order and in certain forms). Children's experience with and acquisition of oral language vocabulary is essential to being able to use context clues. Children must be able to generate many relevant words that may possibly make sense and fit the graphophonic clues. As well, listening to stories read aloud provides the foundation to their understanding and use of syntax and semantics in written language.

Activities (The focus is on language and meaning clues matched with phonics clues.)

- Cloze — remove words from the text or story that the context provides clues for, model process by thinking out loud, use oral cloze and oral/print cloze (similar to the activity on p. 85, Concept of Word, only now the focus is on actually reading the correct word not just matching spoken to printed word).
- Predict and Sort — predict words that may be found in a reading selection or used in a theme study. Sort into categories, show relationships. This develops vocabulary and helps with using context clues which is, in fact, brainstorming words associated with a particular topic.
- Reread stories and sing songs so the language becomes internalized (memorized), encourage "chiming-in" with familiar and repetitive phrases.
- Focus on, Collect, and Discuss — idioms, expressions, colloquialisms, literary structures (e.g. similes, metaphors), this develops familiarity with language structures, expected word order, and vocabulary.
- "Mad-Libs" — prepare a cloze passage (see box), without reading it to the children ask them for words belonging to the same category as the missing words (e.g. fruit, vehicle, adjective or describing word, verb, colour), write the word in the appropriate blank, then read passage out loud. Children love the nonsensical story that results. They can do this activity in pairs or on their own to provide independent rereading practice. This leads to discussion of using appropriate context clues.

"Mad-Lib" — based on *Goldilocks and the Three Bears*

One day a ____1____ girl named _____2_____ went for a walk in

describing word (adj.)   *girl's name*

the ____3____. Soon she came to a _____4_____ house. Then she

place (noun)   *describing word (adj.)*

saw the ____5____ was open, and she _____6_____ right inside the .

thing (noun)   *action word (verb)*

____7____ _____8_____ house. As she _____9_____ through

number   *animal (noun)*   *action word (verb, past tense)*

the house, she saw ____10____ ____11____.

number   *things (plural noun*

Don't read the passage until after the children have given you words. For example start by asking for

1. a describing word or adjective (e.g. <u>shiny</u>)

2. a girl's name (e.g. <u>Pam</u>)

3. a place or noun (e.g. <u>lake</u>)

4. a describing word or adjective, etc. (e.g. <u>puffy</u>)

Reading the passage aloud, putting in the words given, creates a nonsense passage which leads to discussions of context clues and making sense when reading.

"One day a <u>shiny</u> girl named <u>Pam</u> went for a walk in the <u>lake</u>. Soon she saw a <u>puffy</u> house . . . ." and so on.

• Discuss signal words and punctuation and prepare cloze activities based on these (see box).

Signal Words (Irwin, 1986)

Conjunction	and, also, in addition to
Disjunction	or, either . . . or
Cause	because, so, as a result
Purpose	in order to, so that
Concession	but, although, however, yet
Contrast	similarly, on the other hand, in contrast
Condition	If . . . then . . . , unless, except
Time	before, during, after, always, while
Location	there, where

- Web texts and discuss referents (Irwin, 1986)
  e.g.

  1. The three little pigs went to the market. Only two came home.

  2. Tom was hurt at the game. It was really rough play. He can't play tomorrow.

  3. They decided to go to the beach for a swim. Susan ran faster than her friend, Peter. He ran as fast as he could but this time she got there first.

Strategies for word recognition

1. Familiarity with Letters and Phonemic Awareness

2. Concept of Word

3. Sight Words

4. Context Clues

5. **Phonics Clues**

5. Phonics Clues

Activities (The focus is on using phonics in reading and in spelling; see Appendix B: Phonics Patterns.)

- Teach children to use phonics along with context clues by using cloze activities and encouraging children to say the initial sound (and last sound) and to keep reading or reread. Having them say the initial sounds is more effective than substituting a nonsense word like "teakettle" or "blankity" because this more closely resembles a "normal reading" strategy— phonics clues used along with context clues.

- Demonstrate how to blend sounds to approximate pronunciation of new words as they read. For example, using letters tiles (or cards), have the children say the sound of the first letter as it is moved towards the next letter. As it touches the second letter, blend that sound with the first, then extend the sounds to next letter. In this way the children see and hear the blending. They enjoy adding the sound as the letter tiles meet (see Figure 31). If sounding out the word results in a mispronunciation, encourage the children to suggest the correct pronunciation.

- Word Study

  - match words to picture cards based on initial and final sounds

  - find word in text or book when given the spoken word

  - compare word families and rhyming words (put words on cards or on a chart)

  - sort and classify words according to spelling, write on a chart

  - make words from letters, e.g. how many words can be made from the letters "p o t s r" ? Make 2-letter words, then make 3-, 4-, and 5-letter words (see box on p. 89).

- Writing about what they have read, brainstorm story words that relate to the phonics patterns being studied, have children write about the story after reading it using some of these words.

- Other ideas are found in Section III: C, Focusing on Print, Phonics, and Beginning Reading.

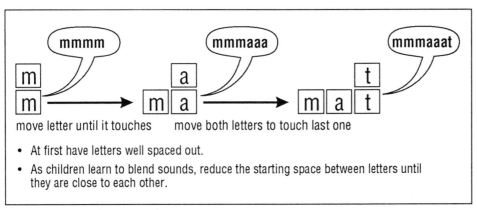

move letter until it touches   move both letters to touch last one

- At first have letters well spaced out.
- As children learn to blend sounds, reduce the starting space between letters until they are close to each other.

Figure 31. Blending Sounds.

- Help children become aware of articulation clues that they are using or could use when they begin to construct spelling. Some children at this stage will benefit from learning to use articulation correctly when sounding out (segmenting) words for spelling or when blending sounds to decode words (see box on page 90). These can be supplemented with "picture stories" that help them remember letter/sound relationships.

Making words given a selection of letters (Cunningham & Cunningham, 1992)

- choose letters/sounds to work with (e.g. in a story being read in class there are many words with short **o** and blends, therefore, you might decide to choose **p o t s r** because words with blends and short o can be made)
- before the lesson print on cards all the 2- to 5-letter words that can be made from the letters
- to begin the lesson have children pick out letter tiles (**p o t s r**)
- ask children to make 2-letter words (you can either ask them to make "to," then "so," or you can have them figure out the 2-letter words themselves depending on their ability)
- after they make the words, put the words cards (prepared earlier) in the pocket chart, discuss similarities/differences, read
- next, have them make 3-letter words one at a time
- after students make each word with the tiles, put the word card in the chart and read (e.g. **top pot sop rot**)
- do the same with 4-letter words (e.g. **post, stop, pots, tops, rots, port**)
- challenge them to make 5-letter words using all the letters (**ports, sport**) or the longest word they can, add to chart
- have children put away letter tiles
- read and sort the words in the pocket chart into phonics patterns (e.g. blends, vowel sounds, plurals)

This activity can be used at various grades and levels by varying the difficulty, for example: the kinds of phonics patterns focused on (e.g. short a, digraphs ch and th, vowel patterns au and aw, syllable patterns "tion" or "age,"); the length of the words to be made; and the amount of guidance given by the teacher (e.g. step-by-step, or "make as many 4-letter words as you can").

Children's initial constructed spellings often reflect their use of articulation to decide which letters to write. They may substitute incorrect but similarly articulated letters. For these children, decoding words based on phonics will be difficult.

Articulation Clues

The following information is for teachers. It is not meant to be studied and memorized by children. When aware of how letter sounds are articulated, you can understand why certain spellings occur in children's early writing. It will also help in modelling correct articulation for sounding out words.

Consonant pairs
(these are usually focused on at different times to avoid confusion)

Unvoiced*	Voiced**	
p	b	lips pop open
t	d	tongue is against upper teeth
f	v	upper teeth placed lightly on lower lip
k	g	tongue in bottom of mouth
ch	j	lips extend out, tongue behind lower teeth
s	z	teeth lightly closed, tongue behind lower teeth
th	th	tongue between teeth (think — then)

* voiced — air pushed out, vocal cords vibrate
— noisier (if you cover your ears)

** unvoiced — air let out slowly, whisper, vocal cords not vibrate
— quieter (if you cover your ears)

Some consonants borrow sounds

c	/k/ (cook)	/s/ (city)	
x	/z/ (xylophone)	/ks/ (box)	/gz/ (exact)
qu	/kw/ (quit)	/k/ (opaque)	
y	as consonant, uses articulation similar to long /ē/ as vowel, uses long /ī/, long /ē/, short /ĭ/		

Nasal consonants (air resonates in nose, difficult to say the sound with nasal passage blocked, e.g. when you have a head cold)

m	lips closed
n	tongue against back of top teeth
ng	tongue on bottom of mouth
nk	/ng/ + /k

Other consonants

w	lips pushed out, air smoothly flows out, voiced
h	tongue in bottom of mouth, lips open, puff of air, unvoiced
l	tongue behind top front teeth, voiced
r	lips pursed, tongue in bottom of mouth, voiced
sh	lips out, teeth together, tongue down, unvoiced
wh	technically this can be distinguished from /w/; it is not necessary to do so for children

Articulation Cues and "Picture Stories"

a — as in apple

o — as in octopus or as in "Aw, can't I stay up late?" (Aw sounds like short /ŏ/ and mouth makes "O" shape)

i — children learn the word *it* quite easily — so **i** as in *it* will help them.

u — as in *up* (The baby doesn't speak properly but says /ŭ/ instead of up. The arms form the letter u.)

e — as in bed or as in elephant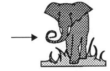

Making up "picture stories" with children who are having difficulty remembering letter-sound relationships will aid their memory.

6. Syllabication and Structural Analysis

Activities (The focus is on syllabication patterns and how to use these to "chunk" multisyllabic words into manageable parts for decoding, and on root words, derivatives, prefixes, suffixes, endings and combining forms and how these help with decoding/spelling and meaning.)

- Decide on the focus of the word study (see Appendices C and D).
- Choose words or have students brainstorm or find words from stories, texts and theme lessons (as whole class, small groups, pairs).
- Sort into patterns, create chart, generalize to other words as they surface in other activities, continue to search for similar words and add them to chart.
- Model when reading how to decode new words by referring to what has been discussed and studied already.
- Model how to determine meaning by using roots, endings, affixes and combining forms.
- Before reading a selection, brainstorm relevant words or have students scan text for new multisyllabic words; list, discuss and decode.
- Use these in other word study/spelling lessons.

Strategies for word recognition

1. Familiarity with Letters and Phonemic Awareness
2. Concept of Word
3. Sight Words
4. Context Clues
5. Phonics Clues
6. **Syllabication and Structural Anlysis**

What to Focus On

Strategies for Word
Recognition

**Strategies for Understanding
and Responding to Literature**

Your mental set influences
what you attend to and how
you interpret sensory input,
that is, perception. It helps
explain the importance of
establishing a purpose for
reading.

Self-concept can be thought
of as a "mental set." Poor
readers often seem to be "set"
to notice what they can't read
or do rather than their
successes.

Establishing a purpose for
reading creates a "set" and
focuses attention on what
may be remembered from
reading.

Strategies for Understanding and Responding to Literature

These teaching and learning activities can be done orally, using text read to students as well as with literature read silently. In this way students can learn comprehension strategies before they can actually use them during independent reading. Before beginning, it is essential to establish purpose for the reading. This is done using activities that involve anticipation, prediction, deciding why the selection is being read, and deciding on strategies to use during reading and on activities to follow reading.

The importance of establishing reading purpose is supported by the concept of "mental set" (Russell, 1984). This concept explains why some information is more easily recognized and remembered. If you have just bought a new car, you begin to notice more of those cars on the road. Out of the thousands of things you could notice, your brain is more tuned at that particular time to notice cars and, in particular, the kind you bought. Psychologists call this "set." If you are expecting a friend to phone, you are likely to recognize their voice more quickly than if you were not expecting them to call. In addition to affecting focus of attention and recognition speed, set plays a role in perception. Magicians rely heavily on this phenomenon — preparing you for a certain happening, while actually doing something else. Your perception of what happened is determined by what the magicians direct you to notice (creating a "set") and not by what they actually did (the reality of events).

The "tip-of-the-tongue" phenomenon is another kind of set. At first you may not be able to think of a particular word you want, but even when you stop trying to think of it, your mind remains "set." Later, the word may be heard or seen in another context or may pass through your mind. You then recognize it as the word you were trying to remember.

Beliefs create a set by which you often notice certain facts and events that support your beliefs and miss those that don't support them. This is why it is so difficult to take a point of view opposite to your beliefs and to find evidence to support it. Some people have suggested that pet owners often have physical traits similar to their pets. Have you ever noticed this? If you begin to look for these similarities, you will indeed see many features that will substantiate this theory. However, did you remember to notice the differences, for example, presence of a tail, shape of the ears, and so on. Set also affects how you see other people and interpret their actions. It can influence your expectations of them and, in turn, their beliefs about themselves. This Pygmalion Effect has been documented by many studies in schools, medicine, business, politics, and so on.

Self-concept could be thought of as a set. Children who feel they are poor readers are "set" to notice what they can't read, rather than what they can read. They often only notice others who read better than they do, and fail to see their own progress, focusing on their difficulties rather than successes. Having children set goals and self-evaluate their progress helps them become more "set" to notice their own abilities.

Establishing a purpose for reading creates a "set" and determines to a great extent what is and is not noticed during reading and, therefore, what may be remembered after reading. Many of the strategies described in the literature are teaching activities that help children establish a purpose for reading. They also encourage children to access prior information and experiences and to decide what else they would like to know or what they expect the reading to be about. This creates a "set" and enhances subsequent understanding during reading and recall.

Read the following passage and be prepared to answer questions and summarize it, connecting it to your prior knowledge.

> With hocked gems financing him, our hero bravely defied all scornful laughter that tried to prevent his scheme. "Your eyes deceive," he said. "It is like an egg, not a table." Now three sturdy sisters sought proof. Forging along, sometimes through calm vastness, yet more often over turbulent peaks and valleys, days became weeks as many doubters spread fearful rumors about the edge. At last, from nowhere welcomed winged creatures appeared, signifying momentous success.

What is this passage about? Who is "our hero?" What is the scheme? If you cannot answer these questions, does it mean you have a reading problem? Note: There is little context for this passage and, therefore, you may have difficulty connecting it to prior knowledge (see p. 94 for background information).

The following lists strategies and activities focused on understanding text.

Before Reading

(Having children share in a group allows each child to hear other students' vocabulary, questions, and ideas.)

- Activate existing prior knowledge
  - Visualizing/Imaging — information, characters, settings, feelings, prior knowledge, prior experiences
  - Brainstorming — associated ideas, concepts, vocabulary questions
  - List or discuss what you already know or think you know, what you want to learn, or think you'll learn, and/or where you might find the answers or information
  - Webbing/Mapping/Advance Organizers — ideas, vocabulary, relationships, questions
- Use text
  - Preview by skimming text or scanning for information illustrations, headings, key words, layout, etc.
  - Questioning — generate questions using text headings or 5 W's and H (who, what, when, why, where, and how)
  - Note the structure of the text — generate outline
  - Read a sample section of the text — decide on strategies
- Provide more background information
  - Other reading about the topic
  - Other experiences — field trips, dramatizations, experiments, films, pictures
  - Discuss key words, idioms, figures of speech
  - Imaging of related ideas/concepts
  - Information about author, topic, text structures

During Reading

(Monitor understanding and comprehension strategies, sharing in a group allows children to learn from others)

- Stop during reading and use text and prior knowledge to predict and confirm, use context clues

Before-reading activities to focus on meaning

During-reading activities to focus on active processing and making meaning

93

- – Make connections, organize, analyze
- – Summarize, recall, ask questions
- – Evaluate

- Make connections with purpose for reading and with prereading or postreading activities (e.g. filling in a chart, making notes, completing plot profiles, semantic maps, or outlines)

After Reading (entire selection)

(Activities will incorporate a variety of communication strategies — written, spoken, and/or representational and verbal/nonverbal)

- Organize, summarize, analyze, evaluate information/story
- Relate activities to purpose for reading
- see Appendix H: Reading Responses

After-reading activities to focus on responding and communicating meaning

Some of the instructional strategies and activities mentioned in the literature are outlined briefly in Part III. They are teaching suggestions for actively involving students in learning to read and to understand the structure of written texts. These suggestions can be categorized as before, during and after reading strategies. Some you will find fall into all three categories, others into one or two. Note the similarities between them and which part of the reading process they focus on (e.g. decoding, thinking skills, fluency). It then becomes easier to make sense of all the suggestions by realizing they often describe similar strategies but are explained and constructed differently by different authors (ReQuest, K-W-L, Reciprocal Teaching, Sketch-to-Stretch, etc.). For example, note that the K-W-L procedure was modified by adding semantic mapping and summarizing to K-W-L and naming it K-W-L Plus. It is not necessary to incorporate each technique into a reading program, nor treat them as entities. Once the basic components are understood, you will be able to evaluate and adapt them and select from the many ideas.

As a teacher, it is important to understand the focus of these techniques and decide which are valuable for the children in your class and why you might include them. As mentioned, on a daily basis children need to be involved in lessons and activities that focus on (1) laying the foundations through providing experiences incorporating all forms of language, (2) learning more about how to read (decoding and thinking/comprehension strategies), and (3) reading independently (using what has been learned). To develop each of these strands, before, during, and after reading activities can be used as needed. To help develop a balanced program — one that ensures students learn to recognize words automatically, to decode unfamiliar words easily, to actively engage in understanding texts, and to willingly read for their own purposes — use the descriptions in Part III along with suggestions for Teaching Reading (see Figure 25, p. 65), the Reading Process Model (see Figure 29, p. 78) and the Summary of Reading Strategies (see Figure 32, p. 95) as a reminder or checklist of components to include.

Background information for passage on p. 93

If you had read the same passage after knowing that it is about Columbus' first voyage to America with his three ships, you would have been set to relate it to what you know already know about this historic voyage. Now, knowing the context, the passage has more meaning and, therefore, will be easier to summarize and remember.

READING STRATEGIES

Prior Experiences and Language Development

- develop vocabulary, concepts, images

Word Recognition (focus on print)

- familiarity with letter and graphemic awareness
- concept of word
- sight words
- context clues
- phonics
- syllabication and structural analysis

Understanding

(active processing, monitoring comprehension, predicting and confirming)

- prior knowledge (language & experiential) — access, connect, revise
- literal and inferential interpretation
- recall/remembering strategies
- establishing purpose — learn, enjoy, evaluate/critique
- using text — context clues, structure, format
- evaluating — text (quality), ideas (fact/opinion/fiction/etc.)

Communicating Understanding and Using Information

(share and reflect upon the meanings constructed, learn from hearing responses made by others)

overt
- write — notes, lists, words, summaries, reports, clustering, overviews, outlines
- sketch, diagram
- dramatize
- discuss, talk about
- represent — fine arts
- demonstrate through one's actions in life
- revise own ideas and thoughts

covert
- reconceptualize
- enhance own knowledge
- modify and create attitudes
- picture, image

Flexibility in using strategies depending on purpose and text
Fluency in reading

Thinking Skills

focusing
   gathering information
remembering
      organizing
analyzing
     generating
integrating
    evaluating

Figure 32. Summary of Reading Strategies.

Assessment and Evaluation of Reading

ASSESSING READING

What

- Product
  - Knowledge
    - Attitude
      - Fluency

- Process
  - Skills
    - Strategues
      - Flexibility

How

- Observing
  - Conferencing
    - Listening to reading
      - Informal and formal tests

When

- more indepth when difficulties noted
- ongoing

Who

- all students
- specific students

Why

- planning teaching, set goals
  - noting progress
    - evaluate difficulties
      - note what child can do

Evaluating Reading

- determine present knowledge, skills, strategies, and attitude
  - relate to what competent reading involves
    - decide what could be learned next
      - establish goals to move towards greater competency
        - identify attainable skills, knowledge, strategies
          - reflect to determine that progress is being made

Accountability

ensuring each child is progressing in reading competency and demonstrates a concept of self as a reader

Standards

the knowledge, skills, strategies and attitudes of an independent, competent reader, the expectation being that each student will gradually approach and eventually attain this standard by developing increased competency and independence over time with consideration of developmental patterns and individual variations

Knowing what is involved in competent reading clarifies the goal of reading instruction and standards for evaluation. A successful reading program will account for every child moving closer to the goal of independence and competency in reading. Evaluation focuses on measuring the progress made toward this goal for each child since the last evaluation rather than comparing to what the "average" child is expected to accomplish.

A standard is defined (Collins English Dictionary) as "an accepted or approved example of something against which others are judged or measured," or "a level of excellence or quality." For reading, competency and independence is the expectation for all students. A competent reader could be described as one who can easily and independently decode a text containing information and ideas new to the reader. A competent reader understands literally and inferentially the main ideas and details, provided the reader has relevant background knowledge pertaining to the topic. As well, the competent reader integrates personal knowledge to help understand the text and attempts to reconstruct the author's meaning. The competent reader willingly initiates reading for learning and for enjoyment and varies his or her reading rate according to the purpose for reading.

It is more difficult to determine the age expectation for reaching this standard and the acceptable deviation from this for students who have difficulties that will keep them from reaching this standard. However, it is expected that each student should continue to approach this standard while in school and that each student will have the skills and desire to continue to improve after graduation. Therefore, the goal of a reading focus within a language arts program is to ensure each student in the class is developing in his or her reading competency.

The purpose of assessment and evaluation is:
- to find out what child knows and can do
  - independently, and
  - with support
- to evaluate progress over time with reference to
  - developmental patterns
  - individual capacities and talents
  - prior learning experiences (oral language, reading, and personal experiences)
  - effective reading strategies and knowledge.
- to decide
  - next goals and expectations
  - kinds of learning activities suitable for student
  - pace of introducing new concepts
  - how much assessment and support is needed

Ongoing evaluation indicates growth or competency in the following areas:
- increasing ease of word recognition and larger reading vocabulary leading to fluent reading
- variety of strategies and skills

Goals and standards

Purpose of assessment and evaluation

- flexible use of strategies
- understanding of increasingly complex and less familiar texts
- positive attitude towards reading for enjoyment and learning

What is considered to be a successful rate of progress is determined by each individual's capacities, talents, and previous experiences. These expectations need to be re-examined regularly throughout schooling in light of questions such as the following. Is this the best the student can do, or is there something else that could be done? Are changes in instructional activities or materials needed? Should the student be allowed to demonstrate learning orally or by drawing rather than writing? Should extra time be allowed for reading and responding? Would extra teaching support improve student progress? The data collected on an ongoing basis together with an evaluation of the students with reference to their abilities, their experiences, and the instruction they receive will help answer these questions.

Assessment Process — Gathering Data from a Variety of Sources

- Types of records that can be kept
  - Student

  - reading log (books read and responses)
  - record of goals set
  - log of strategies learned and used
  - responses to reading in a journal
  - Parent
    - observations of progress and home reading
  - Teacher
    - observations and evaluations
    - reading miscue analyses or running records
    - tapes of oral reading and retelling or summarizing
    - record of types of instructional/learning activities
- Observe children engaged in silent and oral reading and participating in instructional activities. When observing, notice:

  - during quiet, independent reading time if they
    - initiate/engage in reading
    - sustain reading
    - reflect on reading
  - at choice time if they choose to read
  - during instructional activities if they
    - participate actively, willingly
    - demonstrate skills, strategies, knowledge, and understanding
    - use information from reading

- Conference with children about what they have read and their understanding of the text, and their reading strategies. When conferencing:

  Things to consider when conferencing about reading

  − notice their book handling knowledge (title, front/back, use of illustrations, graphs, maps, index, glossary, table of contents, appendices, headings, etc.)

  − determine their reading strategies

    • knowledge and skills for word recognition

    • use of print conventions

    • use of thinking skills

  − ask questions about the strategies student uses

  − ask for their self-evaluation

  − discuss a story with students (e.g. evaluate story, compare/contrast texts, discuss characters, themes, plot, information, conclusions, etc.)

  − ask students to summarize/retell story or information

  − ask students to read part of text and think out loud

  − allow students to "look-back" at text when discussing it

  − have students sequence part of story — sentence strips, paragraphs

- Discuss with parents their children's progress and home reading.

- Listen to children engaged in oral reading (both familiar and unfamiliar texts). When listening to their reading, keep a record of their miscues and reading rate (see Appendix J). Goodman, Burke, and Watson's (1987) Reading Miscue Analysis and Clay's (1985) Running Record are two ways to analyze children's oral reading to gain an insight into their strategies. These two resources provide excellent explanations for evaluating oral reading. Informal Reading Inventories (IRI) are similar in some ways to miscue analyses, but use a series of successively more complex (graded) texts (Johnson, Kress & Pikulski, 1987). There are both advantages and disadvantages to using IRI's.

  Assessment can involve listening to children read.

  Reading Miscue Analysis

  Running Record

  Some advantages: they are easy to use, readily available, and provide a graded reading level as well as some information about students' strategies and their instructional levels.

  Some disadvantages: the passages are short, do not have the appeal of books, have varying levels of interest and connection to students' prior knowledge which directly affect their comprehension scores, as well the comprehension questions are too few to really discriminate (e.g. between 70% and 80%) levels of comprehension.

  Informal Reading Inventories

The advantage of a Reading Miscue Analysis or Running Record is that they can be done using classroom reading material that will interest students more and provide ongoing and more "authentic" assessment of their interests and abilities related to classroom programs. When choosing passages to be read for a Reading Miscue Analysis, students' background knowledge, language, and prior experiences connected with text should be considered because these will influence the ease of reading and comprehension. Keep in mind the following factors when choosing material. Difficulty of a passage is affected by the familiarity of language and topic and whether students have heard/read passage before. In reading unseen passages difficulty is increased if the language structures, vocabulary and topic are unfamiliar. Text features that also contribute to the ease or difficulty are:

- size of print
- presence or lack of illustrations
- sentence length, complexity, and structure
- degree of abstraction and density of concepts
- level of literal or inferential interpretation needed
- author's style
- literary devices
- text organization.

Things to consider when using classroom reading resources for assessment

For emergent readers, selections or books with repetitive or cumulative patterns and high degree of congruence between picture and text can be used to assess book knowledge. For beginning independent readers, the level of vocabulary difficulty in selections can be determined by how many of the words are commonly occurring words (such as **is, like, to, go, the, in**) and how phonetically regular the other words are. Depending on the context and picture clues, the child may be able to predict a fair number of multisyllabic and irregular words. But to assess beginning readers, text containing fewer of these words must be chosen. Selections from anthologies that are compiled for different levels can be used to develop a series of passages with increasing levels of difficulty (see Appendix I which describes examples of such passages). By assessing children's reading using a series of passages, progress can be documented and evaluated.

Reading involves the recreation of the author's meaning in interaction with personal knowledge and this understanding resides in the brain and cannot be directly accessed. Assessment must acknowledge that understanding can only be indirectly evaluated, reflected through both verbal and/or nonverbal responses. As well, it must be acknowledged that children have different capabilities and talents for demonstrating their knowledge and understanding through verbal and nonverbal processes. Therefore, in assessing reading we need to be cognizant of what is actually being evaluated. For example, some children may not be able to communicate as well in writing as they do through speaking. What is thought to be a reading problem could in fact be a speech or writing difficulty, a lack of experience with reading, or a lack of knowledge about the subject matter. What might at first glance appear to be a comprehension problem may not be due to a reading difficulty but rather to difficulties in organizing, analyzing, or integrating information. Or perhaps, as a result of previous experiences, they are reluctant to risk answering for fear of being embarrassed or because they feel they are not capable.

In assessing reading we must be aware of what is really being measured.

Analyzing the Data: Word recognition strategies

Competent readers use a variety of strategies based on print and meaning, and use these fluently and flexibly. From the data gathered during oral reading, children's word recognition strategies can be evaluated (Goodman, Burke & Watson [1987]; Clay [1985], see Appendices I and J) to determine which ones they are using and what would help them improve. Are they overusing one strategy, for example, trying to sound out every word? Do they not have enough phonics knowledge and so do not try to decode new words? Examples of what to note are given below. For a valid assessment, passages in which children can identify 90% or more of the words should be used, otherwise miscues may be due to frustration rather than to a reading difficulty.

★

In my class I have noticed

_____

a. **Familiarity with letters and graphemic awareness, concept of word**

Observations indicating difficulties

No use: students do not know letters, do not relate letters to sounds, are not aware of concept of word (in writing uses string of random letters), do not look at print when memory reading

_____

Minimal use: when memory reading, do not match spoken to written words accurately, obviously guess other words, relate some words to letter sounds

_____

Misuse: say wrong word when pointing to word, use wrong sound for letter (e.g. /f/ for v, /d/ for t), leave sounds out

Overuse: read word-by-word, slowly sounding out each letter even for irregularly spelled words, won't attempt to read or memory read

b. **Sight Words**

Observations indicating difficulties

No use: students are dependent on memory reading or try to sound out each word

_____

Minimal Use: recognize a few words, sound out others or stop reading, do not recognize word even if the same one was read before in the same passage

_____

Misuse: substitute words similar in appearance or try to sound out words that are nonphonetic

_____

Overuse: attempt to recognize words by sight, do not use phonics clues, substitute words that look similar and guess others

_____

c. **Context Clues**

Observations indicating difficulties

No Use: students rely on print clues or sight words, read word-by-word, make nonsense substitutions

_____

Minimal Use: read slowly, stop if can't sound out word

_____

Misuse: guess incorrectly, substitute words that fit function but not meaning, begin to make up story from their own experience

_____

Overuse: rely on context clues, do not attend to print, substitute words that make sense or partial sense but are unrelated to print clues

_____

d. Phonics

Observations indicating difficulties

No Use: students rely on memory and background knowledge, stop reading when word is unfamiliar

Minimal Use: rely on context clues, pictures, background knowledge, guess word with some graphic/sound similarity

Misuse: don't know letter/sound relationships, use incorrect letter/sound relationships

Overuse: attempt to sound out all words, don't use context or language background, don't recognize same word previously read

e. Syllabication and Structural Analysis

Observations indicating difficulties

No Use: students make up word (nonsense or otherwise), mumble, skip words, or stop reading

Minimal Use: use beginning and/or end of word, use word that has some graphic or phonic similarity

Misuse: use incorrect sound associations, incorrect word parts, incorrect pronunciation of syllables

Overuse: decode all multisyllablic slowly, don't use context or language clues to help with pronunciation

Analyzing the Data: Comprehension

In evaluating reading comprehension, it is essential to be sure the assessment task reflects the students' ability to understand. Prior experiences and knowledge or lack thereof, difficulty with writing or speaking, and inability to decode many of the words are some of the things that can interfere with an accurate assessment. Thus, it is important to know the strengths and needs of students. Some things to consider:

• Are they able to identify about 90% or more of the words?

• Do they have difficulty with processing speech and, therefore, find it difficult to retell a story orally?

• Do they have writing difficulties that prevent them writing answers or summaries that express their full understanding?

• Have they learned how to retell a story (e.g. using story grammar as a framework)?

• Do they know what is being requested when they are asked to retell the story?

• If they could dramatize the story, would their understanding be demonstrated better than by writing a summary or by answering questions?

• Does the task assess comprehension, or some other skill or prior knowledge and experiences? Giving a reading passage to all students in a class and evaluating their retelling of it will provide a range of responses. Do the differences in retelling reflect differences in comprehension based on reading abilities, or differences in prior knowledge, in prior experiences with retelling, in speaking abilities, in understanding the task, and so on?

Before students read they must understand the purpose for reading and the task they will be asked to do after reading. In any passage there is a great deal of possible information that could be recounted. All readers attend to specific aspects of the material depending on their purpose or "set" for reading and their personal background. Thus, when being assessed, students need to know the kind of assessment task that will be used. As well, the assessment task needs to focus on finding out what readers know about reading and their reading strategies rather than their ability to score well on a particular task.

Students need a purpose for reading even when being assessed.

In assessing comprehension, the familiarity of the topic and language structures must be considered. For example, if the student has no prior knowledge of the topic and many new words specific to the topic are included in the passage (concept and vocabulary load is high), then they will have more difficulty understanding and recalling information than if the topic is more familiar to them. In this case, it is important to consider what is being assessed — the students' knowledge or their reading comprehension. If questions are asked, to ensure students access reading skills rather than prior knowledge, the questions must have answers that are unfamiliar to the reader. The answers should be "passage dependent," that is, the reader cannot answer the question from prior knowledge alone. As well, the context must be reasonably helpful in providing the answer either explicitly or implicitly (see Part III: E2, Question/Answer/Relationships).

Students need to be some-what familiar with the general topic and language structure.

Comprehension questions can be structured to require different kinds of answers: multiple choice, recall, or "look-back" (readers can refer to text). Each of these requires different skills in addition to comprehension. Multiple choice and "look-back" rely less on memory than recall. With straight recall, readers must remember from one reading and generate an answer. With "look-back," readers are able to reread, but still must generate their own answer. With multiple choice, readers only need to recognize an answer from those provided, and guessing can distort the assessment. Multiple choice also is a less "authentic" task; seldom do children respond to multiple choice questions after reading other than in school. Each of these tasks provides different kinds of data for evaluating reading comprehension and has a difference degree of relevancy to everyday reading tasks.

Comprehension questions can be multiple choice, recall or "look-back." Each format calls on different skills.

In assessing reading comprehension, it is also necessary to provide a variety of ways for students to demonstrate their understanding such as through writing, drama, sketches, semantic mapping, discussing, reporting, making models. The assessment task must be one in which they have had some instruction and opportunity to learn. For example, for writing a summary, they need to have learned what to include in a summary (see Part III: F1, Summarizing); for retelling a story, they must have some idea what this involves (see Part III: F4, Retelling).

Students need to be given a variety of ways to express their understanding.

Oral retellings also provide information about students':

- ability to remember in relation to task difficulty
- familiarity with the topic (how much supplemental information students provide)
- idea of what story is about (student provides global or detailed statements)
- ability to infer and interpret
- ability to integrate reading with their personal knowledge and experiences

- composing behaviours
  - use of own words or words from text
  - order of ideas, retold in sequence or mixed up
  - story grammar or text structure
- ability to verbalize ideas.

Oral reading can provide some information about students' comprehension.

Information about reading comprehension is also obtained from analyzing students' oral reading. Note whether they stop and self-correct their errors when meaning is disturbed and whether they alter their reading rate when they have difficulty recognizing words. Competent readers predict what words might come next based on meaning and monitor their understanding as they read. If something does not make sense they stop and reread, or slow down when there is an increasing number of unfamiliar words. Some students continue to read at the same rate, skipping words and miscuing frequently, an indication they are not reading for meaning and perhaps have difficulty with word identification skills. They will be able to retell a few details but the retelling will not be in sequence and will have only a few details reflecting those parts that were easier to read. Similarly, they will be able to answer questions related solely to these easier parts. Other questions, particularly those relating one part of the passage to another, will remain unanswered. Allowing these students to "look-back" when retelling or answering questions will determine if they just read too quickly, couldn't read the words, or had difficulty understanding. Given a chance to go back and read the words skipped, they may be able to answer the questions. Providing opportunities for students to "look-back" to the text may indicate that they can understand the material but could not remember everything after one reading. Or it may indicate that, although they could not remember the details, they could remember where in the passage the information was and could quickly scan the selection to find it. In ordinary situations this is what good readers do if they can not remember something.

Deciding whether word recognition, comprehension, or reading rate is the difficulty

Providing passages to read and asking students to "think aloud" is another way to assess their understanding and strategies as they read. Students need prior instruction with this so they understand what kinds of comments are expected (see Part III: E4, Think-Aloud). Wade (1990) describes the use of think-alouds for assessing comprehension, and groups students according to five types of comprehenders:

- Good comprehenders — are interactive readers, monitor comprehension, draw on extensive prior knowledge, make reasonable guesses, recognize when more information is necessary to substantiate predictions.

- Nonrisk-takers — don't predict, look for clues from others rather than risk being incorrect, retellings are verbatim from story or they respond, "I don't know," answers are given in a questioning manner.

- Non-integrators — develop new predictions for each section of the text, don't relate new hypotheses to previous information in text, use personal knowledge.

- Schema imposers — hold on to an initial prediction, attempt to make the text fit it despite conflicting information.

- Storytellers — draw on own experience and prior knowledge more than text information, construct meaning that is very different from that of the author's.

Wade's different types of comprehenders

Assessment results that indicate poor understanding may actually be due to a lack of word identification skills and strategies rather than to reading comprehension difficulties. If students cannot easily read about 90 to 95% of the words, then understanding will be more difficult and perhaps not truly reflect comprehension skills. Students may have difficulty remembering from an orally read passage so comprehension should also be assessed after silent reading.

Difficulty with understanding text that students read with 90% to 100% word recognition can be due to students:

In my class I have noticed

a. **Lacking prior (background) knowledge/experience**

  – don't understand vocabulary

  – don't understand concepts

  – haven't had experiences similar to those in text

b. **Not using prior knowledge/experience**

  – don't relate reading to personal knowledge/experience

  – don't self-correct as reads

c. **Lacking relevant language/vocabulary**

  – don't recognize words when decoded

  – don't understand idioms, expressions, sentence structures, signal words

d. **Not using prior language/vocabulary knowledge**

  – don't self-correct mispronunciations, miscues

  – don't use context clues to define new words and concepts

e. **Lacking knowledge of text structures and print conventions**

  – don't know about different text structures, can't use them to help understand

  – not aware of punctuation and other print conventions and how they affect meaning

f. **Not using text structures and print conventions**

  – don't use structure of text to help recall information or retell story

  – don't use punctuation and other print conventions to interpret text (to convey expression, feelings, etc.)

g. **Not imaging/visualizing or using illustrations to help understand**

  – don't associate reading with creating images in head

  – don't use illustrations, diagrams, charts, etc. to help with interpretation

h. **Not making sense of text during reading**

  – don't associate reading with understanding

  – don't monitor understanding or self-correct

  – consider reading a task to say the words as fast as possible

  – don't associate meaning from one part of text with other; read each sentence or paragraph as if independent of others

i. **Imposing own meaning on passage**

- don't understand author's point of view

- construct meaning from own point of view/knowledge and guess words to make sense

j. **Reading with one speed**

- don't adjust reading rate to match purpose (to skim, scan, read "normally", study, memorize)

- don't adjust rate when encounter difficult words

- feel reading should be fast and fluent

- don't use print conventions, appropriate phrasing and expression

Analyzing the Data: Fluency

The process of reading competently involves not just associating print with meaning but doing so with ease (automaticity). This enables the reader to use minimal effort and, therefore, sustain reading over a period of time. Furthermore, it allows the reader to focus attention on thinking and monitoring comprehension.

Competent readers are able to recognize words easily by sight, and also use phonics, syllabication, and structural analysis skills easily. That is, if a word is not recognized by sight, then at least the competent reader is able to quickly sound it out or analyze it.

Difficulties with fluency may be due to:

a. **Inefficient use of context and phonics**

- lack sufficient phonics vocabulary and language skills

- have difficulty analyzing and blending sounds

b. **Unfamiliar vocabulary, concepts, or language and text structures**

- need to slow down or reread to understand

c. **Retaining earlier reading style**

- in beginning to learn to read, children go through a phase of word-by-word reading; they may unwittingly continue to read this way

d. **Invariant rate**

- don't vary reading rate when encountering unfamiliar words, language structures, or concepts; instead, they omit or substitute words and continue reading in order to maintain fluency, even though meaning is lost

e. **Slow processing**

- although readers decode words accurately and understand text, their processing of words takes time and reading rate is slow, they read easy and more difficult material at the same rate

f. **Vocalizing words**

- say every word when reading silently, which slows the reading rate

In my class I have noticed

Analyzing the Data: Flexibility in using different strategies

Competent readers have a variety of strategies they can use to recognize words and gain meaning from the text. They are able to use these strategies easily and fluently. As well they are flexible in their use of these strategies, trying one and changing it if it doesn't work.

Difficulties with flexibility may be the result of:

- not having a repertoire of strategies
- not understanding the need to try different strategies
- not understanding when to try different strategies
- not knowing how to choose strategies

In reflecting on the profiles of many children experiencing difficulty with reading, Phinney (1988) has categorized these readers based on their overall reading strategies. Although they may lack a particular skill, they also lack fluency and flexibility in using skills.

- Strategy dependent readers — use only one strategy, rely on memory, do well on the first part of a familiar story, don't match voice to print.

- Overloaded readers — lack vocabulary knowledge, not accustomed to longer sentences, have patchy fluency, make poor substitutions which have some phonics relationships, attempt to maintain flow of reading and attach some meaning to the nonsense substitutions, get the gist of the text.

- Underpredictive readers — don't use prior knowledge and experience or context clues, don't predict or guess words, use sounding out words as main strategy, remember a few details.

- Overpredictive readers — don't self-correct, frequently substitute and omit words, produce miscues that don't maintain the sense of the story, make up parts of story using personal interpretation and experiences, overuse graphic clues, reflect sketchy comprehension.

- Global readers — have a strong orientation toward meaning, have difficulty retrieving words, lack fluency, demonstrate difficulty with phonemic processing and phonics, continue to reverse words (e.g. says buttons for donuts), prefer oral reading.

Phinney's evaluation of different readers

Evaluation — Making Sense of the Assessment Data

There is an overabundance of data that can be collected about children's reading. To keep the task manageable and focused on its purpose — to guide instruction, provide feedback and document progress — teachers must decide how much data is necessary and what it implies for ongoing instruction. The focus for evaluation is to create from the data, a profile of the children's reading knowledge, skills, strategies and attitudes at a particular time and relate that to progress over time. Not all children will require the same kinds of records, some will need more indepth assessments than others.

Evaluation is making sense of all the assessment data — e.g. creating a profile of the student's reading knowledge, skills and attitudes, and then relating this to instructional and learning activities.

In curriculum-focused programs, assessment and evaluation focuses on the knowledge and skills embedded in the curriculum and attempts to determine if children have reached certain curricular goals by certain ages or grades. Children are then graded according to their success with demonstrating those skills and knowledge — above average, average, or below average in their achievement. Sometimes achievement gets confused with ability and some children feel less able than they actually are because they have not reached an expected level of achievement by the end of a certain grade. What is often overlooked is that within one grade level, children vary up to one year in age and, as well, in experience. They also vary in developmental growth and personal capacity. By definition they all cannot reach the average level by the end of a particular grade.

The focus is on progress toward independent, competent reading.

In learner-focused programs, assessment and evaluation focus on what knowledge, skills, strategies and attitudes learners have acquired and whether growth has occurred, reflected by their increasing independence and competency in reading. The focus is on ensuring for every child that there is progress in reading. It is accepted that there will be variations in the rate of progress and in the level of competence that different learners will achieve as they progress through school.

Evaluation of the assessment data creates a profile of the child's knowledge, skills, strategies and attitudes. Summaries or reading profiles can be kept and compared over time.

From ongoing instruction and assessment, data about the students' reading can be gathered from a variety of activities and reading materials. Summarizing and evaluating the data creates a profile of their reading abilities and needs — what they can do now and what needs to be learned next at a particular time (see Figure 33). Keeping the profiles of their achievements and needs during a year and over the years in a portfolio helps students, teachers and parents to evaluate progress accurately and within a broader time frame. These portfolios might contain two *profiles* a year which summarize the assessment data and include one or two samples of reading miscue analysis data (e.g. see Figure 33 and Appendix I). Too much raw data stored in a portfolio becomes overwhelming and is not as meaningful once the immediate context of it is lost. To be useful similar tasks should be compared over time and an evaluation made about the knowledge, skills, strategies and attitudes the students exhibit with word recognition, understanding and responding. By comparing an earlier profile to a later one, progress can be evaluated and kept in perspective.

The guidelines for assessing and evaluating children's reading in this book reflect a learner-focused philosophy. By taking into consideration the ongoing assessment and evaluation of each student's reading, and using the information presented earlier about learning and reading processes, how children learn, and individual differences in learning, decisions can be made to match reading instruction and activities to the needs of the students.

Reading Evaluation Profile

Student: _____ Date: _____

Student's attitude: _____

Student knows about and uses:

_____
_____
_____
_____
_____

Progress since last report:

_____
_____
_____
_____

Next goals to enhance competency and independence:

_____
_____
_____
_____
_____

* For another Reading Profile, see Appendix I, BLM A
* For keeping a record of teaching and learning activities, see BLM B

Things to Keep in Mind

attitude   skills

knowledge   strategies

awareness of print
memory reading
sight words
phonics   → picture clues
context   ————————→ semantics
                              → syntax
syllabication
structural analysis
prior knowledge
print conventions
fluency and flexibility
understanding and responding

Refer to:
  learning process
  reading process
  components of reading process
  general developmental trends
  individual talents, abilities, interests
  elements of text

Figure 33. Summarizing Reading Competency and Progress.

Part III: Teaching/Learning Strategies Described in the Literature

This section gives brief overviews of strategies for teaching and learning. The reference source is provided for those who wish to obtain more indepth information.

A 1-3   Strategies for planning and teaching lessons to help students actively focus on reading strategies

B   Establishing purpose for reading, acknowledging its direct impact on the reader's focus during reading, on the prior knowledge accessed, and on recall of the story and information

C 1-5   Focusing on print, phonics, and beginning reading

D 1-6   Active processing and understanding before, during and after reading

E 1-4   Questioning and inferencing, including think-aloud strategies to help with understanding literature

F 1-4   Responding during and after reading to demonstrate understanding

G 1-3   Developing students' reading fluency and creating flexible groupings depending on purpose and activity

A. Strategies for Planning and Teaching Lessons

Note the similarities between these procedures. Although they have different names, they seem to be variations of a basic teaching strategy and lesson plan. There are many other variations with different names in the literature.

A1. Model for Teaching Strategies (Gordon, 1985)

Procedure

To teach a new strategy, the teacher demonstrates the steps, explicitly modelling and explaining. The teacher and/or students read a story or text passage. The teacher asks questions to which answers are given along with the evidence from the text. This is supplemented by the teacher explaining the line of reasoning used. Over the next few sessions, students practise parts of the strategy with close guidance from the teacher.

Gradually the students independently use the strategy, taking over the teacher's role as well. The table below illustrates the teaching sequence (T = teacher and S = student).

STAGES	ASKS QUESTIONS	ANSWERS QUESTIONS	FINDS EVIDENCE	LINE OF REASONING
1. Modelling	T	T	T	T
2. Guided Practice	T	T	S	S
3. Guided Practice	T	S	T	S
4. Practice/Application	T	S	S	S
5. Student Control	S	S	S	S

A2. EMQA — Explication, Modelling, Questioning, Activities (Irwin, 1986)

Procedure

1. Explication — the teacher explains directly the knowledge or the skill, or strategy and why it is important.

2. Modelling — the teacher shows how the knowledge, skill, or strategy is used and talks about the thinking processes and skills.

3. Questioning — students ask questions about the process and the text after reading and are encouraged to refer to the text.

4. Activities — students complete the activities and/or reading that require the use of the knowledge and strategies taught.

A3. Informed Strategies for Learning (ISL) (Cook, 1986; Paris, 1985)

Procedure

• State explicitly what the strategy or goal is

• Relate to previous lessons or activities

- Discuss strategy how it works, its importance, when and why to use it, when it is not effective
- Model effective use of strategy, demonstrating some examples
- Explain why the strategy promotes reading and learning
- Have students practice new strategies on relevant material (e.g. related to the theme or content area goals)
- Provide corrective feedback during and after practices
- Fade support so students use strategy and self-correct on their own
- Bridge the strategy to other areas of the curriculum by referring to it in other situations and lessons.

B. Establishing Purpose for Reading
(Blanton, Wood & Moorman, 1990)

Establishing purpose for reading makes a significant difference to what is focused on during reading. Simply skimming or scanning the material may be sufficient for one's needs, or the material may be read purely for enjoyment, or to learn how to do something, or to remember facts and ideas. Purpose creates the criteria for what information is relevant or irrelevant. Purpose for reading is closely connected with the kinds of responses made to the reading.

Blanton et al. (1990) discuss different purposes for learning activities and relate them to instructional strategies. Some are listed below.

PURPOSE	INSTRUCTIONAL STRATEGY	POSTREADING ACTIVITY
To access prior knowledge and develop vocabulary and/or concepts	• Semantic Maps (F2) • Graphic Organizers (F2) • Content Guides (F2) • Concept Guides (F2) • K-W-L (D1) • Semantic Feature Analysis (F2) • SQ3R (D4)	Revise during and after reading
To verify accuracy of predictions and monitor understanding	• DRTA (D3) • K-W-L, K-W-L Plus (D1, D2) • Previewing • Reciprocal Teaching (D6) • ReQuest (D5)	Discuss and confirm predictions with reference to text
To learn about text structure	• Story Maps (F2) • Text Feature Maps (F2)	Discuss and compare stories and genre
To apply strategy and understand how it works	• DRTA, DLTA (D3) • Model for Teaching Strategies (A1) • ISL, EMQA (A2, A3)	Discuss as passage is read

C. Focusing on Print, Phonics and Beginning Reading

Beyond whole class lessons that focus on phonics, some children need more individualized or small group lessons and opportunities to read and write with guidance. The following lessons and activities look at ways to teach phonics explicitly while presenting it in the context of reading and writing (Appendix B outlines the phonics patterns to teach).

C1. Reading Recovery (Clay, 1985; Pinnell, Fried, & Estice, 1990)

Reading Recovery is a program that requires extensive teacher training and is intended to be an early intervention program for beginning readers experiencing difficulty in their first year of reading instruction. The focus of the program is to help children move into beginning independent reading by providing instruction closely matched to their particular needs. As the child reads a passage/story, the teacher notes what needs to be taught (e.g. phonics, voice/print matching, context clues) and then teaches it to the student during and after reading. The children selected for this program receive individual, 30-minute lessons daily in addition to classroom reading activities. The program is meant to be short term (e. g. 3 to 5 months).

In a classroom and in most education systems, there is not the luxury to provide such intensive individual reading instruction to more than a few children. However, the structure of the lessons used in Reading Recovery exemplify good instructional processes for teaching reading and can perhaps be modified to a classroom setting. The procedure integrates reading, writing, lessons about spelling and word recognition, and rereading for fluency.

The following is a modified procedure suitable for a small group (e.g. 2 to 4 students) based on the lesson structure and activities suggested by Clay for Reading Recovery.

1. **Students reread familiar stories.** As books are introduced they can be kept handy for rereading. Students (or teacher) choose favourite, familiar books to be reread by students each day.

2. **Without help students orally read the book that was introduced the day before.** The students should be able to read this book with 90-95% accuracy. As students read, teacher notes reading strategies and difficulties.

3. **Work with letters or words.** Teacher provides lesson focusing on letter recognition and/or sounds related to students' decoding needs as observed in Step 2. Teacher ensures there is a link between the lesson and miscues in the students' story reading. Other reading strategies may be focused on as needed.

4. **Students write a message or story daily.** As the students write the teacher makes connections with decoding and spelling focused on in steps 2 and 3 and with the content of story.

5. **Reading a new book.** Teacher introduces a new book, with students looking through it, discussing pictures, predicting what it may be about, and employing other prereading activities. Depending on their level students may listen to the story, read the story with assistance, or just be involved in the prereading discussions. (This is the story that is read independently the next day at step 2.)

C2. Early Intervention in Reading Program (EIR)
(Taylor, Short, Frye, & Shearer, 1992)

This is an alternative to Reading Recovery that focuses on preventing reading problems with first graders in a small group setting. The program uses quality literature, develops phonemic awareness, and teaches students to use phonic and context clues as they read. The procedure incorporates repeated reading of stories and opportunities to write. The teacher works with the students for 15 to 20 minutes daily as a small group in the classroom. The materials used in this program included 36 picture books, summaries of those books on a chart and in booklet form, and 14 other easy-to-read books.

Procedure

Children spend three days on each story. The teacher reads a story to the entire class, modelling fluent reading. Before, during and after this reading, the teacher chooses to focus on aspects of reading suitable to the whole class. Then, while other students work independently, a summary of the story written on a chart is read to a selected group of children. These students then read the summary. The teacher stops at different words to focus on developing phonemic awareness and model decoding based on context and phonics. Children write up to five words from the story that the teacher has chosen as appropriate focus for decoding and spelling. On the next two days the children reread the summary individually, applying the decoding strategies they have learned. They also write about the story. The children also have 5 to 10 minutes with a teaching assistant or volunteer to reread the story summary in their personalized booklet which they have illustrated and to reread favourite stories. After three days they take the booklet home to read to their parents.

After using this procedure with a number of stories, children are given easy-to-read books to read independently which the teacher has chosen so that the students are successful (for easy reading books see Appendix G). This procedure ensures students are introduced to quality literature, are included in whole class activities that may focus on understanding and responding to literature read to them, and are provided with reading material at their reading level. It also focuses on print, phonics, and other decoding strategies and provides for review of whole class lessons and development of reading fluency. Preteaching could be built in to this procedure by teaching phonics patterns, sight words and so on to the small group before it is introduced in the whole class context.

Structure of the Program

Children listen to the full story when it is read to whole class, then read summaries of the story on the chart, and in their personalized "summary" books.

- Level A has 40-60 word summaries
- Level B has 60-90 word summaries
- Level C has 90-150 word summaries, and 50-150 word unseen, easy-to-read books
- Level D has 100-200 word unseen, easy-to-read books

Some of the stories used (and summaries made for Levels A-C) were:

Level A   Ask Mr. Bear
               You'll Soon Grow into Them
               Herman the Helper

Level B	Three Kittens
	Good Night, Owl
	Round Robin

Level C	Hattie and the Fox
	The Doorbell Rang
	The Chick and the Duckling (independent reading)

Level D	Noisy Nora
	The Bear's Toothache
	Just for You

C3. Shared Reading — Using Enlarged Print (Big Books, language experience charts, and messages, poems, songs on board, charts or overheads)

Teaching beginning reading using enlarged print (such as Big Books) was largely inspired by the work of Holdaway (Strickland & Morrow, 1990). These materials allow groups of children to see the printed page as it is read out loud. Fundamental concepts about print can be demonstrated as the children enjoy the story. Repeated readings provide students with the opportunity to assimilate the pattern of written language and vocabulary. Strickland and Morrow list several activities that can be used with Big Books (or any enlarged print):

Tracking Print

After reading a story once or twice, move hand or pointer smoothly under the words. This demonstrates the directionality of print and matching spoken words to print. Children like to imitate this when they use the books on their own.

Think Aloud

Occasionally use a think-aloud process as you read a story, demonstrating a strategy and the active nature of the reading process (decoding words, self-correcting miscues, using context clues, predicting what will happen, etc.).

Cloze Activities

Pause and let children fill in the next word. This helps them develop and use context clues (see C5, Cloze Procedure).

Examining Text Features

After several readings, focus on aspects of the print such as repeated words, letter sounds, consonant clusters, punctuation marks, and so on (see What to Focus on, pp. 77-95).

C4. Quality Phonics Instruction (Trachtenburg, 1990; Stahl, 1992)

The debate about the importance of teaching phonics, and when and how to teach it, continues in the literature. Research presents considerable evidence for the importance of phonics instruction in early reading achievement (Chall, 1987; Adams, 1990). All programs, including those based on a Whole Language philosophy, focus some attention on helping young readers use phonics to decode words. The problem is that the word "phonics" conjures up many contrasting images to different people. What some critics may be responding to is not the usefulness of phonics in reading but rather the ways being used to teach phonics. To some it means children learn to "bark at print;" to others it is associated with worksheets or skills presented in a certain sequence, or having children sound out words in lists; to still others it means learning rules and decoding words without a reading context.

Phonics actually refers to the use of phonetics to teach reading, with emphasis on the relationship between letter and sound patterns in words. Not all children need detailed instruction in phonics. However, some children do require explicit instruction and more reading practice using what they learn. Phonics can be explicitly taught within a meaningful context by using instruction that demonstrates reading strategies which integrate phonics with other decoding strategies (context clues, picture clues, sight words, structural analysis, syllabication). A meaningful context also refers to learning activities in which children relate phonics to reading and spelling. They are actively trying to use what was discussed and practised in a lesson while they read and write independently. The learning activities may involve decoding words in stories, in sentences, or in phrases. They may involve comparing words to one another and reading them. For clarity of instruction and learning, the words may need to be taken from stories and put on cards or on the board. This helps some students focus better and more clearly see the letter/sound relationships. A meaningful context means more than the words being in a "sentence or story context." It also means the words and phonics focused on are related directly to the reading and writing being done in the classroom, not just taken from a preplanned program and presented as "separate phonics lessons."

When learning to read, all students learn about letter/sound correspondences. Because some children seem to intuitively figure out these relationships and how to decode words, not all will require the same degree of instruction. For some students, informally pointing out the relationships as they attempt to read and write stories will be sufficient; whereas for others, more systematic instruction focusing on letter/sound relationships is necessary. Teachers need to make decisions related to individuals in their classes and to provide the appropriate kind and amount of instruction.

Some guidelines for quality phonics instruction are listed by Stahl (1992):

- Build on children's rich language background and knowledge of print. Read to children, provide opportunities for exploring books, writing, and language.

- Build a foundation of children's phonemic awareness (see pp. 82-84).

- Provide instruction that is direct and clear. An "explicit approach" shows the word in context *and* in isolation. The teacher points out that it begins with the letter __ and that the letter has the sound /__/ and provides other examples of printed words with the same initial letter. Children read the words and name the initial letter. Then they can return to the story to find similar words and letter/sound patterns.

- Integrate phonics instruction into the total language program. Have children listen for the sound that is being focused on. Read stories and look for words with that letter or sound. Have students write about the stories, and check for the spelling of words containing the sound. For example, some quality children's stories (Trachtenburg, 1990) have a high frequency of certain common phonic elements (e.g. short /ā/ — *The Cat in the Hat, Who Took the Farmer's Hat? There's an Ant in Anthony*). One story could be read, with instruction focusing on short **a**. The children could then read the other stories using the knowledge of the short **a** sound to help decode new words. They could also write about this story using the short **a** words that were brainstormed after reading the story. Note that Clay's (1989) Reading Recovery Program (see C1) includes instruction on phonics related to writing that is done after reading familiar and new books.

- Focus on reading (and writing) words, not learning rules. Teach phonics connected to the texts and stories children are reading and to their writing. Point out patterns and compare new words to words that they already know.

- Include a focus on rimes (the part of the word from the vowel onward, also referred to as word families such as -at, -an, -ack, -ead, -ean). Adams (1990) points out that letter/sound correspondences are more stable when the pattern includes the final consonants (e.g. "ea" has 2 sounds, but in "ean" it generally has the long /$\bar{e}$/ sound).

- Include frequent opportunities to write using constructed (invented) spelling.

- Develop word recognition strategies that require children to examine the internal structure of words.

- Develop fluency in decoding so it becomes an automatic process and attention can be given to understanding. Children need to learn to analyze the graphic clues and patterns of words quickly and easily.

Other activities that focus on phonics are described in the section on Phonics (see pp. 71, 88-90). The patterns and suggested teaching sequence are listed in Appendix B. The purpose of the instruction is not to memorize these relationships, but to help children notice the patterns and use them in their reading and writing. In learning about phonics, children are learning both to decode new words and to spell words. Instruction needs to highlight this connection and provide both reading and writing opportunities that use the letter/sound relationships focused on during instruction.

C5. Cloze Procedure

As an instructional procedure, cloze can be used to help focus on context clues to identify a target word. It can also be used to teach phonics for decoding words. There are variations in using this technique that serve different purposes.

- Ways of presenting cloze:
  - **Aural/oral cloze** — when reading aloud stop and let children provide the next word
  - **Print/oral cloze** — have students follow print as it is read out loud, and then say missing word
  - **Print/print cloze** — students read on own and write in missing word (or choose word on card).

- To focus only on context clues:
  - when reading without text in front of students, pause, skip word and keep reading, then go back and read sentence again pausing for students to give missing word
  - when reading with text in front of student, in place of the word, put line for each letter or put a blank unrelated to length of word.

- To focus on phonics and context clues:
  - when reading out loud, say the initial consonant(s), pause briefly and continue reading, then reread pausing for students to finish the missing word
  - when reading with the text in front of the students, in place of the word, print the initial consonant and blank, or print the initial and final consonants separated by a blank.
- Ways to substitute the word in the cloze passage:
  - put a line for each letter left out (with or without phonics clue) e.g. Rosie, the _ _ _, went for a w _ _ _ in the f _ _ m y _ _ d.
  - put a blank related to the length of the missing word (with or without phonics clue) e.g. Rosie, the ___, went for a w___ in the f_____.
  - put a blank unrelated to the length of the missing word (with or without phonics clue) e.g. Rosie, the ____, went for a w___ in the f___.
- Choosing words to be left out will depend on the instructional purpose, for example:
  - words with certain phonic pattern that is being focused on
  - certain parts of speech
  - words that are defined by the context
  - signal words (see p. 87), referents, or parts of idioms or common expressions, e.g. if . . . then, but, however, first, last, after, as a matter of fact, he, they, it.

D. Active Processing and Understanding Before, During and After Reading

D1. Know, Want to Know, Learn Strategy (K-W-L) (Ogle, 1989)

Purpose

- to help students take an active role in reading and learning from expository text
- to actively involve students before, during and after reading

Suggestions

- Teacher should model brainstorming, categorizing, anticipating, and questioning in other settings and activities before the students are asked to go through the whole procedure.
- Teach these using teaching strategies (see A1-3).

Procedure

- Students brainstorm what they know about a topic and categorize information gathered.
- Students predict categories of information that may be presented and list questions they want answered.
- During and after reading, they use personal worksheets to record what they are learning and what else they want to know.

K-W-L- STRATEGY SHEET		
What we know	What we want to find out	What we learned

Categories of information we expect to use:

1.   4.
2.   5.
3.   6.

Variations of K-W-L (Palinscar et al., 1986)

What I think I know	What I want to know	How I will find out	What I have learned

What do you . . .			
know you know?	think you know?	think you'll learn?	know you learned?

D2. K-W-L Plus (Carr & Ogle, 1987)

K-W-L strategy *plus* mapping text and summarizing information

Procedure

- Start as with the K-W-L strategy.
- After reading the selection and filling in the K-W-L chart, students then create semantic or concept maps showing relationships between words and ideas (see F2), using the categories listed in the K-W-L chart to help with the semantic map.
- Students create a written summary from the concept or semantic map that they just developed (the map provides the outline).
- As students gain experience with the K-W-L Plus strategy, they write their summary from the chart, omitting the mapping stage.

D3. Directed Reading and Thinking Activity (DRTA)
(Stauffer, 1969)

Purpose

- to direct the reading of narratives

Prerequisite

- model appropriate predictions and effective questions

Involves

- predicting what a story will be about and what will happen at each stage of the plot
  - using text information to reject or revise predictions
  - developing habit of making and verifying predictions and explain their reasoning by referring to the text and to prior knowledge

Basic procedure

- Choose short, interesting stories with three to four clear divisions in their plot development.
- Before students read, ask questions such as:
  - "Based on the title, what do you think the story might be about?"
  - "How do you think the story will begin?"
- Students read the first page and then close books.
  - "What do you think now? What in the story makes you think that?"
  - "Do you need more information? If so, what?"
- Direct students to read to page __.
  - "Now what do you think the story will be about?"
- Shift to focusing on the next event.
  - "What do you think will happen next?"
- Direct students to read to p.__ and tell them to be prepared to discuss what in story confirms or contradicts their prediction.
- Repeat procedure for next section, predict what will happen, discuss what in story confirmed or contradicted prediction.

- Encourage students to provide evidence from the story.

Adaptations to this procedure

- During the process students may write or draw predictions, or tell them to a partner, rather than discussing in a class or small group.
- Rather than predicting, students might ask questions they feel need to be answered by the text, then read to answer their questions.
- The number of stopping points depends on the story (natural breaks in plot), on the students' abilities (how much they can read their on own), and on the instructional focus (story grammar, character development, etc.).
- The teacher could read the story out loud (**DLTA** — Directed Listening Thinking Activity) or the teacher could read one part, and the students could read the next section, etc.
- Could be adapted to science and social studies expository texts, rather than just narratives.
- Silent DRTA (Richek, 1987)— teacher hands out selection with stopping points marked, and students read passage silently, stopping to make their predictions in writing.
- DRTA SOURCE (Richek, 1987) — when making a prediction, students identify which part was engendered by the text and which by student's prior knowledge.

D4. Survey, Question, Read, Recite, Review (SQ3R)
(Forgan & Mangrum)

Procedure

Integrate this with instruction about the structure of expository texts, e.g. classification (Science), sequential/episodic (History), compare and contrast (Science, Socials), cause-effect (Science, Socials), etc. (see F2, Text Structures on pp. 130,132).

- Survey — quickly read headings, read beginning and final or summary paragraphs, examine illustrations, and diagrams, etc., if there are no headings, skim paragraphs for topic sentences.
- Question — change major headings or points into questions.
- Read — to answer the questions, skim, skip, or reread depending on purpose (e.g. to get the gist, find specific information, study to remember details).
- Recite — say answer out loud, share with partner.
- Review — answer questions following completion of reading.

This strategy is useful for reading and studying expository text. When studying, review should occur after reading the first time as well as the following day. Before introducing the entire procedure, teach each strategy using teaching strategies described in A1-3.

D5. ReQuest (Manzo, 1969, cited in Rhodes & Dudley-Manning, 1988)

Purpose

- to teach students to independently ask questions before and during reading
- to help them set their own purpose for reading (after reading a few paragraphs)
- to develop questioning skills

- to share information and strategies with others

Procedure

- Students and/or teacher choose passage, book, article.
- Each student has copy.
- Students silently read part of text (sentence, few sentences, paragraph).
- Teacher asks questions first to model questioning skills. (Also teacher has discussed effective questioning skills in other lessons and contexts.)
- Students request clarification of question, if necessary.
- Students give well-thought out answer and give evidence to support it from the text and/or their prior knowledge.
- Teacher may also answer some of the first questions to demonstrate different kinds of question-answer relationships (see E2, Question/Answer/Relationships).
- Students can take the role of teacher, and ask questions.

(Note the similarities of this procedure to those generic lessons outlined in A1-3.)

Modifications

This can be a laborious technique if applied to every few sentences or paragraphs. However, it can be used to teach active reading strategies and to start a reading session. The reading after this introduction can be completed by independent or buddy reading.

D6. Reciprocal Teaching (Palincsar & Brown, 1985; 1986)

Procedure

- Initially the teacher models four tasks:
  - summarizing paragraph or segment in a sentence
  - asking one or two high level questions
  - clarifying hard parts
  - predicting what the next paragraph or segment will discuss.
- After a few demonstrations the teacher has student take over role of "teacher." The other students must help revise the summary, answer questions, clarify unclear parts, and concur or disagree with the prediction (note the similarity to teaching strategies in A1-3).
- After turning the reins over to the students, the teacher:
  - takes regular turn as "teacher"
  - provides feedback about quality of summaries or questions
  - provides encouragement to student in "teacher" role
  - keeps students on track
  - encourages each student to move beyond present level of competence.
- This method works well for small group activity (e.g. 1 "teacher", 2 students).

E.   Questioning and Inferencing

E1. 5 W's and H (Who, What, When, Why, Where, How)

Materials

- Use short stories, articles, etc.

Purpose

- to teach how to generate questions or make predictions

Procedure

- Teacher asks questions before students read the passage, modelling the kinds of questions (including literal and inferential, see also E3, Teaching Inferences).
- Students then read to find answers.
- Next students ask questions, and read to find answers. (Can be whole class activity, or small groups and pairs can make up questions and then share with class.)
- Integrate this with other techniques that require student to ask questions and make predictions (e.g. DRTA, ReQuest, SQ3R, Reciprocal Teaching).
- Teach difference between asking questions that require one word answers (some teachers call these "skinny questions") and those that require phrases or sentences ("fat questions").

E2. Question/Answer/Relationships (QAR) (Raphael, 1984)

Purpose

- to teach students how to get information for answering questions
- to teach students strategies for answering questions

Procedure

- Teach the following four strategies for answering questions and how to tell the differences between them.
  - First strategy — **RIGHT THERE**

    Find words from the question that are also in the text, read the sentence to find the answer. The answer to the question is in one sentence.
  - Second strategy — **THINK AND SEARCH**

    Question has answer in text, but requires information from more than one sentence or paragraph.
  - Third strategy — **ON MY OWN**

    Answer to question comes from the student's prior knowledge, not from the text.
  - Fourth strategy — **WRITER AND ME**

    Answer requires information from student's prior knowledge but also needs more information found in text.

Suggestions

- Teach each answer strategy using teaching strategies A1-3.
- Start with shorter, simple texts and move to longer, more complex ones.
- Move from group to independent activities.

E3. Teaching Inference (Johnson & Johnson, 1986)

Purpose

- to teach students concept of inferential interpretation

Procedure

- Teach

  The teacher reads a passage. Using a think aloud process, the teacher describes the type of inference and then explains the information from the text and from prior knowledge that is used to reach the conclusion. The teacher identifies and lists any relevant word clues that are used.

- Practice

  Students read passage and then identify word clues that help with making inferences.

- Application

  Students read passage one line at a time, make inferences, and identify the words/information used to make the inferences. The teacher lists word clues on chart or board.

- Extend

  In daily reading activities, the teacher asks children to make and identify inferences.

- Assess

  As students discuss reading, the teacher notes if they are able to make inferences and discuss how they know something, using both text and prior knowledge to answer questions.

Note the similarity in teaching sequence to those outlined in A1-3. Also make connections to E2, QAR, for example, making inferences is similar to finding "Writer and Me" and "On My Own" answers to questions about the story or passage. See also F3, Sketch to Stretch which can be used to focus on inferences.

Inference Types (Johnson & Johnson, 1986)

Inferences can be made about:

- **Location** (e.g. The waitress came as soon as we sat down.)
- **Time** (e.g. Mom woke me up for breakfast.)
- **Action** (e.g. With a bat in hand, the player approached the plate.)
- **Instrument** (e.g. With a loud buzzing noise, the tree was felled.)
- **Object** (e.g. The heavy ball fell silently to the ground exploding as it landed.)
- **Category** (e.g. The ketch and yawl were docked beside the schooner.)
- **Occupation or Pastime** (e.g. Her job was to sweep up the hair and put away the scissors.)
- **Cause-Effect** (e.g. After six days, water was reaching up to the rooftops.)

- **Problem-Solution** (e.g. It was late in the afternoon and the baby was crying.)
- **Feeling-Attitude** (e.g. As I ran across the finish line, my parents cheered.)

Also, inferences can be made based on 5W's & H questions

E4. Think-Aloud (Davey, 1983; Wade, 1990)

The teacher and eventually students verbalize their own thoughts out loud while reading. This provides opportunities to develop metacognitive strategies which help students learn to monitor their own thinking and reading comprehension. As well it is a way to teach thinking skills (comprehension) through modelling.

Procedure

- Select passage that contains points of difficulty (e.g. predicting what comes next, ambiguities, using context to identify unknown words).
- Read passage and think out loud, students follow along listening to the thinking strategy (see thinking skills on p. 26).
- Make predictions about what the entire selection will be about using the title and illustrations.
- Model ways to cope with variety of difficulties relevant to the students' needs.
- Describe images (pictures, sounds, feelings, etc.) created during reading.
- Demonstrate how prior knowledge is linked to information in text (e.g. relate to own experience, make comparisons or analogies).
- Verbalize confusion and monitoring comprehension (e.g. "This doesn't make sense." "I wonder why it says . . . ?").
- Model "fix-up" strategies, self-correcting — reread, read ahead, use illustrations, look up word meaning.
- Model how other reading strategies can be incorporated (e.g. story grammar, text structure, selecting schema from prior knowledge).

After modelling this process several times, have students practise think-alouds with a partner. Teacher can circulate to provide feedback. This process is also effective as a strategy during conferences.

Using Think-Alouds to assess comprehension (Wade, 1990)

- Preparing text
  - Choose short (80–200 word) passage, new to student but familiar topic and at student's instructional level.
  - Remove title, change topic sentence to end.
  - Divide into segments of 1 to 4 sentences each.
- Administering Think-Aloud assessments
  - Tell student that he or she will read a story/passage in short segments and will be asked to tell what it is about after each section.
  - Student reads out loud, and then explains what is happening in the story (fiction) or what information is presented (nonfiction). Question student to encourage hypotheses "What do you think this is about?", and to support their hypotheses, "What in the story/text makes you think so?"

- Continue through sections, then have student retell entire passage in own words (student can reread, if necessary).
- Analyzing data
  - Does the reader hypothesize and what information from text is used to support hypotheses?
  - Does the reader relate the material in the text to prior knowledge?
  - Does the reader develop an overall schema for integrating information?
  - How does the reader deal with unfamiliar words?
  - How confident is the reader in predicting and confirming?

Wade (1990) identifies four types of comprehenders that he describes as good comprehenders, non-risktakers, schema imposers, and storytellers (see p. 104).

- In analyzing the students' think-aloud responses, keep in mind that:
  - the strategies the reader uses depend on type of passage and amount of prior knowledge,
  - the think-aloud process is not a normal process so students may not describe what they usually do, and
  - verbal reports are only indications of the readers' stated awareness of comprehension process. Students may not report everything they are aware of and also they cannot understand and put into words everything they do.

F.   Responding During and After Reading

F1. Summarizing (Taylor, 1986)

This is an effective postreading technique that fosters increased understanding and recall. Students need to be taught strategies for making summaries.

What to teach first (Use teaching strategies described in A1-3)

- story grammars and expository text structure (see F2)
- semantic maps and graphic organizers (see F2)
- guidelines for condensing information (teach separately at first):
  - deleting trivial information
  - deleting redundant information
  - thinking of categorical term to replace lists of details
  - using topic sentences of paragraphs (if none create them)
  - identifying good summaries from variety of examples
  - learning how to rate summaries (eventually their own included)

Procedure for teaching summarizing

- Model the summarizing process more than once, thinking aloud as you demonstrate it
- Provide guided practice with all the students
- Go through process several times with different materials
- Provide feedback
- Chunk into smaller lessons (don't begin with students trying to write full summary

(Note that D2, K-W-L Plus is another strategy for teaching summarizing.)

F2. Semantic Mapping, Semantic Feature Analysis, Webbing, Clustering, Plot Profiles, Story Grammar, Expository Text Structures, Story Maps, Sociograms, Structured Overviews, Graphic Organizers, etc.

Diagrams and tables can be used before, during and after reading to help prepare children for reading, to teach story grammar and text structures, to represent information and concepts, to organize information and to show relationships between words and ideas (see accompanying diagrams and Appendix H). These are also useful for lessons on preparing overviews, studying, note-taking, organizing research and prewriting activities.

Webbing

Semantic Mapping

Concept Item

Story Grammar/Story Maps

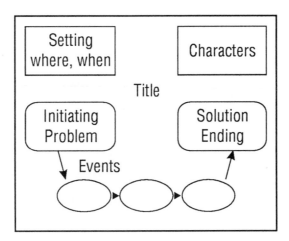

Linear

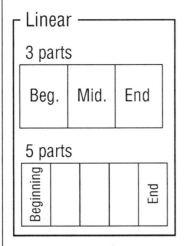

Circular

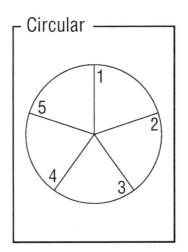

Repetitive

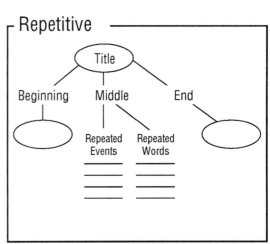

Flash Back

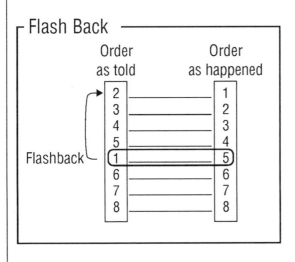

Cumulative

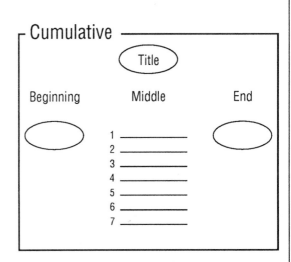

Purposes for using maps/webs/diagrams

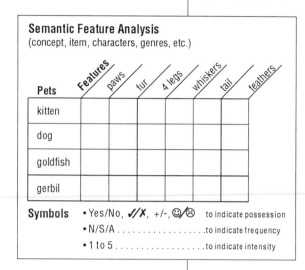

- Preparing for learning and reading — advance organizers, structured overviews

- Vocabulary expansion, brainstorming and organizing information — clustering, webbing, semantic mapping (Johnson & Pearson, 1984)

- Vocabulary development (analyzing how words and concepts are the same or different) — semantic feature analysis (Johnson & Pearson, 1984; Pittelman, Heimlich, Berglund, & French, 1991)

- Diagramming relationships of concepts and vocabulary in a story, making graphic organizers such as: time lines, structured overviews, flow charts, outlines, semantic maps, etc. (Moore, Readance & Rickelman, 1982)

- Diagramming story structures

  - story grammar/story webs (show key elements of the story including characters, setting [where, when], initial problem, events, turning point, and solution/conclusion)

  - plot profiles, story graphs — identify and rate importance of events

  - story maps — diagram structure of plots (circular, linear, repetitive, cumulative, flashback). Variations may focus on giving evidence for literal and inferential interpretations, diagramming cause-effect, mapping comparisons/contrasts, or providing evidence for drawing conclusions as related to a particular story (Davis & McPherson, 1989)

- Identifying characters and illustrate their relationships and interactions with each other — sociograms

- Diagramming expository structures for reading and pre-writing activities (Armbruster, Anderson & Ostertag, 1989; Sinatra, Stahl-Gemake & Morgan, 1986)

  - descriptive/thematic

  - sequential/episodic (temporal)

  - comparison/contrast

  - classification (see p. 132)

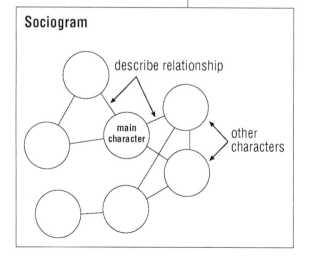

Variations of Story Maps

Cause & Effect Map

```
┌─────────┐        ┌────────┐        ┌─────────┐
│         │    →   │ Effect │    →   │         │
│  Cause  │        │   ↓    │        │ Effect  │
│         │        │ Cause  │        │         │
└─────────┘        └────────┘        └─────────┘
     │                                ┌─────────┐
     └──→  (  Effect  )    →          │         │
                                      └─────────┘
```

Character Summary Map

```
                    (  traits  )  ──  ┌──────────┐
                                      │ Evidence │
        ( character )                 │ from text│
                                      └──────────┘
              │        (       )  ──  ┌──────────┐
              │                       │          │
        (       )  ──  ┌──────────┐   └──────────┘
                       │          │
                       └──────────┘
```

Inferential Map

```
              →  ┌──────────────┐  →  ( inference )
  ( Event      ) │ words from text│
  ( or         ) →  ┌──────────────┐  →  ( inference )
  ( Character  )    │ words from text│
              →  ┌──────────────┐  →  ( inference )
                 │ words from text│
```

Mysteries

Clues/Observations	Suspect	Motive
( )	☐ ☐	____ ____
( )	☐ ☐	____ ____
( )	☐ ☐	____ ____

Reaching a Conclusion

Evidence	Suspect	Motive
☐	☐	☐

Drawing Conclusions

```
  ( Event )  ──→   Conclusion  ──→  Reason
      │
   (     )  →  ┌────┐  →  (     )
      │        └────┘
   (     )  →  ┌────┐  →  (     )
               └────┘
```

* Based on Davis & McPherson, 1989

Expository Text Structures

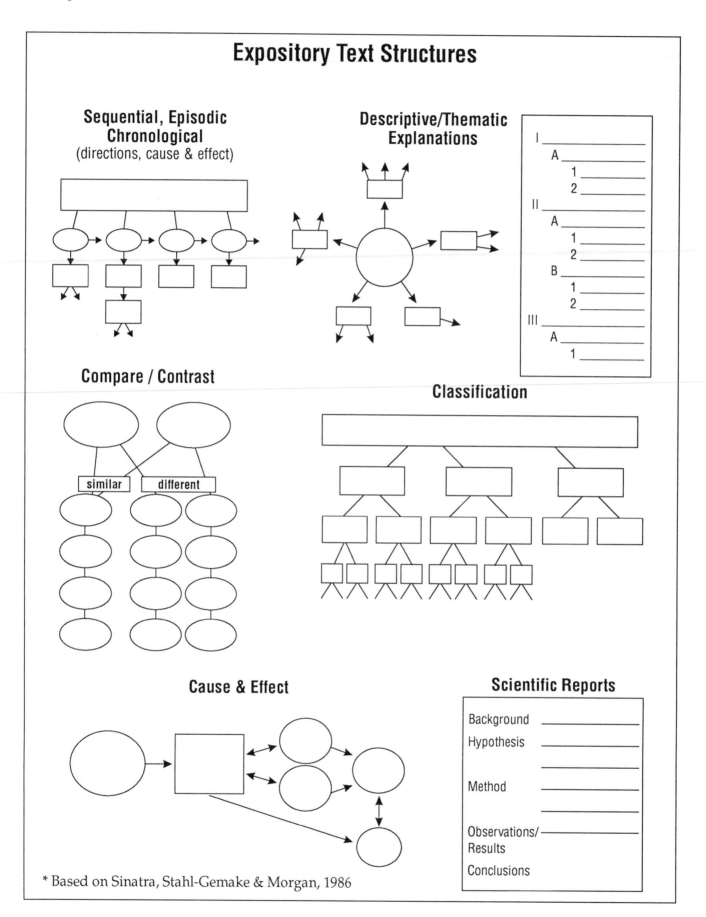

Sequential, Episodic Chronological
(directions, cause & effect)

Descriptive/Thematic Explanations

Compare / Contrast

similar   different

Classification

Cause & Effect

Scientific Reports

Background

Hypothesis

Method

Observations/
Results

Conclusions

* Based on Sinatra, Stahl-Gemake & Morgan, 1986

F3. Sketch to Stretch (Seigel, 1984; cited in Shanklin & Rhodes, 1989)

Children sketch their interpretations of a text and share them with other students during and after reading. They may focus on representing what the text meant to them, what it made them think about, what they learned from reading it, their favourite part, inferences about the story or what characters think, predictions, and so on. This can be incorporated into DRTA (D3), in which part of the story is read and students draw what they think will happen next. It also can be part of teaching story grammar (F2) in which children identify the stages in the plot and draw their interpretations, and retelling (F4).

Verbally explaining their sketches becomes an important part in extending comprehension. The teacher encourages students to explain why they sketched what they did, how it relates to the text, and to talk about the personal meanings they have constructed. Sharing allows students to understand how they comprehend text in ways similar to and different from each other.

"Speech balloons" and "thinking bubbles" can be added to the sketches to indicate what the characters may be saying and/or thinking. In this way main ideas are identified and inferences such as what the reader thinks can be illustrated.

F4. Retelling (Morrow, 1989; Goodman, Watson & Burke, 1987)

Retelling is usually an oral postreading or postlistening activity in which students recreate what they understand and remember about a text. Retelling indicates the readers' or listeners' assimilation and reconstruction of text information and reflects their understanding and what was of interest to them.

If used as a teaching procedure, pre- and postdiscussions help, as well as feedback on the quality of the retelling (see also F1, Summarizing). Students can tape their own retellings and listen to them to self-evaluate.

Procedural guidelines

Unaided Retelling

- Ask student to retell story or summarize text. (e.g. "Retell the story as if you were telling it to a friend who has never heard it", "Tell me what this passage was about. What was important?" "What information did it give you?")

Aided Retelling

- If student is having difficulty, suggest how to start "Once upon a time . . .", " This passage was about . . ."
- If student stops before the end of the story, or there is still more information to retell, encourage him or her to continue by asking, "What comes next?", "Then what . . . ?", "Tell me more about (already mentioned)", "Why do you think _____?", "Anything that gave you trouble?"
- If the student stops retelling and prompting doesn't help, then ask questions relevant to specific points in the text.
- If the student is unable to retell, or retelling lacks sequence and detail, prompt step by step by asking specific questions (5 W's & H) about the story/information.

Teaching Retelling

- Story grammar, text structures and K-W-L (D1) strategy provide the student with frameworks for retelling. Demonstrate the connection between story grammar and expository text structures (F2) and retelling/summarizing (F1). Model retelling using these frameworks.

- Provide prompts or ask questions as the student learns to retell the story/text. This "scaffolding," providing models and prompts, helps the student learn what is involved in retelling.

- Texts for retelling should have easy to follow story lines or have clearly written exposition. Elements that add to predictability will make the initial experiences in learning to retell easier, e.g.

  - repetitive phrases
  - familiar language and sentence structure
  - familiar sequences and plots
  - clearly organized information.

- Alternative strategies for retelling
  - Flannel Boards — retell story with flannel props
  - Chalk Talks — draw as retell story
  - Props — use different props from story
  - Puppets — student has puppet retell story
  - Sound Effects — retell adding appropriate sounds
  - Dramatize — student enacts part of story
  - Creating Story Maps — draw and summarize

Retelling as an Assessment Tool

After teaching students ways to retell what they have read, this process can be used to assess the students' reading strategies and understanding of the passage read (see also Appendix J). Ensure students are able to recognize about 90% or more of the words. Before reading the passage, they need to be told what the focus of the retelling will be (e.g. recall sequence of events, make inferences and support with evidence, integrate with prior knowledge). For assessment, unaided retelling should be used first. If they get stuck encourage them to continue, "Is there anything else you can remember?" If prompts are necessary, note on the assessment which was aided or unaided retelling. By analyzing the retelling, you can get an idea of the students':

- sense of story or text structure (whether the same structure and sequence is used to retell the story)

- vocabulary level (ease of retelling, use of words from text, use of own words, use of specific terms rather than using "something," or "this thing")

- literal recall (general idea or details given, the sequence in which events are given, descriptions of characters and setting, etc.)

- inferential interpretation (how the information is organized, classified, integrated, etc. with their own prior knowledge, whether they use their own words rather than the vocabulary from text)

G. Developing Reading Fluency and Flexible Groupings

G1. Repeated Reading (Dowhower, 1989)

Purpose
- to increase reading fluency
- to develop reading in phrases and with expression
- to increase comprehension of text

Assisted Repeated Reading
- read-along with live or audiotape reading

Unassisted Repeated Reading
- independently reread text

Procedure
- Preparation
  - keep passages short, 50 — 300 words
  - passages can be taken from any kind of reading material
  - monitor word recognition level (beginning accuracy should be around 85% to 90%, otherwise it is too difficult).
- As students read, record miscues and reading time.
- Graph the reading rate and word recognition accuracy with each rereading so students can see progress, usually students read the same passage 3 times in succession. (Note: the procedure suggested in the literature is to graph reading rate and *number of errors*; however, it is a more positive approach to show progress using increasing word recognition accuracy; young students understand this format better.)

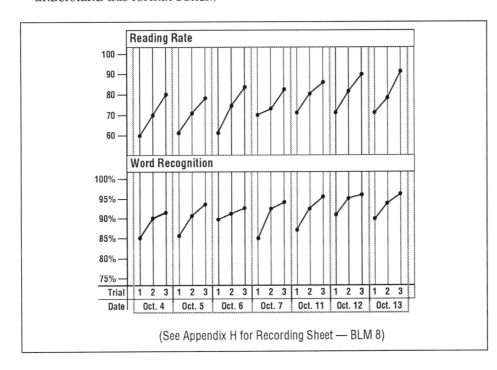

(See Appendix H for Recording Sheet — BLM 8)

- Keep practice passages at same level of difficulty until acceptable rate and accuracy is achieved on the first or second reading. (The stories do not need a high degree of shared words from one day to the next.)
- Use read-along approach (assisted reading) if student reads accurately but slower than 45 words per minute.
- When student reaches 60 words per minute on first reading of assisted reading, use the unassisted (independent) procedure.
- Set a specific number of rereadings (e.g. 3) rather than a speed criterion for children who are reading at "relatively" high rates and accuracy.
- For very slow readers set a mastery level for a particular passage after which they move to a new passage, rather than just reading the passage 3 times and moving on to a new passage (e.g. Dowhower (1987) suggests a goal of 85 wpm for older remedial students and 100 wpm for Grade 2 students who are reading accurately but word-by-word at 50 wpm).

Incorporating Repeated Reading into Classroom

Direct Instruction (with children who need extra help with reading)

- Teacher reads story first and discusses it with students. Then children choral read or echo read. Finally they independently practice segment of text to meet criterion of rate and accuracy (e.g. 75 wpm, 95% accuracy) with expression. Procedure is repeated next time with another passage which is a little more difficult.

Centre Approach

- Assisted repeated readings — students read along with tape and record how many times they follow along.
- Unassisted repeated readings — students time themselves and record their time (parent volunteer may help with this).

Paired Repeated Reading

- Students select and read silently a 50 word passage from a story used in a reading lesson.
- They choose partners and one student rereads passage 3 times, the other student records time
- The second student takes turn rereading their selected passage and the first student records the time.

At Home

- Students can take passages home to practice with parent.
- Parent listens to child read.
- Next day at school child reads to teacher and records rate and accuracy.

(If parent is unable to help at home, perhaps a teaching assistant or parent helper at school could be the person who listens to that student read.)

G2. Developing Reading Fluency in the Classroom
(Rasinski, 1989)

Several methods have been used successfully to develop reading fluency, such as:

* repeated readings
* echo reading or reading along with another reader or tape
* neurological impress method

However, these were generally intended for use with small groups or one to one. With modifications, some of the benefits of the above methods can be carried into the classroom setting.

Activities suggested by Rasinski

* Repetition — children love to hear their favourite stories more than once and can work in pairs on repeated reading tasks.
* Putting on plays or reader's theatre is another way to provide repetition in an interesting format.
* Practising and then reading to a buddy is yet another.
* The teacher can model fluent reading by reading aloud daily. Opportunities can be made to discuss the difference in fluent and nonfluent reading and to help children become aware of their reading style by providing feedback.
* Children can tape themselves reading and self-evaluate. Every few months they can tape their reading to note changes and progress.

Ways to provide support to develop reading fluency

* Choral reading with other fluent readers
* Neurological Impress Method (Heckelman, 1969; cited in Rasinski, 1989) The teacher begins by reading slightly ahead and louder than student. As student gains in fluency, the teacher's voice fades and shadows student reading. (Volunteers or parents can help with this.)
* Reading while listening, or echo reading (teacher reads or use a taped story)
* Providing easy material — students need to be able to choose easy reading materials and have time available to reread these. Rereading books allows students to focus on expression, phrasing and fluency rather than decoding.

These suggestions for developing fluency are not meant to be isolated lessons, but rather to be incorporated into lessons that also focus on other aspects of reading. For example, before teaching comprehension strategies for a particular story, students might first listen to it on tape, read along with the tape, and then read it to themselves and/or a partner. When the lesson is presented using the story, they will be able to read it more fluently and focus better on learning and using the comprehension strategy. Further repeated reading can be done by rereading the story at home, or reading to a teaching assistant, volunteer or buddy at school.

G3. Flexible Groupings for Instruction
(Flood, Lapp, Flood & Nagel, 1992)

- Purposes for creating flexible groupings for instruction in a classroom
  - whole class, small groups — direct instruction of a strategy or skill
  - interest groups — projects, sharing reading
  - heterogeneous groups — based on ability, work habits, strengths, knowledge or strategies
  - social groups — random selection or student choice
- Size of groups
  - individuals, dyads, small groups (3-4), larger groups (7-10), whole class
- Activities/Materials
  - same material/activity for all groups (to teach a specific strategy and/or knowledge, to introduce theme and share ideas)
  - different level of materials on same topic/theme within a group or for different groups (to match reading levels of students while they study the same theme)
  - different topics and similar activities within a theme (to match students' particular interests while all students learn the same strategy)
  - different topics and different activities within a theme (to match interests and preferences for responding, to encourage self-motivation and decision-making)

In teaching one story, many of these variations may be used:

- Preparing for reading — whole group listening
- Reading the story — whole group listening, individual reading, buddy reading, or some read on own, while others listen to tape
- Demonstrating story map — whole class
- Completing story map — individuals and/or pairs
- Reader's Theatre — choice of groups
- Responding to the story — individual student choice of activity and/or group work

References

Adams, M. J. (1990). *Beginning to read: Thinking and learning about print. A summary*. Cambridge, Mass.:MIT Press.

Armbruster, B. B., Anderson, T. H., & Ostertag, J. (1989). Teaching text structure to improve reading and writing. *The Reading Teacher, 44*(3), 130-137.

Beck, J. L., & Juel, C. (1992). The role of decoding in learning to read. In S. J. Samuels & A. E. Farstrup (Eds.), *What research has to say about reading instruction (2nd ed.)* (pp. 101-123). Newark, DE:IRA.

Blanton, W. E., Wood K. D., & Moorman, G. B. (1990). The role of purpose in reading instruction. *The Reading Journal, 43*(7), 486-493.

Brown, A. L., Day, J. D., Jones, R. S. (1983). The development of plans for summarizing texts. *Child Development, 54*, 968-979.

Brownlie, F., Close, S., & Wingren, L. (1988) *Reaching for higher thought: Reading, writing, thinking strategies*. Edmonton:Arnold Pub.

Brownlie, F., Close, S., & Wingren, L. (1990) *Tomorrow's classrooms today*. Ontario:Pembrooke.

Cairney, T. H. (1990). *Teaching reading comprehension*. Bristol, PA:Open University Press.

Cambourne, B. (1988). *The whole story: Natural learning and the acquisition of literacy in the classroom*. NSW, Australia:Ashton Scholastic.

Carr, E., & Ogle, D. (1987). K-W-L plus: A strategy for comprehension and summarization. *Journal of Reading, 30*, 626-636.

Chall, J. S. (1983). *Learning to read: The great debate (rev. ed.)*. New York:McGraw-Hill

Chall, J. S. (1992/93). Research supports direct instruction models. *Reading Today, 10*(3), 8-10

Clay, M. M. (1985). *The early detection of reading difficulties*. Portsmouth, NH:Heinemann

Cunningham, P. M., & Cunningham J. W. (1992). Making words: Enhancing the invented spelling-decoding connection. *The Reading Teacher, 46*(2), 106-115.

Davis, Z. T., & McPherson, M. D. (1989). Story map instruction: A road map for reading comprehension. *The Reading Teacher, 44*(4), 232-241.

Dowhower, S. L. (1989). Repeated reading: Research into practice. *The Reading Teacher, 43*(7), 502-507.

Flood, J., Lapp, D., Flood, S., & Nagel, G. (1992). Am I allowed to group? Using flexible patterns for effective instruction. *The Reading Teacher, 45*(8): 608-616.

Fogarty, R. (1990). *Designs for cooperative interactions*. Illinois:Skylight Publishing, Inc.

Forgan, H. W., & Mangrum, C. T. (1989). *Teaching content area reading skills*. New York:Charles E. Merill.

Gardner, H. (1983). Frames of Mind. New York: Basic Books.

Goodman, K. S. (1992/93). Gurus, professors and the politics of phonics. *Reading Today, 10*(3), 8-10.

Goodman, Y., Watson, D., & Burke, C. (1987). *Reading miscue inventory: Alternative procedures*. New York:Richard C. Owen.

Gordon, C. (1985). Modelling inference awareness across the curriculum. *Journal of Reading, 28*(5), 444-447.

Griffith, P. L., & Olson, H. W. (1992). Phonemic awareness helps beginning readers break the code. *The Reading Teacher, 45*(7): 516-523.

Harris, T. L., & Hodges, R. E. (1981). *A dictionary of reading and related terms*. Newark, DE:IRA

Irwin, J. W. (1986). *Teaching reading comprehension processes*. N.J.:Prentice Hall.

Johnson, D. D., & Johnson, B. V. H. (1986). Highlighting vocabulary in inferential comprehension instruction. *Journal of Reading, 29*(7), 622-625.

Johnson, M. S., Kress, R. A., & Pikulski, J. J. (1987). *Informal reading inventories (2nd ed.)*. Newark, DE:IRA.

Johnson, T. D., & Louis, D. R. (1990). *Bringing it all together*. Toronto, ON:Scholastic.

Juel, C. (1988). Learning to read and write: A longitudinal study of fifty-four children from first through fourth grade. *Journal of Educational Psychology, 80*, 437-447.

Laberge, D., & Samuels, S. J. (1985). Toward a theory of automatic information processing in reading. In H. Singer & R. B. Ruddell (Eds.), *Theoretical models and processes of reading* (3rd ed.). Newark, DE:IRA.

Lombard, M. A. (1989). ReQuest a fact. *The Reading Teacher, 43*, 548.

Manzo, A. U. (1986) *Improving reading comprehension through reciprocal questioning*. Unpublished doctoral dissertation, Syracuse University, N.Y.

Marzano, R. J., Brandt, R. S., Hughes, C. S., Jones, B. F., Presseisen, B. Z., Rankin, S. C., & Suhor, C. *Dimensions of thinking: A framework for curriculum and instruction*. Alexandria, Virginia:Assoc for Supervision and Curriculum Development.

Moore, D. W., Readence, J. E., & Rickelman, R. J. (1982). *Prereading activities for content area reading and learning*. Newark, DE:IRA.

Morrow L. M. (1989). Using story retelling to develop comprehension. In K. D. Muth, (Ed.), *Children's comprehension of text: Research into practice* (pp. 37-58). Newark, DE: IRA.

O'Brien, M. (1987). Whole language, the resource teacher and intervention. *Reading-Canada-Lecture, 5*(3), 165-170.

Ogle, D. M. (1989). The Know, Want to Know, Learn Strategy. In K. D. Muth, (Ed.), *Children's comprehension of text: Research into practice* (pp. 205-223). Newark, DE:IRA.

Palinscar, A. S., & Brown, A. L. (1985). Reciprocal teaching: Activities to promote "reading with your mind." In T. L. Harris & E. J. Cooper (Eds.), *Reading, thinking, and concept development* (pp. 147-158). New York:College Board Publications.

Palinscar, A. S., & Brown, A. L. (1986). Interactive teaching to promote independent learning from text. *The Reading Teacher, 39*(8), 771-777.

Paris, S. G. (1985). Using classroom dialogues and guided practice to teach comprehension strategies. In T.L. Harris & E.J. Cooper (Eds.), *Reading, thinking, and concept development* (pp. 133-146). New York:College Board Publications.

Pearson, P. D., Roehler, L. R., Dole, J. A., & Duffy, G. G. (1992). Developing expertise in reading comprehension. In S. J. Samuels & A. E. Farstrup (Eds), *What research has to say about reading instruction (2nd ed.)* (pp. 145-199). Newark, DE: IRA.

Phinney, M. Y. (1988). *Reading with the troubled reader*. Ontario:Scholastic.

Pinnell G. S. (1989). Reading recovery: Helping at risk children learn to read. *The Elementary School Journal, 90*(2), 160-183.

Pinnell, G. S., Fried, M. D., & Estice, R. M. (1990). Reading recovery: Learning how to make a difference. *The Reading Teacher, 43*(5), 282-295.

Pittelmann, S. D., Heimlich, J. E., Berglund, R. L., & French, M. P. (1991). *Semantic feature analysis: Classroom applications*. Newark, DE:IRA.

Raphael, T. E. (1984). Teaching learners about sources of information for answering comprehension questions. *Journal of Reading, 27*(4), 303-311.

Rasinski, T. V. (1989). Fluency for everyone: Incorporating fluency instruction in the classroom. *The Reading Teacher, 43*(9), 690-693.

Reutzel, D. R. (1989). Using a literature webbing strategy lesson with predictable books. *The Reading Teacher, 43*(4), 208-215.

Rhodes, L. K., & Dudley-Manning, C. (1988). *Readers and writers with a difference*. Portsmouth, NH:Heinemann

Rhodes, L. K., & Shanklin, N. L. (1990). Miscue analysis in the classroom. *The Reading Teacher, 44*(3), 252-254.

Richek, M. A. (1987). DRTA: 5 variations that facilitate independence in reading narratives. *Journal of Reading, 30*(7), 632-636.

Robinson, F. P. (1941). *Diagnostic and remedial techniques for effective study*. New York:Harper Collins.

Rosenblatt, L. (1985). The transactional theory of literary work: Implications for research. In C. R. Cooper (Ed.), *Researching response to literature and the teaching of literature: Points of departure*. Norwood, NJ: Ablex

Russell, P. (1984). *The Brain Book*. NAL-Dutton.

Samuels, S. J., Schermer, N., & Reinking, D. (1992). Reading fluency: Techniques for making decoding automatic. In S. J. Samuels & A. E. Farstrup (Eds), *What research has to say about reading instruction (2nd ed.)*(pp. 124-144). Newark, DE:IRA.

Shanklin, N. L., & Rhodes, L. K. (1989). Comprehension instruction as sharing and extending. *The Reading Teacher, 42*(7), 496-500.

Cochrane, O. Cochrane, D. Scalena, S. & Buchanan, L. (1984). *Reading, Writing and Caring*. Winnipeg, MB: Whole Language Consultants.

Sinatra, R., Stahl-Gemake, J., & Morgan, N. W. (1986). Using semantic mapping after reading to organize and write original discourse. *Journal of Reading, 29,* 4.

Sloan, P., & Whitehead, D. (1986). Reading theories explained: Answers to questions teachers ask. *P.E.N., 55.* Rozelle, NSW, Australia:Primary English Teaching Assoc.

Smith, F. (1990). *To think.* Teachers College Press.

Smith, F. (1992). Learning to read: The never-ending debate. *Phi Delta Kappan, 73*(2), 432-441.

Spiegel, D. L. (1992). Blending whole language and systematic direct instruction. *The Reading Teacher, 46*(1), 38-44.

Stahl, S. A. (1992). Saying the "p" word: Nine guidelines for exemplary phonics instruction. *The Reading Teacher, 45*(8), 618-624.

Stauffer, R. G. (1969). *Directing reading maturity as a cognitive process.* New York:Harper and Row.

Strickland, D. S., & Morrow, L. M. (1990). Sharing big books. *The Reading Teacher, 43*(5), 342-343.

Tarasoff, M. (1990). *Spelling strategies you can teach.* Victoria, BC:Active Learning Institute.

Tarasoff, M. (1992). *A guide to children's spelling development.* Victoria, BC:Active Learning Institute.

Taylor, B. M., Short, R. A, Frye, B. S., & Shearer, B.A. (1992). Classroom teachers prevent reading failure among low-achieving first-grade students. *The Reading Teacher, 45*(8), 592-597.

Tough, J. (1976). *Listening to children talking.* London:Schools Council Pub.

Trachtenburg, P. (1990). Using children's literature to enhance phonics instruction. *The Reading Teacher, 43*(9), 648-654.

Uhry, J. K., & Shepherd, M. J. (1993). Segmentation/spelling instruction as part of a first-grade reading program: Effects on several measures of reading. *Reading Research Quarterly, 28*(3), 219-233.

Wade, S. E. (1990). Using think alouds to assess comprehension. *The Reading Teacher, 43*(7), 442-451.

Appendix A
Sight Words

1044 Most Frequently Occurring Words

115 most commonly used words

a	could	her	look	on	that	went
about	dad	here	love	one	the	were
after	day	him	made	only	them	what
all	did	his	make	or	then	when
an	do	how	many	other	there	where
and	does	I	may	out	these	which
are	down	if	me	over	they	who
as	each	in	mom	people	this	will
at	find	into	more	said	three	with
be	first	is	most	saw	to	would
been	for	it	my	say	two	yes
big	from	its	name	see	up	you
brother	go	just	no	she	very	your
but	had	know	not	sister	want	
by	has	like	now	so	was	
can	have	little	of	some	way	
come	he	long	off	than	we	

Next 365 most commonly used words

able	back	came	don't	feet	gone	however
above	ball	can't	done	felt	good	hundred
across	beautiful	Canada	door	few	got	I'll
add	became	car	draw	field	great	I'm
again	because	care	dry	final	green	ice
against	become	carefully	during	fine	ground	idea
ago	before	carry	early	fire	group	important
air	began	cat	earth	fish	grow	inside
almost	begin	center	easy	five	half	instead
alone	behind	centre	eat	floor	hand	it's
along	below	certain	either	follow	happen	itself
already	best	change	else	food	hard	job
also	better	check	end	foot	head	keep
although	between	children	English	form	hear	kept
always	black	city	enough	found	heard	kind
am	blue	class	even	friend	heart	knew
American	boat	close	ever	front	heavy	land
among	body	common	every	full	held	language
animal	book	complete	everyone	fun	help	large
another	both	course	everything	game	high	last
answer	bottom	cut	example	gave	himself	later
any	box	dark	face	get	hold	lay
anything	boy	deep	fact	girl	home	learn
area	bring	didn't	fall	give	horse	learned
around	brought	different	family	glass	hot	least
asked	build	distance	fast	going	hour	leave
away	built	dog	feel	gold	house	leaves

left	new	possible	school	state	thought	watch
less	nothing	power	sea	stay	through	weather
letter	notice	probably	seen	still	tiny	well
life	number	problem	sentence	stood	today	whether
light	often	put	set	stop	together	while
line	oh	question	several	story	told	white
list	old	quite	shall	strong	too	whole
live	once	rain	ship	such	took	why
lived	open	ran	short	suddenly	top	wide
living	order	read	should	summer	toward	wild
longer	our	ready	show	sun	town	wind
low	outside	real	side	sure	tree	winter
man	own	really	simple	system	true	within
matter	page	red	since	table	try	without
mean	paper	remember	six	take	turn	work
men	part	rest	size	talk	turned	world
mixed	past	right	sky	tall	under	write
moon	pattern	river	small	tell	understand	year
morning	perhaps	road	snow	ten	until	yet
mother	person	rock	someone	that's	upon	young
move	piece	room	something	themselves	us	
much	place	round	sound	thing	usually	
must	plant	run	space	think	voice	
near	play	sad	special	third	walk	
need	point	same	stand	those	walked	
never	poor	sat	start	though	warm	

Next 564 most commonly used words

according	baseball	business	clean	cover	dress	explain
act	basic	busy	clear	cross	drink	express
action	bear	buy	cloth	crowd	drive	eye
addition	beat	cabin	coal	current	drop	fair
afraid	bed	cake	coast	dance	drove	familiar
afternoon	being	called	coat	danger	dust	famous
age	believe	camp	cold	dead	east	far
ahead	beneath	cannot	color	deal	edge	farm
alive	beside	capital	colour	dear	effect	farmer
amount	beyond	captain	column	death	eight	farther
ancient	bird	case	community	decide	electric	father
angry	bit	catch	company	describe	electricity	fear
anyone	blood	cattle	compare	desert	empty	feed
apart	blow	caught	compound	desk	energy	fell
appear	board	cause	consider	develop	engine	fence
arm	born	cent	contain	development	enjoy	fight
army	bottle	centimetre	control	die	entire	figure
art	bought	century	cool	difference	equal	fill
ate	bread	chair	copy	difficult	especially	finger
attention	break	chance	corn	dinner	evening	finish
average	breakfast	chart	corner	direction	everybody	fit
baby	breath	cheque	correct	discover	everywhere	flat
bad	bright	chief	cost	divide	except	flew
bag	broke	child	cotton	doctor	exercise	flight
band	broken	choose	couldn't	doesn't	expect	fly
bank	brown	church	count	double	experience	fixed
base	bus	circle	country	Dr.	experiment	force

forest	history	lake	meat	natural	particular	public
forth	hit	late	meet	nature	party	pull
forward	hole	law	member	necessary	pass	purpose
four	hope	lead	mental	neck	path	push
fourth	huge	led	met	neither	paw	quick
free	human	leg	method	nest	pay	quiet
fresh	hungry	length	metre	next	period	race
fruit	hurt	let	middle	nice	phrase	radio
further	I'd	level	mile	night	pick	raise
future	I've	lie	milk	nine	picture	range
garden	imagine	liquid	million	noise	plain	rate
gas	inch	listen	mind	none	plan	rather
general	include	litre	mine	nor	plane	reach
glad	indeed	lost	minute	north	please	reason
government	industry	lot	miss	northern	poem	record
grass	information	loud	modern	nose	popular	region
gray	interest	machine	moment	note	population	regular
grew	iron	main	money	noun	position	report
grown	island	major	month	object	practice	represent
guess	isn't	map	motion	ocean	present	result
guide	join	mark	mountain	office	pressure	return
gun	jump	market	mouth	oil	pretty	rich
hair	key	mass	movement	onto	process	ride
happy	kilometre	master	Mr.	opposite	produce	ring
hat	king	match	Mrs.	original	product	rise
he's	kitchen	material	music	oxygen	proper	rode
heat	knowledge	maybe	myself	paid	protect	root
herself	lady	meant	narrow	pair	proud	rope
hill	laid	measure	nation	paragraph	provide	rose

row	shore	south	stream	throughout	value	wire
rubber	shot	southern	street	thus	variety	wish
rule	shoulder	speak	strength	till	various	woman
safe	shown	speech	string	time	verb	women
salt	sight	speed	study	tomorrow	village	won
sand	sign	spend	subject	total	visit	won't
scale	silver	spent	sugar	touch	vowel	wonder
science	similar	spoke	supply	track	wagon	wood
season	sing	spot	support	trade	wait	wooden
seat	single	spread	suppose	train	wall	word
second	sit	spring	surprise	travel	war	worth
section	skin	square	symbol	trip	wasn't	wouldn't
seem	sleep	stage	tail	trouble	water	wrong
sell	slow	star	teacher	truck	we'll	wrote
send	soft	statement	team	tube	we're	yard
sense	soil	station	teeth	twelve	wear	yellow
sent	sold	steam	television	twenty	week	you'll
separate	solid	steel	temperature	twice	weight	you're
seven	solution	step	tent	type	west	yourself
shape	solve	stick	test	unit	wet	zipper
share	son	stone	their	United States	wheel	zoom
sharp	song	store	therefore	unless	whose	zoo
sheep	soon	storm	thick	use	wife	
sheet	sort	straight	thin	useful	win	
shook	soup	strange	thousand	valley	window	

Appendix B
Phonics Patterns

This appendix presents common phonics patterns. It provides a general sequence, not a strict hierarchy, for focusing lessons and activities. For example children may be able to learn the short a and o vowel sounds before they know all the consonant sounds (e.g. those for h, y, q). They may be able to learn the sounds of ee, ay, ow, oo before they know all the short vowel sounds (especially short i and e). So rather than following a strict sequence, you can choose from a group of phonics patterns to match

- what the children need to learn in order to read a particular story
- what they are attempting to spell in their writing
- what your assessment indicates they might be able to learn.

For example, if they know most of the consonants and are writing words with initial and final consonants, they could focus on short vowel sounds. If they know the consonants, consonant digraphs, and most of the short vowels, they could focus on long vowel patterns and some diphthongs (ow, ou, oo, oy). The sequence laid out in this appendix indicates that au, aw, and ew tend to be more difficult and less common in early reading than ow, ou, ay, etc.

From practical experience, the sounds of consonants b, t, s, m, n, p, d, z, k, j, f, and c are easier for children to learn than r, g, h, l, w, v, x, y, and q. Also the consonant digraphs th, sh, and ch are sometimes easier than blends. (Note: this sequence is also found in *Spelling Strategies You Can Teach* (Tarasoff, 1990). Learning these letter/sound relationships is basic to both decoding and spelling words.)

Sound/Letter Sequence Relationships

(To be used as a teaching resource for spelling, not to be memorized by the student.)

	Sound/Letter Sequence		Morphology

I

consonants
b c d f g h j k l m n p r s t v w z

digraphs	**short vowels**	
ch sh th wh	a o u	

II

qu y x	**short vowels**	-ing, -s
	i e	
blends	**long vowel patterns**	-ed
st sp sn sm sl sc sk sw	ay ai	
bl cl fl gl pl br cr dr fr gr	ee ea	contractions
pr tr spl str spr scr squ	oa	
	vowel & silent e	compounds
	y as a vowel	

III

-ll -ss -ff	ar or er	-er
	ou ow	est
-ck -ke	oo	
-nk -ng	oi ay	

		irregulars
		plurals

IV

hard and soft c		possessives
hard and soft g		capitals
	ir ur	
kn- wr- -ight	ear are	syllables
	au aw ew	affixes
ph gh	ie ei	root words

-le		hyphens
-tch		
-dge		abbreviations
-tion		combining forms
-ture		more irregular plurals
-age		

Sections I to IV indicate groups of phonics patterns to choose from
as children move from memory reading to competent, independent reading.

Appendix C
Syllabication Patterns

1) A syllable is a speech unit; syllables are thus related to how words are spoken. Have children listen to be aware of each "beat" or part, for example:

    - One syllable: *each, fish, did, run, catch*
    - Two syllables: *learn· ing, be· come, ex· pand*
    - Three syllables: *syl· la· ble, rep· re· sent, un·der· stand*

2) Every syllable has one vowel sound (represented by 1 or 2 vowels): *an· i· mal, cour· age, cau· li· flow· er.*

3) Patterns for spelling sounds in syllables differ from those in one syllable words: *sta· tion* (not **stay**· *tion*), *at· tic* (not *at·* **tick**), *re· main* (not **ree**· *main*), *al· ways* (not **all**· *ways*).

4) In identifying syllables, patterns can be seen in the letter sequences where the syllables join, for example, the vccv or **vcv** patterns (v = vowel, c = consonant):

    a) Divide between consonants **vc· cv**

        can· dy, sil· ver
        (the middle consonants are different)

        pr**et· ty,** d**if· fer**
        (the middle consonants are the same)

    b) Divide between first vowel and consonant **v̄· cv**

        ho· tel, o· pen
        (the single consonant is placed with the second syllable; in these cases, the vowel sound in the first syllable has its long sound)

    c) Divide between consonant and second vowel **vc· v**

        riv· er, man· age
        (the single consonant is placed with the first

syllable; in these cases, the vowel sound in the first syllable has its short sound)

    d) A **consonant** + **le** at the end of a multi-syllabic word forms a syllable, for example: cir· **cle, gig· gle, ta· ble.**

        The vowel sound in the first syllable will help determine whether there will be one or two consonants in the middle:
        short /a/ sound
        two consonants: *rat· tle can· dle*
        long /ā/ sound
        one consonant: *cra· dle sta· ple*

        Note, this is the same pattern as seen for the above **v· cv** and **vc· v** syllable patterns:

    - When syllables end in a vowel, that vowel has its long sound. This is called an open syllable, for example: bē· gin, ō· pen, stā· ple.

    - When syllables end in a consonant, the vowel has its short sound. These syllables are called closed syllables, for example: rĭv· er, măn· age, răt· tle.

Common Patterns

-age	village bandage advantage damage
-tion	station mention fiction
-ture	picture nature adventure future
-ic	picnic attic
-le	rumble battle title

-ia -ious	India curious	
-ian -ier	Victorian funnier	(i sounds like /ē/)
-iest -io	happiest radio	

Appendix D
Structural Analysis

Contractions

is not . . . . isn't	they are . . . . .they're	
did not . . . . didn't	I am . . . . .I'm	we have . . . . we've
do not . . . . don't	he is . . . . .he's	you have . . . . you've
does not . . . . doesn't	she is . . . . .she's	they have . . . . they've
was not . . . . wasn't	it is . . . . .it's	I have . . . . I've
can not . . . . can't	that is . . . . .that's	
could not . . . . couldn't		we had (would) . . . we'd
would not . . . . wouldn't	we will . . . . .we'll	you had (would) . . . you'd
should not . . . . shouldn't	you will . . . . .you'll	they had (would) . . they'd
have not . . . . haven't	they will . . . . .they'll	I had (would) . . . . . I'd
will not . . . . won't	I will . . . . .I'll	he had (would) . . . . he'd
	he will . . . . .he'll	she had (would) . . . she'd
we are . . . . we're	she will . . . . .she'll	
you are . . . . you're	it will . . . . .it'll	let us . . . . let's

Some Compound Words

afternoon	birthday	grandmother	someone
ago	birthday	hillside	something
airplane	cannot	himself	Sunday
along	cowboy	inside	sunrise
anything	daytime	inside	sunshine
anywhere	dishrag	mailbox	today
around	downtown	makeup	tonight
away	everybody	maybe	uphill
bagpipes	everyone	maybe	upon
baseball	everything	myself	upset
bedtime	fireman	myself	without
beehive	football	outside	
behind	grandfather	raindrop	

Patterns for Adding Inflectional Endings

Patterns for adding ed, ing, er and est to single syllable words

	WORD PATTERN (c=consonant v=vowel e=silent e)			
	cvc	**vce**	**vcc**	**vvc**
ROOT WORD	drop pat	hope trade	jump land	join clean
PATTERN	double the consonant	drop the e	no change	no change
ing	dropping patting	hoping trading	jumping landing	joining cleaning
ed	dropped patted	hoped traded	jumped landed	joined cleaned
ROOT WORD	red	fine	fond	clean
er	redder	finer	fonder	cleaner
est	reddest	finest	fondest	cleanest

Patterns for adding ed, ing, er and est to multisyllabic words ending in cvc pattern

	TWO SYLLABLES		THREE SYLLABLES
	ACCENT ON FIRST SYLLABLE	**ACCENT ON SECOND SYLLABLE**	
ROOT WORD	profit	refer	benefit
ed	profited	referred	benefitted
ing	profiting	referring	benefiting

For some words, doubling the final consonant is optional, for example,

    focus: focussing or focusing
    label: labelling or labeling
    cancel: cancelled or canceled

Patterns for adding ed, ing, er and est to words ending in y

ENDING	ing	er
ROOT WORD	carr<u>y</u>	happ<u>y</u>
ing	carr<u>y</u>ing	-
ed	carr<u>i</u>ed	-
er	carr<u>i</u>er	happ<u>i</u>er
est	-	happ<u>i</u>est

Patterns for adding s (es)

ROOT WORD ENDS WITH	PATTERN	EXAMPLES
s x ch sh ss	Add es	mix — mixes, glass — glasses
y	change y to i and add **es**	worry — worries
ey ay oy	Add s	monkey — monkeys, day — days, toy — toys
f	sometimes change f to v and add es sometimes no change (pronunciation provides the key)	loaf — loaves, thief — thieves roof — roofs, chief — chiefs
other words	Add s	jump — jumps, picture — pictures

Some words do not change in their plural form: one fish — two fish
Some words change spelling in their plural form: one mouse — two mice
Oral language experience provides knowledge of which words change spelling or remain the same.

Commonly Used Prefixes and Suffixes

PREFIXES

re	again
dis	not, reversal
pro	in favour of
in	into, not
en, em	in, into, cover
pre	before
ad	to, toward
com, co, con	with, together
e, ex	out of, former
sub	under, beneath
ab	away from
be	make, thoroughly
de	downward, undoing
un	not, opposite
tri	three
super	above, beyond
anti	against, opposed
non	not
mis	wrongly
auto	self
post	after

SUFFIXES

ation, ment	state of
ture	result of
ive	that which
ness	state of being
ic	dealing with
ous	full of
able	can be done
less	without
ish	like
ly	in manner of
ful	full of
er, or, ar	one who
age	state of
ism	belief in
let	little
ory, ery	where it is made
ward	in direction of
al, ial	related to
logy	study of
en	made of
y	marked by

Common Roots and Combining Forms

meter	measure	flec, flex	bend
mit, miss	send	cred	believe
tel(e)	far	chron(o)	time
duc(t)	to lead	flor	flower
phon	sound	man	hand
scop(e)	view	bio	life
the(o)	god	cent	hundred
scrib, script	write	dict	say
pend	hang	duc(t)	lead
graph, gram	write	morp	form
port	carry, harbour, entrance	ped	foot
		phob	fear
ply	fold	photo	light
sign	sign, mark	spect	look

Appendix E
Functions of Oral Language

This list of ways children use oral language is taken from *Listening to Children Talking* (Tough, 1976). Note the similarity between functions 3 to 7 and the skills for reading comprehension and responding to literature.

1. **In self-maintaining, the child**
   - refers to physical and psychological needs and wants
   - protects self and self-interests
   - justifies behaviour
   - criticizes others
   - threatens others

2. **In directing, the child**
   - monitors own actions
   - directs self
   - directs actions of others
   - collaborates in action with others

3. **In reporting on present and past experiences, the child**
   - labels components
   - refers to details/attributes
   - refers to incidents
   - refers to sequence of events
   - compares
   - recognizes related aspects
   - analyzes using above features
   - recognizes central meaning
   - reflects on meaning and own feelings

4. **In logical reasoning, the child**
   - explains process
   - recognizes causal/dependent relationships
   - recognizes problems and solutions
   - justifies judgements and actions
   - reflects on events and conclusions
   - recognizes principles

5. **In predicting, the child**
   - anticipates and forecasts events
   - anticipates details of events
   - anticipates sequence of events
   - anticipates problems and solutions
   - anticipates and recognizes alternative actions
   - predicts consequences of action

6. **In projecting, the child projects into**
   - experiences of others
   - feelings of others
   - reactions of others
   - situations never experienced

7. **In imagining, the child imagines**
   - situations based on real life
   - situations based on fantasy
   - original stories

Appendix F
Teaching Beginning Reading —
20 Lesson Outlines

Goals

- To help students progress from "memory reading" to beginning independent reading.
- To develop word recognition strategies so that students can read a new story or text passage without help.
- To develop context (syntax, semantic) clues and background knowledge through oral/aural language activities (the foundations of reading).

These lessons are for students who:

- can recognize and name most of the letters of the alphabet,
- know many of the consonant letter/sound relationships,
- can "memory read" short stories, matching voice to print accurately,
- can locate a few words in a story either by using initial consonant clues or by tracking words as they repeat the story until they come to the word, and

- need a more direct teaching approach to become independent readers.

The lessons consist of two components which need to be developed concurrently.

1. **Oral and Aural Language Activities (in whole class setting)**

    - listening to stories read aloud for enjoyment and for learning (theme studies)
    - responding to the stories and information (see Appendix H: Reading Responses)
    - participating in learning experiences

2. **Focusing on Print (in small group setting)**

    - learning letter/sound relationships
    - blending sounds together
    - using phonics to decode words
    - recognizing sight words with automaticity
    - reading short stories independently using context and graphophonics clues to identify new words

Components of Beginning Reading Lessons

Focus on

- Sight words
  - high interest
  - frequently occurring
  - nonphonetic
- Decoding words
  - phonics
  - letter/sound relationships
  - blending sounds
  - context clues

20 Lessons, 20-30 minutes daily (10-15 minutes instruction, 10-15 minutes paired practice, independent reading and follow-up writing). Each lesson may take from 2 to 4 days depending on the students. For example, the first few lessons may take longer because the students are learning new skills (e.g. blending sounds, concept of word) not just the words and letter sounds presented in the lessons.

Home practice four times per week is strongly recommended to provide the extra exposure to the words and skills. If this is not possible, another student, parent volunteer or teaching assistant may be scheduled to review the words and read with that student the following day.

Planning Lessons

Suggested words and phonic elements are given in the 20 lesson outlines. However, to match the program more closely to your students you can choose sight words from the list in Appendix A and also those they are writing frequently in their journals and reading during lessons and independent reading time (easy reading books, language experience charts, daily news, etc.)

When choosing books for them to read independently, ensure that the vocabulary in the books have some relation to the decoding skills/strategies you are teaching. For example, if the short /ā/ sound is being focused on, ensure there are new words with this sound in the text (see Appendix G for easy reading books). To make connections with stories read to the whole class, a summary could be made using many of the words the students know (see Part III: C2, Early Intervention in Reading). These can be reread and illustrated by the students as a reading response activity. New words from the story that they may not remember can be under-

lined, cuing them that it is a word from the story. Encourage them to use both phonics and context clues for decoding these words. In the beginning you may need to make up sentences for the students to read, a task the students can soon contribute to. Once they have some sight words and beginning phonics, there will be some beginning reading books they can use.

Research is beginning to indicate that children who are encouraged to use invented, or "constructed" spelling, also become better at decoding words as measured by their ability to use phonics knowledge to decode nonsense words and real words (Uhry & Shepherd, 1993). They suggest that along with frequent reading and writing experiences in the classroom, explicit instruction in segmenting and spelling words (e.g. developing phonemic awareness and phonics) helps develop stronger decoders.

Teaching Strategies

— Sight Words

- Have focus words prepared on word cards.
- Present and read text to students.
- Read text together.
- Students match word cards to words in text.
- Students place word cards in order to make sentence from text.
- Mix up word order and students read new sentence (may not make sense).

- Reconstruct sentence and students reread .
- Students make sentences and read.
- Present slightly different text for students to read (provides chance to recognize words in new text).
- Search for words in story books read to class and in "morning message/news," charts, etc.
- Teach students to visualize words (Tarasoff, 1990).

— Phonics and Phonemic Awareness

- Present text that has words containing the letter/sound relationship to be focused on.
- Present words on cards with the letter/sound relationship.
- Students brainstorm more words, teacher adds to cards or list on chart.
- Demonstrate blending sounds together (see p. 89) — using letter cards spaced apart, sound first letter (e.g. mmmmmmm) and move it towards second letter, as it joins the second add that sound (maaaaaa) and move both letters to join the third sound (maaaat). In this way students see and hear how to blend sounds together to identify words. Repeat with the students blending the sounds as teacher moves the cards. When they are able to do this easily, they can then move the cards themselves as they blend the sounds.

- Students identify (point to or say) words from the text being read that have the letter/sound relationship
- Provide students with letter tiles to make words with the letter/sound relationship (see p. 89), focus on segmenting the word into phonemes and then blending them together. As they become able to remember and print letters easily, they can spell words on chalkboards or paper instead of using letter tiles.
- Sort words from text according to phonic patterns (can use cards in pocket chart, or write words on chart).
- Teacher dictates some words chosen from the text that have the letter/sound relationship for the students to print.
- Search for other words in books, charts, etc.

Learning Activities after Teacher-led Lessons

1. **Paired practice**
   - Reading buddies take words cards and read them to each other. If student reads one incorrectly, the other student says the word and puts the card at the bottom of the deck. Correct words go in a separate pile.
   - When all words have been read by both buddies, students make sentences with cards.
   - Students reread text that was used during the group lesson.

   - Students make words using letter tiles, blending sounds together and print words on chalkboard or on paper; they can check to see if they made any words different from those on the chart.
   - Students complete a cloze activity using text that was read and new text using words known (place word cards on an enlarged version of a cloze passage, or print words on prepared cloze worksheet).

2. **Independent reading**
   - Students read sentences containing the words and requiring the skills taught .
   - Students read summaries of the story read to the whole class structured to focus on certain words.
   - Students read easy reading books which have a more controlled vocabulary .

3. **Writing**
   - Students write words dictated by the teacher or chosen from chart by a student; the words focus on the sounds taught.
   - Brainstorm ideas and words to be used to re-spond to a story.
   - Students write about story, using "constructed" or invented spelling. Trying to sound out words to spell them aids in developing phonemic awareness and learning phonetic relation-ships which are also used for decoding words

4. **Home reading**
   - Students should read the words presented each day at home and review words learned earlier.
   - Students should take home sentences/short story to read. It is best if they do some home reading 4 times a week.

(For other teaching ideas see Section III, C1-5 and pp. 71, 82-95)

These 20 lessons present the following:

   - a review of consonants as part of other words focused on
   - short vowels a, o, i, u
   - consonant digraphs sh, th, ch
   - long vowel patterns ay, ee
   - vowel diphthongs oo, ow, and
   - word families (rimes) -at, -an, -am, -ap, -ad, -ot, -og, -on, -ug, -it, -in, -ip, -ig, -een, -eep, -oon, -ool, -ow, -ay
   - 86 sight words

Sight words presented in each lesson

I	IV	VII	X	XIII	XVI	XIX
the	not	no	Review	but	they	who
I	here	yes		had	are	think
go	is	come		has	do	say
to	big	help		stop	away	went
can	see	we		must	saw	out

II	V	VIII	XI	XIV	XVII	XX
look	Review	this	one	did	where	Review
you		was	two	our	going	
play		in	three	eat	brown	
with		black	yellow	came	ate	
and		he	blue	from	get	

III	VI	IX	XII	XV	XVIII
have	will	run	now	all	soon
alike	up	funny	down	his	too
jump	me	make	by	him	under
little	for	said	into	of	there
my	it	she	good	what	ask

Lesson Outlines

(Use strategies as outlined to present the following sight words and phonics patterns.)

I.   **Sight words** — *the, I, go, to, can*
    Make and read sentences such as:

    I can go to the _____

    Can I go to the _____?

    I go to the _____

    (Words will need to be added by students to complete sentences).

II.   **Sight words** — *look, you, play, with, and*
    Phonics — blending short a words

    use word family "at" — mat, pat, fat, rat, hat, bat, cat

- With each lesson, sentences can be made up for students to read. Having the words on cards makes it easy for them to make up their own sentences. Words of interest that they already know (e.g. names of friends and pets, mom, dad, love, nintendo, etc.) can be added.

    Example sentences to read:

    Look at the cat and the rat.

    I can play with the bat.

    You can pat the cat.

    Look at the fat rat.

    You can play with the cat.

III.   **Sight words** — *have, a, like, jump, little, my*
    Phonics — blending short a words

    use word family "an" — can, man, fan, ran, pan, van

    Example sentences:

    I have a fan and a pan.

    Can I go with the man and the cat?

    I like to go to the _____ with the cat.

    Look at the cat with the hat.

    My little cat ran to the van.

    My cat can run and play.

IV.   **Sight words** — *not, here, is, big, see*
    Phonics — blending short a words

    use word families "am" and "ap" — am, ham, jam, Pam, Sam, cap, tap, map, lap, nap, rap

V.   **Review Progress**
    Graph words known and/or colour in words known (see BLM's B,C, and D in Appendix I)
    Review reading log book and graph number of "books" read

VI.   **Sight Words** — *will, up, me, for, it,*
    Phonics — blending short o words

    use word family "ot" — not, hot, pot, lot, jot, dot

VII.   **Sight words** — *no, yes, come, help, we*
    Phonics — blending short o words

    use word family "og" — dog, log, fog, bog, hog, jog

VIII.   **Sight words** — *this, was, in, black, he,*
    Phonics — blending short o, introduce digraph "th"

    use word family "on" and "ob" — on, Ron, Don, cob, rob, sob

    brainstorm "th" words including — the, this, that

IX.   **Sight words** — *run, funny, make, said, she*
    Phonics — blending short u words, introduce digraph "sh"

    use word family "ug" — tug, rug, bug, dug, mug, lug

    brainstorm "sh" words including — she, shop, shut

X.   **Review** — /ā/, /ō/, /ū/, /th/, /sh/ and sight words
    Note progress
    Graph words known and/or colour in words known
    Review reading log book and graph number of "books" read

XI. **Sight words** — *one, two, three, yellow, blue*
Phonics — review digraph "th", introduce "th" at end of word

> this, that, with, path, bath (brainstorm other words especially those involved with other reading and lessons in the classroom)

XII. **Sight words** — *now, down, by, into, good*
Phonics — introduce "ow" — now, cow, bow, wow, how, pow

XIII. **Sight words** — *but, had, has, stop, must*
Phonics — review short /ă/, /ŏ/, /ŭ/ words

XIV. **Sight words** — *did, our, eat, came, from*
Phonics — blending with short i

> use word families "it" and "in" — bit, fit, hit, kit, lit, mit, pit, sit, bin, fin, pin, tin, win

XV. **Sight words** — *all, his, him, of, what*
Phonics — review digraphs /sh/ and /th/, blending with short i

> use word families "ip" and "ig" — dip, flip, nip, sip, tip, ship, big, dig, fig, pig, wig

Note progress

> Graph words known and/or colour in words known

> Review reading log book and graph number of "books" read

XVI. **Sight words** — *they, are, do, away, saw*
Phonics — introduce long vowel sound concept and /ee/

> use words with "ee, een, eep"— bee, see, three, tree, green, been, teen, seen, queen, sheep, jeep, peep

XVII. **Sight words** — *where, going, brown, ate, get*
Phonics — introduce digraph ch

> brainstorm words including — chip, chop, chat, chin

XVIII. **Sight words** — *soon, too, under, there, ask*
Phonics — introduce /oo/

> use word families "oon" and "ool" — soon, moon, spoon, loon, school, pool, tool, cool, fool, spool

XVIX. **Sight words** — *who, think, say, went, out*
Phonics — introduce /ay/

> use word family "ay" — play, may, say, day, pay, way, tray, pray

XX. **Review Progress**
Graph words known and/or colour in words known

Review reading log book and graph number of "books" read

Once students have begun to use these sight words and phonics skills easily, they will have moved from memory reading into beginning reading independence. Further lessons can continue to develop reading strategies suggested in this book using other resources available in the classroom.

Appendix G
Easy Reading Storybooks and "Chapter" Books

Beginning Reading Books

These are short stories, have few words (1 or 2 lines on page), generally have larger print, focus on sight words and phonics, illustrations on every page

Start to Read — Rhyming Readers

This series has entertaining stories using many rhyming words and colourful illustrations, a few words per line, 1 to 3 lines per page, large print, 16 pages per book. In each set the reading level increases in difficulty over the 10 books (e.g. beginning reading through early grade 2 or later grade 1 through mid-grade 2). Focus is on decoding using phonics patterns (e.g. vowel patterns and consonants) and sight words.

Set A	Up Went the Goat
	I Want a Pet
	The Gum on the Drum
	The Fox on the Box
	Jog, Frog, Jog
	Beep, Beep
	My Friend Goes Left
	Nine Men Chase a Hen
	Say Good Night
	Sue Likes Blue
Set B	Good Bad Cat
	Get Lost, Becka!
	I Want to be a Clown
	Foolish Goose
	Benny's Baby Brother
	Elephant and Envelope
	Jace, Mace and the Big Race
	That's Not All
Set C	The New Bike
	Bumble Bear
	Peter's Dream

Fabulous Principal Pie
Hanna's Butterfly
The Last Game
I Don't Like Peas
The Lost Puppy

Get Ready, Get Set, Read!

This series has colourful illustrations, large print, one or three lines per page, rhyming words that focus on specific word families and vowel sounds, 32 pages per book.

Find Nat	short a
The Tan Can	
The Sled Surprise	short e
The Best Pets Yet	
Sometimes I Wish	short i
A Mop for Pop	short o
Frog Knows Best	
The Bug Club	short u
Bub and Chub	
What a Day for Flying	all short vowels

Phonics Beginning Reading Series

Each set has 10 short, 8-page stories, focusing on different word families and phonetic patterns, one or two lines per page, larger print, difficulty overlaps between sets.

Short Vowels — Set A, B, C, D
Long Vowels — Set A, B, C, D
Consonant Blends — Set A, B, C
Consonant Digraphs — Set A, B, C

Ladybird Key Words Reading Scheme

This series has colourful illustrations, each set begins with a few words per page and short sentences, 50 pages per book. Each book in the series increases in difficulty and in the

number of words on the page (e.g. spanning beginning reading to about mid-grade 2 level). Focus is on sight words through controlled introduction of vocabulary and repetition.

Set A   Play With Us
We Have Fun
Things We Like
Things We Do
Where We Go

Set B   Look at This
Have a Go
Boys and Girls
Fun at the Farm
Out in the Sun

Set C   Let's Play
The Dragon Boat
The Space Boat
Sam to the Rescue
Kate and the Crocodile

Easy Reading Storybooks

These books have larger vocabularies and longer stories for beginning independent readers

Little Rooster Read-a Story Series

These books have one to three lines per page, a few words per line, larger print, basic sight words, 32 pages, colourful illustrations.

Are We There Yet?
Go Away Crows
Good Dog, Rover
Ready, Alice?
Two Good Friends
Winter Coats

Hello Reading Series

These books have one to five lines per page, a few words per line, larger print, basic sight words, 32 pages, colourful illustrations.

Cat Games
Dark Night, Sleepy Night
Dr. Cat
Good Luck, Bad Luck
Harry Goes to Camp
How Big is Big
Strike Four
Lunch Boxes
My Tooth is Loose
Please Let It Snow

The following sets of stories have larger vocabulary, more pages and smaller print than above sets, coloured illustrations on most pages.

Bank Street Ready-to-Read Level 1

These books have 32 pages, colourful illustrations on every page, two to several lines per page, few words per line, medium-size print, larger vocabulary than other sets listed here, some have rebus. Good for reading aloud to beginning readers before they try to read them on their own.

Who Goes Out on Hallowe'en?
Yoo Hoo Moon
Good News
Dozen Dirty Dogs
The Gruff Brothers
Things That Go
Eency Weency Spider

Bank Street Ready-to-Read Level 2

Annie's Pet
Moon Boy
Hedgehog Bakes a Cake
Too Many Mice
Beavers Beware
The Monster From the Sea
Follow That Fish!
Show-and-Tell Frog
"Not Now!," Said Cow

Dial Easy to Read Series

These books have 56 pages, coloured illustrations on most pages, three to several lines per page, few words per line, medium-size print, most words are from the 200 to 300 most commonly occurring words or can be sounded out.

Swamp Monsters
Grizzly Riddles
Lionel in the Spring
Fox All Week
Fox and His Friends
Fox in Love
Fox on the Job
Tales of Amanda Pig
More Tales of Amanda Pig

"An I Can Read Book" Series

These books have 64 pages, coloured illustrations on most pages, three to several lines per page, few words per line, medium-size print, most words are from the 200 to 300 most commonly occurring words or can be sounded out.

Arthur's Hallowe'en Costume
Arthur's Loose Tooth
Big Max
Danny and the Dinosaur
Days With Frog and Toad
Dolphin
Grasshopper on the Road
Here Comes the Strikeout
Kick, Pas and Run
Mice at Bat
No More Monster for Me!
Oscar Otter
Red Fox and his Canoe
The Smallest Cow in the World
Ten Copycats in a Boat and Other Riddles

Beginning to Read Series

Just Beginning to Read Collection

These sets have 6 books with colourful illustrations, 40 to 65 sight words in each 28 page story. Within interesting stories the vocabulary is repeated, few lines per page, almost regular sized print

Sets A, C, E, F

Dear Dragon and Dinosaur Collection

These sets have 6 books with colourful illustrations, 60 to 75 sight words in each 32 page story. Within interesting stories the vocabulary is repeated, few lines per page, almost regular sized print

Sets B, M, W, X

Step into Reading Series — Step 1

These books have 32 pages, coloured illustrations on most pages, three to several lines per page, few words per line, medium-size print, most words are from the 200 to 300 most commonly occurring words or can be sounded out.

Beef Stew
David and the Giant
Dinosaur Babies
Five Silly Fishermen
Noah's Ark
Toad on the Road
Teeny Tiny Woman
TMNT — Pizza Party
Railroad Toad
Follow the Monsters

Easy Storybooks and "Chapter" Books

Bank Street Readers Level 3

storybooks, colourful illustrations on most pages, medium sized print, 48 pp

The Magic Bus
A Horse Called Starfire
Lion and Lamb Step Out
Lo-Jack and the Pirates
Mr. Baseball
Mr. Monster
Noah and the Flood

Step into Reading Series — Step 2

storybooks, colourful illustrations on most pages, medium sized print, 48 pp

Baseball Ballerina
Best Mistake Ever
Dinosaur Days
Happy Birthday Little Witch
Hungry, Hungry Sharks
Tom the T.V. Cat
Whales, the Gentle Giants
Wild, Wild Wolves
Dolphins!
Norma Jean, Jumping Bean
Pretty Good Magic

Step into Reading Series — Step 3

storybooks, colourful illustrations on most pages, medium sized print, 48 pp

Amazing Rescues
Cannonball Chris
Deputy Dan and the Robbers
Mystery of the Pirate Ghost
Pompeii — Buried Alive!
Secret of Foghorn Island
Soccer Sam
Titanic: Lost ... and Found
Treasure of the Lost Lagoon
Tut's Mummy: Lost ... and Found
20,000 Baseball Cards Under the Sea
Aladdin and the Magic Lamp
Little Mermaid
Space Rock

Step into Reading Series — Step 4

colourful illustrations on most pages, medium sized print, "chapter" book, 48 pp

Baseball's Best: Five True Stories
Baseball's Greatest Pitchers
Comeback! Four True Stories
Dinosaur Hunters

Moonwalk: The First Trip to the Moon
Trojan Horse: How the Greeks Won the War
Witch Hunt: It Happened in Salem Village
True Life Treasure Hunts
To the Top! Climbing the World's Highest
Mountain

Dell Young Yearling

illustrations on every page, storybooks

The Pancake	48 pp
The Tree Angel	40 pp
The Cats' Burglar	80 pp
To Many Rabbits	48 pp
How Big is a Foot	48 pp
Nate the Great	64 pp
Nate the Great and the Lost List	48 pp
Nate the Great Goes Down in the Dump	
	48pp

chapters, fewer illustrations

Little Soup's Birthday	64 pp
Little Soup's Bunny	64 pp

Stepping Stone Books

"chapter" books, fewer black and white illustrations, 48 pp

Aliens for Lunch
Great Uncle Dracula
Aliens for Breakfast
Adventures of Ratman
Elaine and the Flying Frog
Dinosaurs Before Dark
Daring Rescue of Marion the Pig
Ghost in Tent 19
Pioneer Cat
Pizza Pie Slugger
Soccer Mania
Marvin Redpost: Kidnapped at Birth
Mummies in the Morning
Knights at Dawn

Kids at Polk Street School

some black and white illustrations on a few pages, 80 page novels, pages have fewer words than Step Up novels and Stepping Stone books

The Candy Corn Contest
December Secrets
In the Dinosaur's Paw
Lazy Lions, Lucky Lambs
Say "Cheese"

The New Kids at Polk Street School

some black and white illustrations on a few pages, 80 page novels, pages have fewer words than Step Up novels and Stepping Stone books

Fancy Feet
All About Stacey
B-E-S-T Friends
Spectacular Stone Soup

Step Up Classic Chillers

several black and white illustrations, more words per page, regular sized print, 96 pp

Dr. Jekyll and Mr. Hyde
Dracula
Frankenstein
Mysteries of Sherlock Holmes
Phantom of the Opera
The Vampire
Mummy Awakes
Return of the Werewolf

Step Up Classics

several black and white illustrations, regular sized print, 96 pp

Black Beauty
Knights of the Round Table
Peter Pan
Robin Hood
Treasue Island

Ladybird Classics

small print, colourful illustrations on every page, 52 pp

Alice in Wonderland
The Invisible Man
Journey to the Centre of the Earth
Kidnapped
Swiss Family Robinson
Three Musketeers
Tom Sawyer
Treasure Island
Hound of the Baskervilles
The Lost World

For more information on books and ordering, contact Active Learning Institute.

Appendix H
Reading Responses —
Black Line Masters

There are many ways students can respond to literature and demonstrate their understanding. The following presents a list of ways students can respond to reading as they are involved in both learning to read and using text to learn. Black line masters that can be used for **responding** are included in this appendix. Suggestions for using the BLM's are given on the back of each one. However, there are many ways these can be used, so try your own ideas, or better yet, let the students invent new ways. Many of these can also be used for **prewriting** activities (brainstorming, clustering, organizing, outlining, etc.) or for research projects (recording information, organizing, etc.). Using similar techniques for prewriting and for responding to text helps students see the connections between reading and writing. Instead of putting the title of a book and the author at the top of the response sheet when used as a prewriting activity, the students would put their own title and their name as author.

These BLMs can be duplicated for students in your class and used as a whole class activity when you are introducing strategies. They could also be made available so that students choose the way to respond to their reading. Also you may want to laminate a BLM filled in as an example to keep in a "reading centre."

Ways to respond:
- read and predict — oral or written activity
- create a reader's theatre from the story, practice and perform; create a news report or interview, tape record or video
- dramatize — act out, create puppet show
- discuss — explain answers or interpretations, make comparisons with other texts, take a character's point of view to discuss story
- retell orally — without props, with props (puppet, flannel board, drawings), retell individually or in group with students taking turns
- represent visually — drawings, models
- write responses — summaries, answer questions, written retelling, rewrite story from different point of view or incorporating characters or events from other stories, write a review of the book to encourage others to read it, write questions, clues, riddles about story for others to answers, write a letter to a character, write a journal entry as if student was one of the characters
- illustrate, diagram, web, map, etc.

More BLMs can be found in "Blackline Masters for Reading Instruction that Makes Sense" (published by Active Learning Institute). See also suggestions given in Brownlie, Close, & Wingren (1988, 1990), and Johnson & Louis (1987).

Date			Name			

Author

2.

4.

Title

1.

3.

Narratives

Use before, during and after reading for focusing on prediction and plot

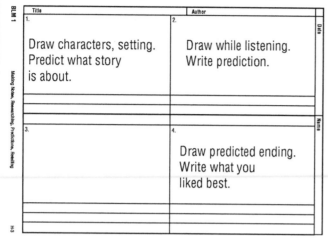

1. Show pictures — draw characters, setting, important artifacts. Write prediction.

2. While listening, draw interesting ideas/events. Stop reading, predict what will happen next.

3. Read next part, do as in #2.

4. Draw predicted ending, write why you think so.

Use before, during and after reading for focusing on character development

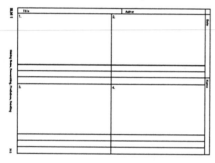

1. Draw character. Write predicted qualities.

2. Draw event. Write qualities.

3. Draw event. Write additional qualities.

4. Draw character. Describe how character changed.

Use after reading for retelling

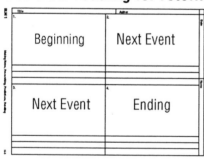

1. to 4.   Retell by writing main events, then illustrate.

Use after reading for summarizing

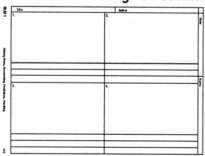

1. to 4.   Write main idea in space.

Write details on lines.

Title/Theme _____   Name _____

Author _____   Date _____

Non-Fiction

Use during reading and researching
— make notes

Use for prewriting activity
— make outline

Title/Theme _____ Name _____ Author _____ Date _____	
Write Main Idea	details
Main Idea	details
Main Idea	details

BLM 2   Making Notes, Researching, Predictions, Retelling, Prewriting Activity   H-5

Narratives

Use during reading — predict and confirm while listening

Title/Theme ____ Name ____ Author ____ Date ____	
Draw prediction	Write what happened

BLM 2   Making Notes, Researching, Predictions, Retelling, Prewriting Activity   H-6

Title/Theme ____ Name ____ Author ____ Date ____	
Draw what happened	Write prediction for next part

BLM 2   Making Notes, Researching, Predictions, Retelling, Prewriting Activity   H-6

Use after reading — retell

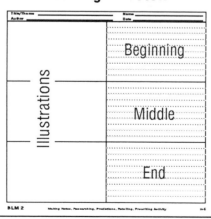

Title/Theme ____ Name ____ Author ____ Date ____	
Illustrations	Beginning
	Middle
	End

BLM 2   Making Notes, Researching, Predictions, Retelling, Prewriting Activity   H-6

Use after reading or for prewriting activity

Title/Theme ____ (student) ____ Name ____ Author ____ Date ____	
Characters	Write beginning or key words
Setting	Write middle or key words
Brainstorm words	Write end or key words

Action words, describing words →

BLM 2   Making Notes, Researching, Predictions, Retelling, Prewriting Activity   H-6

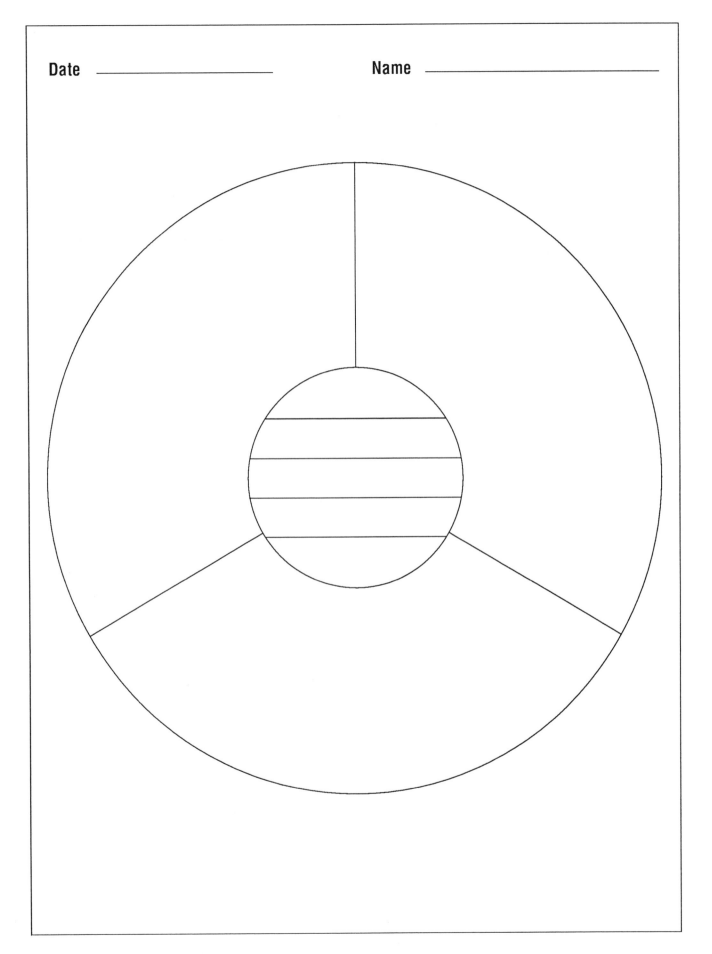

3-Part Story Wheel

Narratives — Circular Journey — 3-part Retell
Use before, during and/or after reading

★ Illustrate beginning, middle, end, showing events/setting/characters. Use them to retell story orally.

★ Draw main characters at end of story — include speech balloon and/or thinking bubbles to indicate what they would say and think.

★ Write action, describing interesting and/or exciting words from (1) beginning, (2) middle, (3) end. Use these to orally retell story.

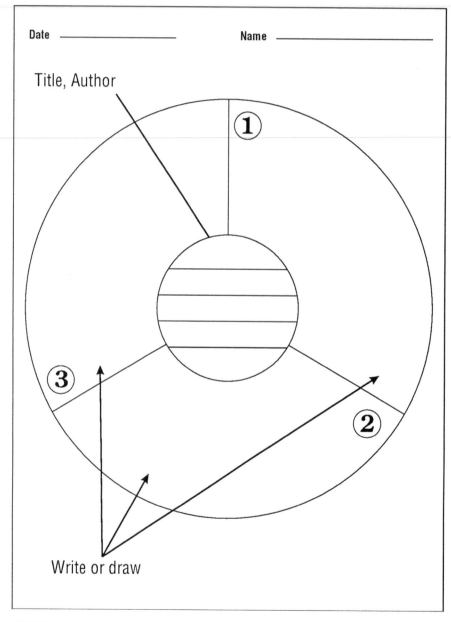

Date ——————— Name ———————

Title, Author

① ② ③

Write or draw

Name _____

Date _____

Title _____

Author _____

Characters

Descriptive Words

_____
_____
_____
_____
_____
_____
_____

Descriptive Words

Settings

_____
_____
_____
_____
_____
_____
_____

Beginning	Middle	End

Story Grammar

Use during and after reading to focus discussion

draw favourite part
draw main character
draw most important event, etc.

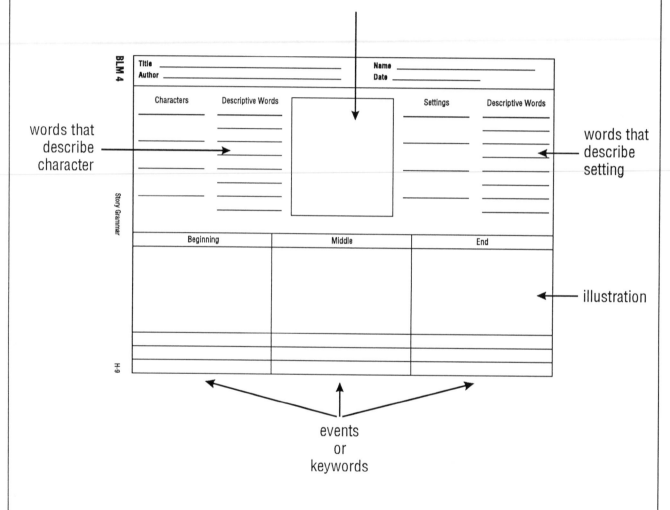

words that
describe
character

words that
describe
setting

illustration

events
or
keywords

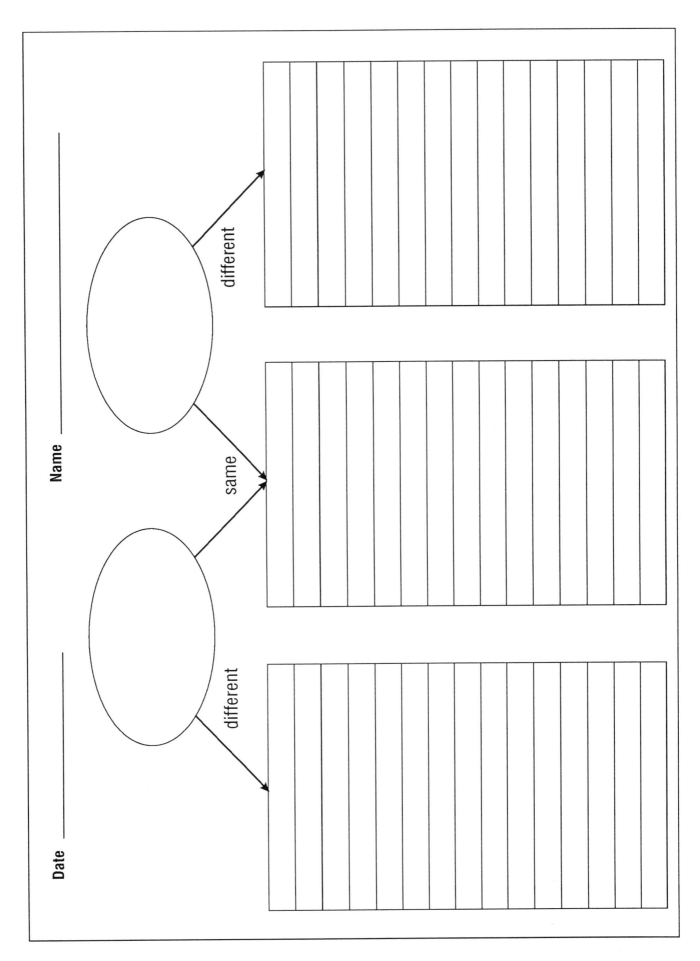

Name

Date

different

same

different

Reading Log

Name _____

Date _____

Title _____

Author _____

Best Part _____
_____
_____
_____

Nifty Language _____
_____
_____

Date _____

Title _____

Author _____

Best Part _____
_____
_____

Nifty Language _____
_____
_____

Date _____

Title _____

Author _____

Best Part _____
_____
_____

Nifty Language _____
_____
_____

Date _____

Title _____

Author _____

Best Part _____
_____
_____

Nifty Language _____
_____
_____

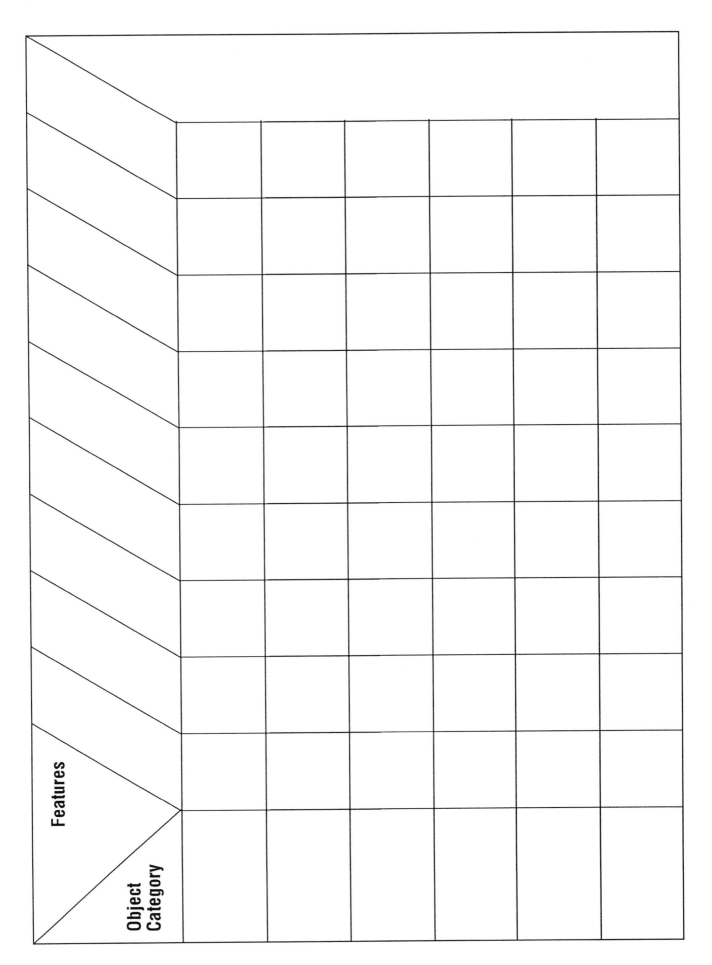

Features

Object Category

Semantic Feature Analysis

Use before, during and/or after reading to develop concepts and vocabulary

Symbols

to denote possession of the feature	to denote frequency of the feature	to denote relative intensity or quantity of the feature
✓ or ✗ + or − Y or N ☺ or ☹	A (almost) always S sometimes N (almost) never	rate **1** through **5**

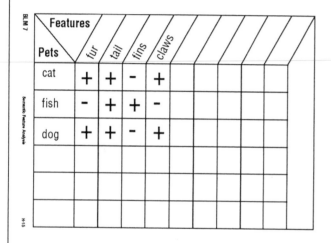

Features / Pets	fur	tail	fins	claws			
cat	+	+	−	+			
fish	−	+	+	−			
dog	+	+	−	+			

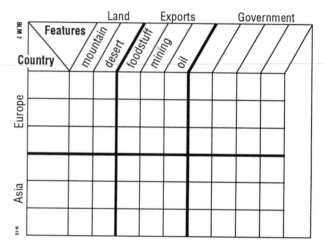

Features / Country		Land		Exports		Government
	mountain	desert	foodstuff	mining	oil	
Europe						
Asia						

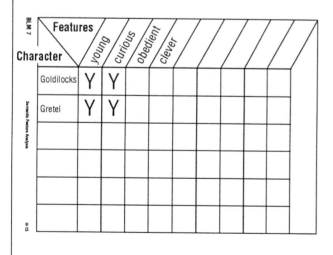

Features / Character	young	curious	obedient	clever			
Goldilocks	Y	Y					
Gretel	Y	Y					

Characters / Feelings	John	Papa	Susan				
annoyed	✓	✗	✗				
unhappy	✗	✓	✓				
worried	✓	✓	✗				

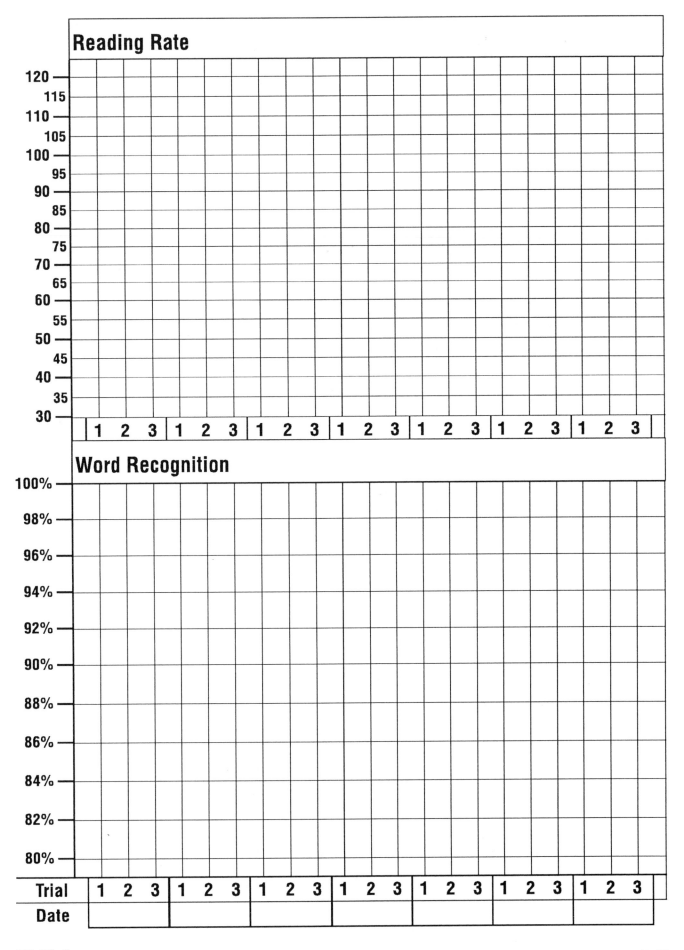

Reading Rate

120
115
110
105
100
95
90
85
80
75
70
65
60
55
50
45
40
35
30

| 1 | 2 | 3 | 1 | 2 | 3 | 1 | 2 | 3 | 1 | 2 | 3 | 1 | 2 | 3 | 1 | 2 | 3 | 1 | 2 | 3 |

Word Recognition

100%
98%
96%
94%
92%
90%
88%
86%
84%
82%
80%

| Trial | 1 | 2 | 3 | 1 | 2 | 3 | 1 | 2 | 3 | 1 | 2 | 3 | 1 | 2 | 3 | 1 | 2 | 3 | 1 | 2 | 3 |
| Date | | | | | | | | | | | | | | | | | | | | | |

Reading Fluency — Repeated Reading

- Before student reads model fluent and non-fluent reading, discuss difference in word-by-word reading and reading in phrases.

- Begin with passage student can read with 90% *or more* accuracy, since focus is on developing fluency.

- Student reads same passage 3 times.

- Graph reading rate and word recognition accuracy.

- Next day student repeat reads a different passage of similar difficulty.

- Progress can be noted in beginning rate and accuracy over time.

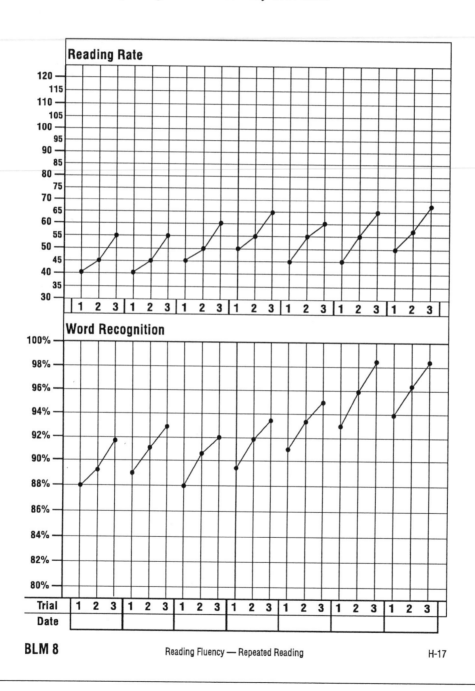

BLM 8   Reading Fluency — Repeated Reading   H-17

Appendix I
Assessment and Evaluation —
Using Classroom Literature

As suggested in the section on assessment and evaluation and in Appendix J, a great deal of information about children's reading knowledge, strategies and development can be determined through listening to their oral reading and analyzing the reading miscues and retellings. As well, observations of their reading behaviours and attitudes in the classroom setting supplements the data. The concept of authentic assessment suggests that a more accurate profile of students' reading ability is obtained when they are assessed under conditions as close to "real reading situations" as possible. That is, they have a purpose for reading and are interested in the text, and the act of reading as well as the result of reading is evaluated. Using an informal reading miscue analysis of the students' oral reading is one way of obtaining data. Although silent reading does not provide as much information about word recognition and reading strategies, we need to remember that it is the main goal of teaching reading. Understanding of texts read silently should also be evaluated.

Using classroom books for assessment enables the teacher to evaluate the students' reading using texts similar to those they will be reading every day. Using books rather than passages from published tests allows the assessment to resemble "real reading" (e.g. coloured illustrations and book formats are not found in published reading inventories and miscue analysis materials). This appendix suggests how to choose stories and passages for reading miscue analyses at different reading levels.

Having a series of passages with different reading levels provides the means for demonstrating students' progress. For example, the student may have been able to read the first passage fairly easily, and only the beginning of the second passage with 70% accuracy (too difficult to finish). A few months later the same student may be able to read the first passage very quickly, to finish the entire second passage with fewer miscues, and read the beginning of the third passage with 85% accuracy (see BLM A in this section for recording page and example).

Selecting Stories and Passages

★ For emergent readers, there should be some repetitive or cumulative short stories that they may be able to attempt to "memory read" after hearing it once or twice. (For students who find this too difficult, ask them to pick their favourite story from books in the class to read to you and observe what they know about book handling and the function of print.)

O'Brien (1987) suggests books similar to the following:

Level I

One Bright Monday Morning. Baum, A. & J., Pinwheel Books.

Goodnight Moon. Brown, M. W., Harper and Row.

The Very Hungry Caterpillar. Carle, E., Scholastic

The Bus Ride. Wagner, J. (illus.), Scott Foresman.

Rosie's Walk. Hutchins, P., Collier Books.

Where Have You Been? Brown, M.W., Scholastic

Level II — more varied and lengthier text

Chicken Soup with Rice. Sendak, M., Harper Row

Ask Mr. Bear. Flack, M., MacMillan Co.

Over in the Meadow. Keats, E. J. (illus), Scholastic

Play with Me. Ets, M.H., Puffin Books.

The Carrot Seed. Krauss, R., Scholastic.

Level III — much lengthier text, illustrations don't explicitly match text, less patterned but contain repeated sections

The Gingerbread Boy. Galdone, P., Clarion Books

The Three Billy Goats Gruff.
Brown, M. (illus), Harcourt, Brace, Jovanovich.

The Three Little Pigs. Galdone, P., Clarion Books.

The Little Red Hen. Galdone, P., Clarion Books.

Millions of Cats. Gug, W., Coward, McCann & Geoghegan.

★ For assessing students who are able to memory read, stories should be short with one line per page. There should be some variation in sentence structure and vocabulary (that is, not so repetitious that the child uses the first two sentences to predict the others and does not need to follow the print closely). Vocabulary should be drawn from sight words such as the Preprimer Dolch

list or the most commonly used 115 words (see Appendix A). As well the unknown words should be no more than 10% of the text and be mostly phonetically regular.

Small books with one line per page such as:

"My Home" in the *Sunshine* Series (Ginn)

"My Home" in the *Storybox* Series

"Play With Me" in the *Read with Me* Series (Penguin)

If individual books are not available, many of the anthologies now produced for different reading levels contain some stories that will be suitable. For example, *Fly Away Home*, the first level of the Impressions Series (published by Holt, Reinhart & Winston), contains the story "Go Away Dog" which can be use for the beginning readers.

Level 1 "Go Away, Dog"
(*Fly Away Home* Anthology, Impressions Series)

• about 40 words on a page with illustration, 3 to 6 words per line, frequent repetition of words, familiar vocabulary and topic

> Go away, dog.
> Go away, you bad old dog.
> I don't like dogs.
> I don't like dogs at all.
> Big dogs, little dogs.
> Any dogs at all.
> I don't want that stick.
> Don't give it to me.

★ For students able to read the beginning short stories, passages from stories with more words per page and a higher level of vocabulary are needed. To ensure the vocabulary is not too difficult, choose common topics and story structures. In this way, prior knowledge and vocabulary will support the students' reading. Again anthologies of children's literature at the next level provide a source for finding suitable passages because the editors have already chosen stories that they feel are within a certain readability and interest. Not all stories in an anthology are of equal readability and, therefore as you choose, you need to consider such things as familiarity of topic and sentence structures, vocabulary, size of print, accompanying illustrations, interest to students, density of information, events, and concepts.

Some examples of text passages chosen for different reading levels from the Impressions Reading Series follow. Part of each passage is provided so that you can get the gist of what the vocabulary, sentence structure, and so on would be at the different levels. You can then choose passages from books and anthologies that are available to you. Passages should be about 300-500 words, increasing in length as reading level increases. During assessment if students find the passage too difficult, stop before they are too frustrated. Note how many words they were able to attempt. This adds data for later comparison (e.g. perhaps a month later they are able to read the passage with little difficulty, see example on BLM A).

Level 2a "The Butterfly Friend"
(*East of the Sun* Anthology, Impressions Series)

- about 80 words on a page with accompanying illustration, 4 to 9 words per line, higher level of sight words and vocabulary, familiar topic, note that the repetitive phrase "on this flower and on that flower" is difficult for some children who find it an unusual pattern and do not easily recognize those words

> There were once three butterflies —
> an orange one, a red one, and a blue one —
> who played in the sunshine,
> and who danced on this flower
> and on that flower.
> They were so happy
> that they never grew tired.
> One day it started to rain
> and they got wet,
> so they tried to fly home.
> The door was shut,
> and they could not get in, ,
> so they had to stay out in the rain,
> and they got wetter and wetter.

Level 2b "Split Pea Soup"
(*West of the Moon* Anthology, Impressions Series)

- mostly 5 to 11 words per line with illustrations on almost every page, 45 to 125 words per page depending on size of illustration, some unfamiliar vocabulary, dialogue, smaller print

> Martha was very fond of making split pea soup.
> Sometimes she made it all day long.
> Pots and pots of split pea soup.

> If there was one thing that George was not fond of,
> it was split pea soup. As a matter of fact,
> George hated split pea soup more than anything else,
> in the world. But it was so hard to tell Martha.
> One day after George had eaten ten bowls
> of Martha's soup, he said to himself, "I just can't stand
> another bowl. Not even another spoonful."
> So, while Martha was out in the kitchen,
> George carefully poured the rest of his soup
> into his loafers under the table.

Level 3a "Yummers"
(*Over the Mountain* Anthology, Impressions Series)

- mostly 5 to 12 words per line, illustration not on every page, pages have up to 225 words, more multisyllabic words, less commonly occurring words, all students don't understand the humour

> Emily Pig was upset.
> She was gaining weight and she didn't know why.
> "Maybe I should get more exercise," she said to herself.
> The next day Emily jumped rope.
> "I don't really like this," she said, huffing and puffing.
> "I have a better idea," said her friend Eugene.
> "Why don't you come for a nice long stroll with me?
> Walking is the best exercise of all."
> Emily was delighted. "Walking is more fun," she said.
> "It doesn't seem like exercise."
> "And there are so many lovely things to see," said Eugene.
> But walking made Emily hungry.
> "Do you think we have time for a little snack?" she asked.

Level 3b "The Young Rooster"
(*Under the Sea* Anthology, Impressions Series)

- mostly 8 to 12 words per line, illustration on separate page, 280 words per page, less familiar vocabulary, more inferences need to be made to make sense of the story

> A young Rooster was summoned to his Father's bedside.
> "Son, my time has come to an end," said the aged bird. "Now
> it is your turn to crow up the morning sun each day." The young
> rooster watched sadly as his Father's life slipped away.
> Early the next morning, the young Rooster flew up to the roof
> of the barn. He stood there, facing the east. "I have never done

this before," said the Rooster. "I must try my best."

He lifted his head and crowed. A weak and scratchy croak

was the only sound he was able to make.

Level 4a "The Witch Who Wasn't"
(*Cross the Golden River* Anthology, Impressions Series)

- mostly 8 to 14 words per line, illustrations not on every page, up to 330 words per page, more complex and less familiar sentence structures and vocabulary

Isabel was a witch!

At least she should have been a witch.

Her mother was a witch. Her mother's mother was a witch. In

fact, all her relatives back as far as she could remember had been

witches, which, if you are a witch is very far indeed.

She had a black cat. And bats in her belfry. A long, twiggy

broom. And a very tall broad-brimmed, pointed-top, brass-buckled,

very black hat.

Yes, Isabel was a witch!

At least she should have been a witch. Her mother ... oh, yes,

you already know that. But Isabel wasn't. She was a witch who wasn't!

Other books to choose from are listed in Appendix G: Books for Beginning Readers and Easy Novels. To evaluate student's reading using passages like these, see section on Assessment and Evaluation (pp. 96-110) and Appendix J for more information about Reading Miscue Analysis.

Once children are reading passages with familiar topics and vocabulary fluently, that is reading smoothly and accurately (e.g. 100 words per minute with 95%+ accuracy), more difficult passages will contain not necessarily more words, but will have topics that are less familiar and more unfamiliar vocabulary. Using these passages, continued progress will also be demonstrated by expression, phrasing, fluency, increasing reading rate appropriate to interesting oral reading.

Following are record sheets that can be used to keep track of students' progress. BLM A is a sheet to record students' word recognition and reading rate of different passages/stories when doing an informal reading assessment. A profile of their progress develops as the data is collected over a period of time (see example given on the back of BLM A). At the bottom, comments can be made about strategies and goals for the next instructional period (refer to BLM B for list of decoding and reading strategies). BLM B is also a checklist for planning a balanced program. As different components are focused on and taught, you can circle or check them off, providing an at-a-glance overview.

On BLM C and D are listed 560 of the most commonly used words. Students can colour in or highlight the words they are able to easily recognize. On BLM E they can graph the number they know, adding to the record sheet and graph during the year. In this way there is a visual representation of their progress with sight word recognition.

Reading Profile

Student _____ School _____ School Year _____ Teacher _____

Informal Reading Assessment

Passage Title																					
Date	Sight Words	Reading Rate (wpm)	% Word Recog.	# words	Reading Rate (wpm)	% Word Recog.	# words	Reading Rate (wpm)	% Word Recog.	# words	Reading Rate (wpm)	% Word Recog.	# words	Reading Rate (wpm)	% Word Recog.	# words	Reading Rate (wpm)	% Word Recog.	# words		

Evaluation/Summary of Strategies Student Uses

Date _____	Date _____	Date _____	Date _____

Goals			

Reading Profile

Student __Mary__   School __Johnston Elementary__

School Year	Teacher
1990-91	Miss Smith
1991-92	Ms. Thomas
1992-93	Mr. Johns

Informal Reading Assessment

Date	Sight Words	Go Away Dog			Butterfly Friends			Split Pea Soup			Yummers			The Young Rooster		
		Reading Rate (wpm)	% Word Recog.	# words	Reading Rate (wpm)	% Word Recog.	# words	Reading Rate (wpm)	% Word Recog.	# words	Reading Rate (wpm)	% Word Recog.	# words	Reading Rate (wpm)	% Word Recog.	# words
Sept. '90	22/220	—	62	29												
May '91	126	42	96	113	28	81	80									
Sept. '91	145	75	100	113	50	87	150	23	59	41						
May '92	207							56	96	224	42	92	225			
Oct. '92	218							72	96	224	58	94	225	35	92	180
June '93	220							80	98	224	70	94	225	70	92	180

Evaluation/Summary of Strategies Student Uses

Date	May '91	Date	Sept. '92	Date	Oct. '92
	sight words, picture clues, stops reading when doesn't know word, many repetitions		sight words, initial consonants, some use of context clues		sight words, phonics, context clues
Goals	phonics skills, fluency in decoding, phrasing in reading		vowel sounds, blending, sounds easily, better use of context, reading in phrases		syllabication/decoding, fluency, expression, phrasing

Record Sheet for Teaching Lessons

(For Teacher Use)

Circle patterns and strategies taught

Sound/Letter Sequence

consonants
b c d f g h j k l m n p r s t v w z

digraphs ch sh th wh

qu y x

blends
st sp sn sm sl sc sk sw bl cl fl gl pl br cr
dr fr gr pr tr spl str spr scr squ

-ll -ss -ff

-ck -ke
-nk -ng

hard and soft c
hard and soft g

kn- wr- -ight

ph gh

-le
-tch
-dge
-tion
-ture
-age

short vowels
a e i o u

long vowels

silent e

ai ay ee ea oa
y as a vowel

ar or er

oi oy
ou ow oo

ir ur
ear are

au aw ew
ie ei

Morphology

-ing, -s

-ed

contractions

compounds

-er
-est

irregular plurals

possessives
capitals

syllables

affixes
root words

hyphens

abbreviations
combining forms
more irregular plurals

Reading Strategies (from Reading Process Model)

Word Identification

pictures, illustrations
print conventions
semantic context clues
syntax context clues

sight words
phonics
syllabication
structural analysis

Thinking Skills

understanding
predict/confirm
prior experiences
prior language

focusing
gathering information
remembering
organizing

analyzing
generating
integrating
evaluating

Fluency and Flexibility ———————— Reading Rate

Ease of
Word Recognition
Stategies

Reading Rate

Use of Strategies

Aspects of Written Text
(see Figure 16, p. 43)

Self-Correcting   Metacognitive Awareness of Strategies

Words I Can Read

a	and	been	build	clean	does	example	friend	hand	how
able	angry	before	built	clear	doesn't	face	from	happen	however
about	animal	began	busy	close	dog	fact	front	happy	hundred
above	another	begin	but	cold	don't	fall	fruit	hard	hungry
across	answer	behind	buy	colour	done	family	full	has	hurt
act	any	being	by	come	door	far	funny	have	I
add	anything	below	call	common	down	fast	game	he	I'll
afraid	are	beside	came	complete	draw	feet	gave	head	I'm
after	arm	best	can	could	drink	fell	get	hear	I've
again	around	better	Canada	couldn't	dry	felt	girl	heard	ice
against	art	between	Canadian	country	during	few	give	heart	idea
age	as	big	can't	course	each	field	glass	heavy	if
ago	ask	bird	cannot	cover	early	final	go	held	important
ahead	at	black	car	cut	earth	find	goes	help	in
air	ate	blue	care	dance	easy	fine	going	her	inch
alive	away	board	careful	danger	eat	fire	gold	here	inside
all	baby	boat	carry	dark	eight	first	gone	high	instead
almost	back	body	catch	day	either	fish	good	him	into
alone	bag	book	caught	dead	else	five	got	himself	is
along	ball	both	centre	dear	end	floor	great	his	isn't
already	bank	bottom	certain	deep	English	fly	green	hold	it
also	baseball	bought	change	did	enough	follow	ground	hole	it's
although	be	box	check	didn't	even	food	group	home	its
always	bear	boy	children	different	ever	foot	grow	hope	itself
am	beautiful	bread	choose	difficult	every	for	guess	horse	job
among	became	bring	circle	dinner	everyone	form	had	hot	jump
amount	because	brought	city	distance	everything	found	hair	hour	just
an	become	brown	class	do	eye	four	half	house	keep

BLM C, D and E

Students can highlight or shade in the words as they show they can read them.
This provides visual feedback on progress. Once or twice a month they can then
graph the number of words known on BLM E.

Words I Can Read

kept	loud	name	outside	quiet	she	story	third	up	where
kind	low	near	over	ran	short	strong	this	upon	whether
knew	made	need	own	read	should	such	those	us	which
know	make	never	page	ready	show	suddenly	though	use	while
land	man	new	paper	really	side	summer	thought	useful	white
large	many	next	part	red	sign	sun	thousand	usually	who
last	matter	night	party	remember	simple	sure	three	very	whole
later	may	no	pass	rest	since	surprise	through	visit	why
laugh	me	noise	past	right	six	table	time	voice	wide
lay	mean	not	people	river	size	take	tiny	wait	wild
lead	men	nothing	perhaps	room	sky	talk	to	walk	will
learn	might	now	person	round	sleep	tall	today	want	wind
least	milk	number	pick	run	small	teeth	together	warm	winter
leave	mixed	of	piece	sad	snow	tell	told	was	wish
left	money	off	place	said	so	ten	too	wasn't	with
less	month	often	plant	same	some	than	took	watch	within
let	moon	oh	play	sat	someone	thank	top	water	without
letter	more	old	please	saw	something	that	toward	way	woman
life	morning	on	point	say	soon	that's	town	we	won
light	most	once	poor	school	sound	the	tree	we'll	won't
like	mother	one	possible	sea	space	their	trip	we're	word
line	mountain	only	power	see	special	them	true	wear	work
list	move	open	problem	seen	stand	then	try	weather	world
little	Mr.	or	probably	sent	start	there	turn	well	would
live	Mrs.	order	pull	sentence	stay	these	two	went	wouldn't
living	Ms.	other	put	seven	still	they	under	were	write
long	much	our	question	several	stood	thing	understand	what	wrong
look	must	out	quick	shall	stop	think	until	when	wrote

BLM C, D and E

Students can highlight or shade in the words as they show they can read them. This provides visual feedback on progress. Once or twice a month they can then graph the number of words known on BLM E.

Words I Can Read

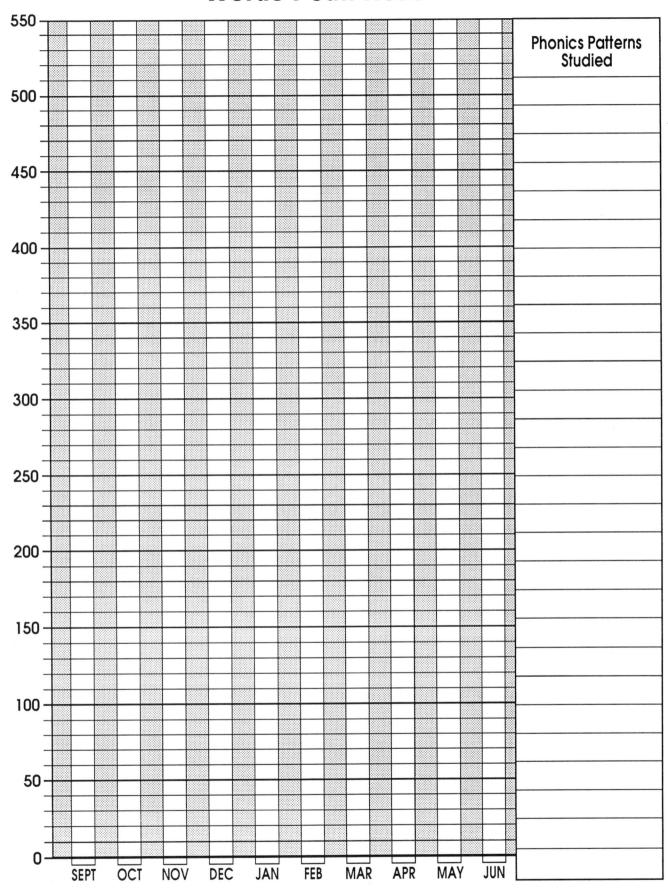

BLM C, D and E

Students can highlight or shade in the words as they show they can read them.
This provides visual feedback on progress. Once or twice a month they can then
graph the number of words known on BLM E.

Appendix J
Informal Reading Miscue Analysis

A Reading Miscue Analysis (RMA) (Goodman, Watson & Burke, 1987) is a more formal way of assessing students' reading strategies and ability. But every time students read out loud, there is an opportunity to assess their reading informally. An informal assessment is similar to a formal RMA and, although not as indepth, it does provide ongoing information for planning instruction.

For formal miscue analysis the passage should be long enough to generate at least 25 miscues in about 500 words (Goodman, Watson & Burke, 1987). However, for informal assessments and for beginning readers shorter passages may be necessary and, depending on the students' frustration level, fewer miscues may have to be accepted. Before the students read, tell them to read the story just as they normally do and that when they don't recognize a word to use whatever strategy they usually use. Let them know they will be asked to retell the story including the important characters and events (or information if it is an expository text). Let the student know that you are expecting him or her to remember as much as they can. Let the student retell as much as possible without prompting. If necessary, prompts can be given (see Part III: F4, Retelling).

To assess word recognition accuracy, calculate % correct:

$$\left(\frac{\text{\# words read less \# miscues disrupting meaning}}{\text{total \# words read}}\right) \times 100$$

To assess word recognition strategies, record miscues (see Table 1 and BLM F). The strategies are evaluated by analyzing the types of miscue, for example:

- do most miscues involve sight words, phonics, or syllabication skills?

- do the miscues have graphic and/or phonic similarities or no similarity to the text words?

- do the miscues change the meaning of the text?

- does the student self-correct most miscues?

To assess fluency, note repetitions, pauses, and rate of reading:

$$\frac{\text{\# words read} \times 60}{\text{\# seconds taken to read the passage}}$$

To assess comprehension and thinking, have student retell story/information and make notes as suggested in the assessment chart (Table 1). From the retelling the teacher can determine such things as the students' recall of characters, setting, plot, theme, character development, the gist of the passage, details, or, for an expository text, the major concepts, generalizations, specific information and logical structuring.

Rhodes and Shanklin (1990) outline a Classroom Reading Miscue Assessment instrument. They state that they traded "off the depth, detail, and extensive quantification of data available from elaborate, formalized miscue analysis procedures for a more manageable, yet still informative, version of the miscue analysis" (p. 252). An indepth miscue analysis is not always necessary and not for every student. However, it is necessary to have informal assessment procedures that provide information on an ongoing basis that do not require extensive time commitments from the classroom teacher.

They suggest that after the student has read a passage, comprehension can be assessed by determining whether each sentence maintained the meaning intended (include self-corrections made by the student). These are counted as semantically acceptable sentences. Comprehension is reflected by the percentage of semantically acceptable sentences

(# acceptable/ total sentences x 100), with 80% indicating adequate and above comprehension. Less competent readers may have 60% or less.

Analyzing the types of miscues reflects word identification strategies. As well they suggest noting

- the ways meaning is being constructed:
  - logical substitutions, self-correction of errors that disrupted meaning, use of picture and text clues, recognizing miscues that disrupt meaning, and
- the ways in which meaning is disrupted:
  - nonsense substitutions, omissions that change meaning, relying too heavily on graphic clues (Rhodes & Shanklin, 1990).

When children are reading in class activities, miscues provide information about their knowledge of word identification and comprehension strategies. Not all miscues need to be responded to in the same way. As long as miscues are not occurring frequently (more than 5 to 10%) they may be responded to as follows:

- No response, student keeps reading when there are:
  - occasional meaningful substitutions, additions, omissions, and the meaning of the passage is not significantly altered
  - self-corrected miscues
  - words read in different order, no change in meaning.
- Short response such as telling the student the word when there are:
  - substitutions that are graphically similar but alter meaning

  - difficulties with decoding words that occur infrequently.
- Longer response such as having the student reread or modelling decoding strategies when:
  - miscues are made and are not self-corrected
  - words are sounded out slowly without the correct pronunciation and meaning is lost
  - words are substituted with nonsense words or other words
  - reading stops because the word has no meaning or student can't decode it, or the text structure is confusing.

Frequent miscuing may indicate that the passage is too difficult or that the student lacks prior knowledge, decoding skills, and/or self-confidence. For these students, a more indepth assessment would be appropriate. Examples of this miscuing are:

- ignoring punctuation, little phrasing, no expression and continuing to read even though reading does not make sense
- sounding out each word, even though it has occurred several times before (slow word-by-word reading)
- stopping and looking at teacher to provide word if it seems difficult or unfamiliar (reading with a questioning manner)
- reading at same rate, no self-correcting, while substituting graphically similar words or nonsense words.

Table 1. Informal Reading Miscue Analysis — Scoring Guide

Scoring Guide	
Type of Miscue	**How to Record Miscue**
1. Substitution • real word is used in place of word in text	Write the substituted word over the text word *licks* .... *me* John likes to play with my dog
2. Mispronunciation / Nonword substitution • distorted pronunciation that doesn't make sense	Write the phonic mispronunciation over the text word *plan* .... *erpart* The plane landed at the airport.
3. Omission • letter, part of word, word, phrase, line, puncuation left out	Circle the omission When I call(ed) to tell (him) about the party, he was busy(o)
4. Insertion • letter, word part, words, puncuation added	Write in the addition, the position marked with a caret *big* The ^old cat sat ^under the tree.
5. Reversals • change order of letters, word, phrases	Draw a line to indicate changes The little girl (was) very upset when the boy (yelled loudly)
6. Hesitation • word that stops fluent reading but is read within 5 seconds	Write in H above word, or put a slash in front of it *H* .... *H* They danced and danced all night long
7. Repetition • word part, word, phrases repeated	Draw wavy line under repetition The doctor began the operation on the animal that had been shot.
8. Self-corrections • correct previous miscue	Write C beside miscue symbol *C fourteen* Did you really eat fifteen cookies?
• abandon previously correct word/phrase	Record miscue and write AC beside it *AC fifteen* Jimmy had collected fourteen different baseball cards.
9. Repeated miscue • same miscue is repeated for same word in text	Record miscue and write R beside it *cream* .... *cream R* . . . nose in the churn. "Get . . . bumped into the churn."
10. Word-by-word reading	Mark with slashes between words, phrases the bunny/settled/into its/new,/ warm hutch/

Table 1 (continued)

Scoring Guide	
Type of Miscue	**How to Indicate**
11. Asks for help	Indicate with ? **?** The most important activity is
12. **Teacher assistance given to get reader back on track** • e.g. reader loses place, reader having difficulty with certain part of text	Write T-A **T-A** They danced on this flower and on that flower.

Retelling Guide

Unaided

- gives general ideas, has gist of story
- tells events in sequence/not in sequence
- gives details
- uses words/phrases from text
- rephrases, uses own words
- relates to personal knowledge
- makes inferences

Aided

- General prompts used
  - Tell me more about ....
  - After....., what happened?
  - Why do you think .....?
  - _____
  - _____

Specific questions asked about

- Setting
- Characters
- Events/Main ideas
- Beginning /Problem
- Solution/Conclusion
- Details/Specific information
  - _____
  - _____

Miscue Analysis

Student _____ School _____ Assessed by _____

Date	Passage	# words read	% word recognition	Reading rate	% sentences semantically acceptable	Miscue	Text	sound similarity	graphic similarity	self-corrected	substitution	omission	hesitation	meaning maintained	loss of meaning

Glossary

A

accent (also referred to as stress) — the degree of relative loudness with which a syllable is spoken. In words of two or more syllables, one syllable is accented or stressed more than the other or others. A shift in accent can affect meaning (e.g. con'tract, con tract', pres'ent, pre sent', ob'ject, ob ject'). Syllables may be spoken with at least three degrees of accent:

>   **primary accent** — the loudest accent or stress, e.g. the first syllable in sec're tar' y

>   **secondary accent** — the next loudest accent or stress, e.g. the second syllable in en cy'clo pe'di a.

>   **no accent** — the syllable said with the least loud accent or stress, e.g. the first syllable in the words ap prove', re main' and the last two syllables in the word con'fi dent are unaccented.

acuity — clarity or keenness of reception of sensory stimuli; the extent to which the senses can detect the duration, intensity, position, and other properties of stimulus (compare this to discrimination)

advance organizer — a passage written to enhance the learning of other material, presented prior to the material.

affix — a prefix or suffix

alliteration — the repetition of the initial sounds in words or stressed syllables, spoken or written closely together

alphabetic writing — a writing system in which one or several letters represent one speech sound (phoneme)

alphabet method — learning to read by naming letters of a word and then pronouncing the word, used from ancient time until early 1800s

analytic approach — method of learning letter/sound relationships by learning whole words and then learning sounds from known words

anaphora — use of a grammatical substitute referring to preceding word or phrase (see referent), e.g. it, they, those

antecedent — word which is replaced by a grammatical substitute (e.g. by a pronoun or by a more inclusive generalized phrase, such as the latter, these reasons)

articulation — movement of the speech organs modifying the air flow to produce of speech sounds

assessment — gathering data through observation, testing, conferencing, etc. with the purpose of understanding something better

assonance — repetition of similar vowel sounds followed by different consonants (e.g. "mad as a hatter")

audience, sense of — awareness of reader, viewer, listener; point of view or responses when writing, performing or speaking

auditory blending — combining discrete phonemes into recognized words (decoding words by sounding them out)

aural — relating to the ear or sense of hearing, having to do with listening

automaticity — without attention or conscious effort

B

background knowledge — total of previous learning and experience

barking at print — usually word-by-word oral reading in which the reader pronounces the words but extracts and conveys little or no meaning; word calling

big book — enlarged book with print and illustrations large enough for a group of children to see and read together

book talk — talk about a book by teacher or student to encourage others to read it

bottom-up processing — reading involves accurate sequential processing, beginning with letters, then words, phrases, sentences, paragraphs

brainstorm — search for many words, ideas and/or solutions without stopping to evaluate

C

capacity — potential to learn; upper limit of actual ability

capacity reading level — inferred upper limit of reading ability determined by student listening to passage read aloud and demonstrating comprehension

choral reading — group reading aloud

chunking — organizing bits of information into a larger group of connected bits, making sense of the bits so that information is easier to remember or process

closed syllable — a syllable ending with one or more consonants

closure — tending to perceive things as wholes, even if part is missing

cloze procedure — omitting portions of an oral or written message, coined to reflect the gestalt principle of closure. Three uses of cloze: 1. to determine readability of a passage, 2. to determine student's reading level, 3. to teach reading skills

cognition — knowing intellectually

cognitive map — pattern/diagram created to show and explain relationships

combining form — a root with which other roots and/or affixes may be combined to form compounds or derivatives, may be at beginning, middle or end of word (e.g. graph — photograph, graphics, telegraph)

competence — ability to perform a given task adequately

compound — a word composed of two or more words that combine their meanings to make a new word. A compound may be written as one word, written as two or more words, or hyphenated (steamboat, dime store, merry-go-round). English compounds are distinguished from phrases mainly by reduced stress on one of the words e.g.

> I saw a bluebird yesterday (bluebird is a compound meaning "a specific kind of bird"). The stress pattern is that of a primary accent on blue and a secondary accent on bird.

> I saw a strange blue bird at the zoo (blue bird is a phrase meaning "any kind of bird that is blue"). The word bird is stressed more strongly than it is in the compound.

comprehension — knowledge or understanding from processing a form of communication or experience

concept — generalized idea derived from distinguishing quality or characteristics of all objects or events in a class and applicable to all members of the class (e.g. concept of tree, concept of dyslexia — which still remains unclear)

concept load or density — the number of different or abstract ideas in relation to the length of the text

confirmation — verification of a prediction by information gained later from a writer's or speaker's language use

consonance — repetition of the final consonant sound in words which do not use the same vowel (e.g. pit, pet, pot)

consonant — speech sound that is produced by interrupting or modifying the outgoing air or breath by some organ of articulation such as the lips, teeth, tongue, or hard and soft palates. Although many letters usually stand for only one sound, (e.g. b and p), some letters may represent more than one sound, (e.g. g as in girl and giant, and s as in sit, his, sure). Still other letters may represent the same sound (e.g. g and j as in gem and jam, and c and s as in city and sent).

consonant blend (also, consonant cluster) — two or more consonant sounds that occur together without intervening vowels, for example, the two initial sounds in please (pl) and in bridge (br) and the three initial sounds in screech (scr), the three medial sounds in astride (str), and the three final sounds in glimpse (mps); common blenders are l, r and s (e.g. bl, cl, fl, gl, pl, cr, dr, pr, sc, sk, sp)

content area — an organized body of knowledge, or discipline, that is reflected in its technical vocabulary, such as mathematics, social studies, literature, science. Note: Reading, an instrument or tool, cuts across all content fields and is ordinarily not considered a content area

content reading — reading in subject or discipline areas such as biology, math, history, geography, chemistry

context clue — sounds, words, phrases, syntax, illustrations, setting, etc. that surrounds a spoken or written word or phrase and helps in identifying new or unfamiliar words and/or their meaning

core vocabulary — words and meanings needed to understand a special field, textbook, topic, etc.

curriculum-based assessment — process of gathering information about students' achievement and progress using materials and tasks derived from the actual curriculum and activities used in the classroom

curriculum-focused instruction — teaching based on predetermined set of knowledge and skills that students are expected to learn by a certain age or grade level

---

D

DEAR — acronym for Drop Everything And Read, a time for silent reading in a classroom (see also SSR or USSR)

decode — identify word (usually pronunciation) from its written form

deep structure — meaning to which a spoken or written message refers which may not be apparent from the surface structure, (e.g. "John insisted Anne stay for dinner" and "John invited Anne to stay for dinner" have similar surface structure but different deep structure)

derivative — word that is composed of a root plus a prefix or suffix or both (e.g. unhappy, happiness, unhappiness)

diagnostic teaching — assessing student's ability and achievement from ongoing instruction

digraph

> **consonant digraph** — two consonants representing one speech sound: ch, th, sh, wh

> **vowel digraph** — two vowels representing one speech sound: ee, ea, oa, ai, ay

diphthong — succession of two vowel sounds that are joined in a single syllable under a single stress. A diphthong is made by a continuous glide of the tongue from one vowel position to the other (e.g. oi, oy, ou, ow)

discrimination — process of noting differences between stimuli (compare this to acuity)

domain — field of action, knowledge, or influence

E

echo reading — oral reading in which student imitates or repeats another's reading while reading together

encode — put message or meaning into symbols (writing, words, mathematical symbols, pictures)

ending — see inflectional ending

evaluation — synthesis of measurements, appraisals and assessments of performance and ability

explicit — clear, specific, unambiguous, overt

expository text — written communication with purpose of explaining and providing information

expressive vocabulary — words a person uses in speaking (compare to receptive vocabulary)

F

feedback — information used or given to change or evaluate a process

Fernald approach or method (VAKT) — technique for learning words that involves looking at a word (Visual) while saying it (Auditory) and tracing it (Kinesthetic, Tactile)

fluency — reading or writing easily, smoothly and readily

frustration reading level — readability or grade level of material that is read with less than 90% word recognition and less than 50% comprehension

G

gist — essential or central meaning aside from details

global approach or method — term for the look-and-say approach, method that emphasizes the recognition of whole words rather than analysis of word parts

Gillingham approach or method — synthetic phonics system reinforced by intensive writing and spelling practice

grammar — description of a language and its morphology, syntax and semantics

grapheme — the written or printed representation of a speech sound (e.g. cow has two graphemes, c and ow, to represent its phonemes, /c/ and /ow/)

graphophonics (also, phonics) — relationship between speech sounds (phonology) and letters or written symbols (orthography) of a language

graphic organizer — a diagram to visually present an overview of material that will be presented later

guided reading — reading instruction in which the teacher provides the structure, including the purpose, for reading and for responding to the material read

H

heteronym — homograph; in popular use word with same spelling but different pronunciation (e.g. I will *read* it tomorrow, and She *read* before I could.)

holistic — whole is greater and different from sum of its parts; recognition of word as a unit, separate from letters and syllables

holistic approach — approach to teaching and learning that emphasizes the whole and integration of parts within the whole

homograph — word with same spelling with different meaning and origin, may or may not be pronounced the same [bow (and arrow) – bow (of a ship), hand (give) – hand (applause)]

homonym — technically, word with same oral or written form [e.g. bear (animal) and bear (carry) and bare (exposed)], includes homophones and homographs; in popular use a word with same pronunciation and spelling but different meaning

homophones — technically, words with same pronunciation whether or not with same spelling e.g. where – wear, spell (a word) – spell (magic); in popular use, two or more graphemes that have same sound, e.g. c in cut, k in kite, ch in choir

I

idioms — expressions that do not have a literal meaning, peculiar to a specific language

image — mental representation of a thing, event, experience; to mentally represent a feeling, thought, event, object, smell, taste, etc.

implicit — implied rather than directly stated

incidental method — instructional approach based on student needs, abilities and experiences identified by a teacher rather than based on long-term pre-planned goals or commercially prepared programs

independent reading level — readability or grade level of material that student can read with better than 98% word recognition (some say 95%) and better than 90% comprehension

individualized reading — approach to reading instruction emphasizing student self-selection of reading material (e.g. trade books), self-pacing in reading; teacher's role is to adjust lessons to student needs in small groups or individual conferences

inflected form — word to which an inflectional ending has been added; an inflectional ending (-s, for example) may be added to a root word (lights), to a derived form (lighters), or to a compound (headlights)

inflectional endings — meaningful word part added to the end of words, -s, -es, 's, ed, ing, er, est

informal instruction — see incidental method

Informal Reading Inventory (IRI) — use of graded series of passages, increasing in difficulty, to make an informal diagnosis of reading performance, resulting in an estimation of student's independent, instructional, frustration reading levels and listening comprehension (reading capacity)

instructional reading level — readability or grade level of material that student can read with 90% to 95% word recognition and better than 75% comprehension; the percentages vary depending on the inventory (IRI) used

interactive processing — theory of reading that proposes the importance of the reader's experiences and expectations interacting constantly with the text (print) information, resulting in word identification and comprehension; processing at many levels occurs simultaneously not sequentially

interest/difficulty levels — the relationship between the appeal of a book and ease of reading; if a student is interested in a particular topic, reading may be easier because of background knowledge or because of more effort made by the student to read

---

K

key vocabulary — words that have immediacy for a child and presumably therefore are easier for the child to learn (Sylvia Ashton-Warner's approach)

kinesthetic approach — any method in which learning takes place through the sense of movement; reading method in which the student traces a word to be learned while at the same time studying the word visually and saying the parts aloud (see also Fernald Method)

kinesthetic feedback — information from muscles, joints, and tendons which helps one repeat a movement or movements, as in articulating words or writing letters easily

---

L

language arts — curriculum areas particularly concerned with the development and improvement of the verbal communication processes (includes reading, writing, speaking, listening, and spelling); used in all content areas and therefore a holistic approach emphasizes integrating language arts instruction with subject areas

language experience approach — approach to learning to read in which the student's or group's own words or oral compositions are written down and used as materials for instruction

learner-focused — teaching planned with consideration for the needs and abilities of students in a class as well as curricular goals

learning activity — an activity that students do which helps them learn, review or refine their knowledge and skills (compare to teaching activity)

levels of processing

>   **sensory** — received by senses

>   **perceptual** — how the brain interprets sensation

>   **automatic** — without attention or thought

>   **cognitive** — attention, thinking

>   **metacognitive** — thinking about thinking, analyzing processes

linguistic approach — beginning reading approach based upon regular sound-symbol patterns

linguistics — study of the nature and structure of language and languages

listening comprehension level (reading expectancy level) — highest level of reading material which a student can understand when it is read out loud to the student

listening vocabulary — see receptive vocabulary

look-back — allowing student to look at text after reading to demonstrate understanding or answer comprehension questions

look-say approach (see analytic approach)

M

main idea — central meaning or topic expressed in a few words; stated or implied major topic stated in one sentence

mastery — demonstrable control over material or behaviours which meets or exceeds an established criterion level

memory — retaining and recalling past impressions and experiences. Types of memory:

  iconic — sensory images, which last briefly

  declarative or semantic — memory of information

  episodic — memory associated with events and personal experiences

  procedural — memory of actions and procedures

  LTM — long term memory

  STM — short term memory

memory reading — student memorizes a selection by hearing it several times before reading, then reads by accurately matching spoken to written words

metacognition — conscious awareness and control of one's own mental processes

metalinguistic awareness — ability to reflect on and talk about language being used

miscue — oral reading response that differs from an accurate reading of the text

miscue analysis — some researchers believe miscues reflect the strategies used by readers to decode and understand text; by analyzing the nature of the miscues, the strengths and weaknesses can be determined and used to provide information for planning instruction

mnemonic — pertaining to memory, especially strategies to aid memory

modality — any of the sensory systems of receiving, processing, and responding to sensation (e.g. visual, auditory, kinesthetic, tactile)

model — standard or example for imitation or comparison (e.g. model of fluent reading); design intended to show how something is formed, or how it functions, by analyzing the relationships of its various parts to each other and to the whole (e.g. a model of reading)

morpheme (meaning unit) — smallest meaningful unit in the structure of words such as root word, prefix, suffix, inflectional ending, combining form (e.g. *rain*, a root word, is a meaning unit or mor-pheme; *rainy* is composed of two morphemes, the root *rain* and the suffix *y*; raincoats, a compound word, is composed of three morphemes, the roots *rain* and *coat* and the inflectional ending *s*)

multi-sensory approach — an instructional approach which uses a combination of several senses, such as visual, auditory, kinesthetic, or tactile

---

N

narrative — writing in which a real or fictional story is told in prose or verse

Neurological Impress Method — method in which the teacher sits slightly behind the student and orally reads the text while one of them points to the part of the text being read; the student attempts to read along as quickly and accurately as possible; in beginning sessions, the teacher reads louder and slightly faster than the student; later, the teacher decreases in volume and speed so that the student will be in the lead; designed to improve fluency.

nonphonetic word — word whose pronunciation cannot be predicted from its spelling and letter/sound relationships

---

O

onset — the part of a syllable preceding the vowel (e.g. st in stop) (compare this to rime)

open syllable — syllable ending in a vowel sound (e.g. /hō/ in hotel) (compare this to closed syllable)

oral — uttered by the mouth or in words; having to do with speaking

oral reading — reading aloud; useful for communicating to another person or audience, and for assessing reading strategies (see silent reading)

orthography — nature and use of symbols in a writing system

Orton-Gillingham approach — see Gillingham approach

P

paradigm — pattern, example

perception — extraction of information from sensory stimulation; perception is an active and selective process and therefore may be influenced by a person's attitude, attention, and prior experience or knowledge

phoneme — smallest unit of sound by which one thing that is said can be differentiated from another in speech (e.g. bet has three phonemes /b/, /e/, /t/; the initial phoneme differentiates words such as bet, pet, met, wet; the medial phoneme differentiates bet bit, bought, but; another kind of phoneme is accent in words such as *permit* in which a shift in accent distinguishes the noun from the verb

phonetic — referring to the nature and production of speech sound and the symbols used to represent the sounds

phonetic analysis — using visual clues in printed words to determine pronunciation including consonant and vowel sounds, syllabication, and accents; hearing phonemes accurately, associating consonant and vowel sounds with letters, blending sounds into syllables and into words with appropriate accent

phonetic spelling — spelling of words according to pronunciation key to indicate phonemes represented by letters and symbols (e.g. feed by /fēd/, fed by /fĕd/); also spelling word incorrectly as though word was phonically regular

phonetic word (phonically regular) — word in which every letter represents the particular sound which is assigned to that letter, and in which every sound is represented by that particular letter and that letter only (e.g. let, hop, fun)

phonics — application of phonetics to teaching reading and spelling, emphasis is placed on sound/letter relationships

phonics method — approach to teaching reading which emphasizes the sound/symbol relationships in word identification

phonogram — letter or group of letters that represent a speech sound or word; a letter phonogram consists of a single consonant or vowel, several letters can be a phonogram [e.g. str, ight, oi, eed (as in feed), at (bat)], a word learned as a sight word can be a phonogram

phonology — study of speech sounds and function in language

picture clue — information from nonverbal illustrations that helps reader identify words or understand text

plot profile — see story graph

pragmatic — practical

prediction as a strategy — using language knowledge and experiences and the context of the text or speech to anticipate what will come next

prefix — meaning element attached at the beginning of a root word or a derived (inflected) form, and combining its meaning with that word's meaning

prereading activities — activities engaged in before reading designed to help with word recognition and comprehension, or to provide a focus for reading and postreading activities

print awareness — noticing that a message is contained in print that can be read and is the same each time; children begin to realize it is the print, not the illustrations, that is read in a specific way

prior knowledge (see background knowledge)

psycholinguistics — study of language behaviour

R

rauding — term introduced by Carver (1977) to refer to the normal process of reading as compared to skimming, scanning, studying and memorizing

readability — ease of reading and understanding, can be affected by such things as text type and font, format, content, style, vocabulary and concept density, illustrations, sentence structure and length, interest, prior knowledge, etc.; an estimation in terms of grade level of the ease of reading a text

read-along — process by which reader follows along, or reads orally, with a competent reader or taped story

reading flexibility — changing reading speed and strategies to suit reader's purpose, prior knowledge and background, and nature of text

reading vocabulary — number of words recognized and understood easily when reading

Reading Recovery Program — a program developed by Marie Clay as short-term, early intervention to reading problems, selected students receive individualized instruction for 30 minutes daily, teachers are trained in the program concepts and procedures

receptive vocabulary — number of words easily recognized and understood when listening

Reciprocal Teaching — an approach developed to enhance student involvement in learning and understanding reading, involves teacher modelling the strategies first with students later taking over the process (Palinscar & Brown, 1985; 1986)

redundancy — extra information provided in a communication that can be removed without loss of meaning, but which helps with ease of decoding the message (e.g. Th_ v_w_ls c_n b_ l_ft __t b_t y__ c_n st_ll r__d th_s s_nt_nc_.); context clues and prediction can be used to identify words and meaning because of redundancy in written English

referent — word referred to by a grammatical substitute (e.g. in the statement "This is mine," *This* refers to some object previously mentioned or pointed to) (also, see anaphora, antecedent)

repeated reading — an activity developed to enhance a student's reading fluency in which student rereads a passage three times attempting to increase fluency and word recognition accuracy

retelling — process of describing what happened in story or what passage was about after reading a text/story

rime — part of a word after initial consonants, includes vowels and final consonants (compare to onset)

root word — base or word to which affixes and inflectional endings are added (e.g. invent is the root word of inventing, invention, inventor, reinvent)

running record — a process used by Marie Clay (1985) to track reading miscues during oral reading

---

S

scaffolding — process in which teacher or more experienced person helps student by first modelling what student cannot do and slowly having student take over more and more of the process as they are able to; concept was first developed by Bruner, word now used in variety of ways

scanning — reading or examining quickly but selectively for a purpose

schema (pl. schemata) — conceptual organization for understanding; generalized plan, structure or description

schwa — vowel sound heard in most unstressed syllables, represented in dictionary by phonetic symbol /ə/

segmentation — dividing words into parts (phonemes, morphemes)

Semantic Feature Analysis — instructional strategy based on the way information is thought to be stored in the memory by categories; features of words are compared in a grid to make their relationships and meaning more apparent (Pittelmann et al., 1991)

semantic mapping (semantic webbing) — diagramming the relationships of words, concepts, ideas

semantics — study of meaning and relations between concepts and names, and referents and names

sensation — reception of sensory stimuli (e.g. seeing, hearing) by the sense organ and nerves

shared reading — reading (or following along with) enlarged print as it is read aloud to a group of students

sight words — words that are nonphonetic (can't be sounded out) and therefore must be recognized as a whole; words that occur frequently and need to be recognized automatically for fluent reading; words that are of high interest to a reader so that they are recognized easily as a whole

silent reading — reading without saying what is read aloud

skill — an ability to perform that can be acquired; part of action that makes up complete performance (e.g. as used in basic skills, reading skills, thinking skills, study skills); note — there is no agreement as to what the actual skills are

skimming — reading rapidly and selectively to get gist of text

sociogram — diagram or chart showing how individuals interact or might choose to interact within a group; **literary sociogram**— sociogram showing interactions and relationships between characters in a story

sounding out (segmenting) — producing the sounds represented by letters or letter combinations in a word in sequence; using phonics to decode a word

speaking vocabulary — total number of words a person normally uses in speech to communicate meaning (see also expressive vocabulary)

SQ3R (survey, question, read, recite, review) — a reading/study technique

SSR (sustained silent reading) — block of time planned for students to read silently, also called USSR (uninterrupted sustained silent reading), or DEAR (drop everything and read)

story board — series of sketches on a page which illustrate in sequence the scenes and events of a story; a way for students to demonstrate their understanding of a story; idea adapted from a panel of sketches which are used for producing T.V. shows and motion pictures

story grammar — analysis of the structure of a narrative to show the main features (e.g. characters, setting, initial problem or initiating event, episodes, climax, solution)

story graph (also plot profile) — a way to illustrate the degree of tension, excitement, and feelings as a story progresses by plotting these against events in a story

strategy — plan or method to accomplish goal; different reading strategies include skills and knowledge organized in different ways

structural analysis — identification of roots, prefixes, suffixes, inflectional endings, and combining forms in words

suffix — meaningful element attached to end of a word, a suffix combines its meaning with that of the word; most suffixes have a grammatical function (e.g. -er added to a verb creates a noun, -y added to a noun creates an adjective)

structured overview — concepts of topic or unit (as illustrated by key vocabulary) identified and organized visually to show patterns and relationships; can be used before reading as an advance organizer, during reading to be revised/confirmed or completed, or after reading to be revised, completed, or used as a study guide

surface structure — sequence of words and their literal meaning (compare this to deep structure)

syllable — word or word part in which a vowel sound is heard, dictionaries divide words into "visual syllables" where a word may be broken at the end of a line; these may or may not correspond to spoken syllables (e.g. making – mak.ing [visual] –/ma/-/king/ [spoken])

synonyms — words with very similar meanings

syntax — sequence of words in phrases, clauses and sentences; grammatical structure of sentences

synthetic approach — teaching reading with emphasis on starting with letters, sounds and syllables and combining them into words

---

T

teaching activity — instructional activity planned by teacher to explain or demonstrate skills and knowledge to students; what the teacher does with the students to help them learn (compare to learning activity)

text — written or printed communication

text analysis — examination of structural features of printed or written communication (e.g. coherence, organization) and their relation to readability

theme — topic broad enough to cover several related concepts or entire scope of a book

theme approach — teaching skills and subjects such as Social Studies, Science, English using the theme as the focus for organizing instruction and resources

theory — general principles as compared to specifics; ideas organized to explain or generate a new understanding

think-aloud — way of demonstrating thinking, logic, or reasoning by talking out loud as process occurs

---

U

USSR (uninterrupted sustained silent reading) — see SSR

V

verbal — having to do with words, written or spoken

vicarious experiences — learning about experiences from others who have had the experience through written or spoken communication

visualization — mentally creating pictures or images of objects or events

vocabulary load — number of difficult words, their frequency and comprehensibility and their effect on readability (see also concept load)

vocabulary control — limiting the number of new words introduced on each page of a reader or in each lesson of a reading program

vocabulary development — increase in student's knowledge of words and their meanings; instructional practices that aid student's learning of vocabulary

voiced — sounds made by vibrating the vocal cords with air forced from the lungs, all vowel sounds and the consonants b d j g v z th (bathe) are voiced [compare — voiceless (unvoiced) sounds are made without vibrating the vocal cords e.g. p t k f s ch th (bath)]

vowel — speech sound produced by air flowing from lungs relatively unobstructed without being cut off at any point; different authorities recognize different numbers of vowel sounds in English (e.g. 19 in some dictionaries); long and short vowels refer to quality of sound, the long vowel sound being the same as the letter name

W

Whole Language — a philosophical approach to teaching language arts which emphasizes using meaningful texts and situations as the starting points for instruction; teaching reading begins with the meaning of the whole text and focuses on the parts within that context

word — speech sound or series of sounds used as a unit of language having meaning

word attack — analysis of word in order to pronounce or identify it

word family — words having common phonic element (e.g. at – bat, cat, mat, sat) or same root or base (e.g. graph – telegraph, graphic, grapheme)

word identification — determining the pronunciation and meaning of an unknown word; some authorities differentiate between this and word recognition

word recognition — quick and easy identification of word

word study — activities to increase vocabulary, word attack skills, spelling

Z

zone of proximal development — concept proposed by Vygotsky referring to the skills and knowledge children do not have mastery of but are able to learn with help; goals that are within child's reach when given instruction or help